Encyclopedia of Dog Breeds

An All-in-One Guide to over 200 Breeds, Cross Breeds and Breed Varieties of Dog

Dog Care Professionals

Copyright © 2012 Author Name

All rights reserved.

Although the author and publisher have made every effort to ensure that the information presented in this book was correct at the present time, the author and publisher do not assume and hereby disclaim any liability to any party for any loss, damage, or disruption caused by errors or omissions, whether such errors or omissions result from negligence, accident, or any other cause.

ISBN:1546526765

ISBN-13: **978-1546526766**

Encyclopedia of Dog Breeds

CONTENTS

Introduction 57

Why Should You Purchase A Dog? 58

    Companionship 58

    Exercise 59

    Watchdog 59

    Nurturing 59

    Empathy 60

A 61

The Affenpinscher 62

    Lifespan 62

    Height and Weight 63

    Breed Characteristics 63

The Afghan Hound 64

    Lifespan 64

    Height and Weight 65

    Grooming 65

Low Pain Threshold 65

Breed Characteristics 66

The Airedale Terrier 67

Lifespan 67

Height and Weight 68

Breed Characteristics 68

The Akita 70

Lifespan 70

Height and Weight 71

Children and Other Pets 71

Breed Characteristics 71

The Alaska Malamute 73

Lifespan 73

Height and Weight 74

Temperament 74

Breed Characteristics 75

The American English Coonhound 76

- Lifespan 76
- Height and Weight 77
- Prey Drive 77
- Breed Characteristics 78
- The American Eskimo Dog 79
  - Lifespan 80
  - Height and Weight (Toy Variety) 80
  - Height and Weight (Miniature Variety) 80
  - Height and Weight (Standard Variety) 81
  - Breed Characteristics 81
- The American Foxhound 82
  - Lifespan 83
  - Height and Weight 83
  - Breed Characteristics 83
- The American Pitbull Terrier 85
  - Lifespan 85
  - Height and Weight 86

Children and other Pets 86

Breed Characteristics 87

The American Water Spaniel 88

Lifespan 88

Height and Weight 89

Roaming 89

Breed Characteristics 89

The Anatolian Shepherd Dog 91

Lifespan 91

Height and Weight 92

Appearance 92

Breed Characteristics 92

The Appenzeller Sennenhunde 94

Lifespan 95

Height and Weight 95

Breed Characteristics 95

The Australian Cattle Dog 97

Lifespan 97

Height and Weight 98

Breed Characteristics 98

The Australian Shepherd 100

Lifespan 101

Height and Weight 101

Coat 101

Breed Characteristics 101

The Australian Terrier 103

Lifespan 103

Height and Weight 104

Coat 104

Breed Characteristics 104

The Azawakh 106

Lifespan 107

Height and Weight 107

Coat 107

Breed Characteristics 108

B 109

The Barbet 110

    Lifespan 111

    Height and Weight 111

    Breed Characteristics 111

The Basenji 113

    Lifespan 114

    Height and Weight 114

    Coat 114

Breed Characteristics 114

The Basset Hound 116

    Lifespan 117

    Height and Weight 117

    General Health 117

    Breed Characteristics 118

The Beagle 119

- Lifespan 119
- Height and Weight.. 119
- Children and Other Pets 120
- Breed Characteristics....................................... 120

The Bearded Collie 122
- Lifespan 123
- Height and Weight.. 123
- Breed Characteristics....................................... 123

The Bedlington Terrier 125
- Lifespan 125
- Height and Weight.. 126

Breed Characteristics 126

The Belgian Malinois... 128
- Lifespan 129
- Height and Weight.. 129
- Breed Characteristics....................................... 129

The Belgian Sheepdog.. 131

Lifespan 132

Height and Weight 132

Breed Characteristics 133

The Belgian Tervuren 134

Lifespan 134

Height and Weight 135

The Other Variants 135

Breed Characteristics 136

The Berger Picard 137

Lifespan 138

Height and Weight 138

Breed Characteristics 138

The Bernese Mountain Dog 140

The Other Breeds of Sennenhund 141

Lifespan 141

Height and Weight 141

Breed Characteristics 142

The Bichon Frise 143

    Lifespan 143

    Height and Weight 144

    Coat 144

    Breed Characteristics 144

The Black and Tan Coonhound 146

    Lifespan 147

    Height and Weight 147

    Breed Characteristics 147

The Black Russian Terrier 149

    Lifespan 150

    Height and Weight 150

    Breed Characteristics 150

The Bloodhound 152

    Lifespan 153

    Height and Weight 153

    Voice 153

Breed Characteristics 154

The Bluetick Coonhound 155

Lifespan 156

Height and Weight 156

Breed Characteristics 156

The Bolognese 158

Lifespan 159

Height and Weight 159

Breed Characteristics 159

The Border Collie 161

Lifespan 162

Height and Weight 162

Breed Characteristics 162

The Border Terrier 164

Lifespan 165

Height and Weight 165

Breed Characteristics 165

The Borzoi 167

    Lifespan 168

    Height and Weight 168

    Breed Characteristics 168

The Boston Terrier 170

    Lifespan 170

    Height and Weight 171

    Breed Characteristics 171

The Bouvier des Flandres 173

    Lifespan 174

    Height and Weight 174

    Coat 174

    Breed Characteristics 175

The Boxer 176

    Lifespan 176

    Height and Weight 176

    Temperament 177

Breed Characteristics 177

The Boykin Spaniel 179

Lifespan 180

Height and Weight 180

Breed Characteristics 180

The Bracco Italiano 182

Lifespan 183

Height and Weight 183

Coat 183

Breed Characteristics 183

The Briard 185

Lifespan 186

Height and Weight 186

Breed Characteristics 186

The Brittany 188

Lifespan 189

Height and Weight 189

- Breed Characteristics 189
- The Brussels Griffon 191
  - Lifespan 192
  - Height and Weight 192
  - Variants 192
  - Breed Characteristics 193
- The Bull Terrier 194
  - Lifespan 194
  - Size and Weight 195
  - Temperament 195
  - Banned 195
  - Breed Characteristics 196
- The Bulldog 197
  - Lifespan 197
  - Size 197
  - Appearance 198
  - Intelligence 198

- Breed Characteristics 198
- The Bullmastiff 200
  - Lifespan 201
  - Height and Weight 201
  - Breed Characteristics 201
- C 203
- The Cairn Terrier 204
  - Lifespan 205
  - Height and Weight 205
  - Breed Characteristics 205
- The Canaan Dog 207
  - Lifespan 208
  - Height and Weight 208
  - Breed Characteristics 209
- The Cane Corso 210
  - Lifespan 211
  - Height and Weight 211

Breed Characteristics 211

The Cardigan Welsh Corgi 213

    Lifespan 214

    Height and Weight 214

    Breed Characteristics 214

The Catahoula Cur 216

    Lifespan 217

    Height and Weight 217

    Coat 217

    Breed Characteristics 218

The Cavalier King Charles Spaniel 220

    Lifespan 220

    Height and Weight 221

    Breed Characteristics 221

The Cesky Terrier 223

    Lifespan 223

    Height and Weight 224

- Coat 224
- Breed Characteristics 224
- The Chesapeake Bay Retriever 226
  - Lifespan 227
  - Height and Weight 227
  - Breed Characteristics 227
- The Chihuahua 229
  - Lifespan 229
  - Size 230
  - Personality 230
  - Children 230
  - Breed Characteristics 231
- The Chinese Crested 232
  - Lifespan 233
  - Height and Weight 233
  - Breed Characteristics 233
- The Chinese Shar-Pei 235

- Lifespan 236
- Height and Weight 236
- Breed Characteristics 236

The Chinook 238

- Lifespan 239
- Height and Weight 239
- Breed Characteristics 239

The Chow Chow 241

- Lifespan 242
- Height and Weight 242
- Breed Characteristics 243

The Clumber Spaniel 244

- Lifespan 245
- Height and Weight 245
- Breed Characteristics 246

The Cockapoo 247

- Lifespan 248

- Height and Weight 248
- Coat 248
- Breed Characteristics 249

The Cocker Spaniel 250
- Lifespan 251
- Height and Weight 251
- The English Cocker Spaniel 251
- The American Cocker Spaniel 252
- Breed Characteristics 252

The Collie 254
- Lifespan 255
- Height and Weight 255
- Breed Characteristics 256

The Coton de Tulear 257
- Lifespan 258
- Height and Weight 258
- Breed Characteristics 258

The Curly-Coated Retriever 260

    Lifespan 261

    Height and Weight 261

    Exercise 261

    Breed Characteristics 262

D 263

The Dachshund 264

    Lifespan 264

    Appearance 265

    Popularity 265

    Breed Characteristics 265

The Dalmatian 267

    Lifespan 268

    Height and Weight 268

    Breed Characteristics 269

The Dandie Dinmont Terrier 270

    Lifespan 271

Height and Weight 271

Breed Characteristics 272

The Doberman Pinscher 273

Lifespan 274

Height and Weight 274

Hierarchy 274

Von Willebrand's Disease 275

Breed Characteristics 275

The Dogue de Bordeaux 277

Lifespan 278

Height and Weight 278

Breed Characteristics 278

E 280

The English Cocker Spaniel 281

Lifespan 281

Height and Weight 282

Temperament 282

Breed Characteristics 282

The English Foxhound 284

    Lifespan 285

    Height and Weight 285

    Breed Characteristics 285

The English Setter 287

    Lifespan 288

    Height and Weight 288

Breed Characteristics 289

The English Springer Spaniel 290

    Lifespan 290

    Height and Weight 291

    Coat 291

    Temperament 291

    Breed Characteristics 292

The English Toy Spaniel 293

    Lifespan 294

- Height and Weight 294
- Breed Characteristics 294

The Entlebucher Mountain Dog 296
- Four Breeds of Sennenhund 297
- Lifespan 297
- Height and Weight 298
- Coat 298
- Breed Characteristics 298

F 300

The Field Spaniel 301
- Lifespan 302
- Height and Weight 302
- Breed Characteristics 303

The Finnish Lapphund 304
- Lifespan 305
- Height and Weight 305
- Breed Characteristics 306

- The Finnish Spitz 307
  - Lifespan 308
  - Height and Weight 309
  - Breed Characteristics 309
- The Flat-Coated Retriever 310
  - Lifespan 311
  - Height and Weight 312
  - Breed Characteristics 312
- The Fox Terrier 314
  - Lifespan 314
  - The Smooth Fox Terrier 315
  - Height and Weight of a Smooth Fox Terrier 315
  - The Wire Fox Terrier 315
  - Height and Weight of a Wire Fox Terrier 316
  - Breed Characteristics 316
  - Lifespan 318
  - Size 319

Frenchie Clubs 319

Personality 319

Breed Characteristics 319

G 321

The German Pinscher 322

Lifespan 323

Height and Weight 323

Breed Characteristics 324

The German Shepherd 325

Lifespan 325

Intelligence 326

Biting 326

Size 326

Breed Characteristics 327

The German Shorthaired Pointer 328

Lifespan 329

Height and Weight 330

- Breed Characteristics 330
- The German Wirehaired Pointer 332
  - Lifespan 333
  - Height and Weight 334
  - Breed Characteristics 334
- The Giant Schnauzer 335
  - Lifespan 336
  - Height and Weight 337
  - Breed Characteristics 337
- The Glen of Imaal Terrier 338
  - Lifespan 339
  - Height and Weight 340
  - Breed Characteristics 340
- The Goldador 341
  - Lifespan 342
  - Height and Weight 342
  - Breed Characteristics 343

The Golden Retriever 344

    The American Type 344

    The British Type 345

    The Canadian Type 345

    Lifespan 346

    Breed Characteristics 346

The Goldendoodle 347

    Lifespan 348

    Height and Weight 348

    Breed Characteristics 349

The Gordon Setter 350

    Lifespan 351

    Height and Weight 352

    Breed Characteristics 352

The Great Dane 353

    Lifespan 353

    Height and Weight 354

- Space 354
- Coat Colorations 354
- Breed Characteristics 355

The Great Pyrenees 356
- Lifespan 357
- Height and Weight 358
- Breed Characteristics 358

The Greater Swiss Mountain Dog 360
- The Other Breeds of Sennenhund 361
- Lifespan 361
- Height and Weight 362
- Breed Characteristics 362

The Greyhound 364
- Lifespan 365
- Height and Weight 366
- Breed Characteristics 366

H 367

The Harrier 368
    Lifespan 369
    Height and Weight 369
    Breed Characteristics 370

The Havanese 371
    Lifespan 372
    Height and Weight 373
    Breed Characteristics 373

I 374

The Ibizan Hound 375
    Lifespan 376
    Height and Weight 377
    Breed Characteristics 377

The Icelandic Sheepdog 378
    Lifespan 379
    Height and Weight 379
    Breed Characteristics 380

The Irish Red and White Setter 381

    Lifespan 382

    Height and Weight 382

    Breed Characteristics 383

The Irish Setter 384

    Lifespan 385

    Height and Weight 385

    Breed Characteristics 386

    Lifespan 388

    Height and Weight 388

    Breed Characteristics 389

The Irish Water Spaniel 390

    Lifespan 391

    Height and Weight 392

    Breed Characteristics 392

The Irish Wolfhound 393

    Lifespan 394

Height and Weight 394

Breed Characteristics 395

The Italian Greyhound 396

Lifespan 397

Height and Weight 397

Breed Characteristics 398

J 399

The Jack Russell 400

Lifespan 401

Height and Weight 402

Breed Characteristics 402

The Japanese Chin 403

Lifespan 404

Height and Weight 404

Breed Characteristics 405

K 406

The Keeshond 407

Lifespan 408

Height and Weight 408

Breed Characteristics 409

The Kerry Blue Terrier 410

Lifespan 411

Height and Weight 412

Breed Characteristics 412

The Komondor 413

Lifespan 414

Height and Weight 415

Breed Characteristics 415

The Kooikerhondje 417

Lifespan 418

Height and Weight 418

Breed Characteristics 419

The Korean Jindo 420

Lifespan 421

- Height and Weight 421
- Breed Characteristics 422
- The Kuvasz 423
  - Lifespan 425
  - Height and Weight 425
  - Breed Characteristics 425
- L 427
- The Labradoodle 428
  - Lifespan 429
  - Height and Weight 429
  - Breed Characteristics 430
- The Labrador Retriever 431
  - Lifespan 431
  - Adult Size 432
  - Official Breed Standards 432
  - Breed Characteristics 433
- The Lakeland Terrier 435

Lifespan 436

Height and Weight 436

Breed Characteristics 437

The Lancashire Heeler 438

Lifespan 439

Height and Weight 439

Breed Characteristics 440

The Leonberger 441

Lifespan 442

Height and Weight 443

Breed Characteristics 443

The Lhasa Apso 444

Lifespan 445

Height and Weight 445

Breed Characteristics 446

The Lowchen 447

Lion Cut 448

Lifespan 448

Height and Weight 448

Breed Characteristics 449

The Maltese 450

Lifespan 450

Height and Weight 451

Coat 451

Breed Characteristics 451

The Maltese Shih Tzu 453

Lifespan 454

Height and Weight 454

Breed Characteristics 454

The Maltipoo 456

Lifespan 457

Height and Weight 457

Breed Characteristics 457

The Manchester Terrier 459

- Lifespan 461
- Height and Weight 461
- Breed Characteristics 461

The Mastiff 463

- Lifespan 464
- Height and Weight 464
- List of Mastiff Breeds 464
- Breed Characteristics 466

The Miniature Pinscher 468

- Lifespan 469
- Height and Weight 470
- Breed Characteristics 470

The Miniature Schnauzer 472

- Lifespan 472
- Height and Weight 473
- Temperament 473
- Breed Characteristics 473

N 475

The Neapolitan Mastiff 476

    Lifespan 478

    Height and Weight 478

    Breed Characteristics 478

The Newfoundland 480

    Lifespan 482

    Height and Weight 482

    Breed Characteristics 482

The Norfolk Terrier 484

    Lifespan 485

    Height and Weight 486

    Breed Characteristics 486

The Norwegian Buhund 488

    Lifespan 489

    Height and Weight 490

    Breed Characteristics 490

The Norwegian Elkhound 492

    Lifespan 494

    Height and Weight 494

    Breed Characteristics 494

The Norwegian Lundehund 496

    Lifespan 497

    Height and Weight 498

    Breed Characteristics 498

The Norwich Terrier 500

    Lifespan 501

    Height and Weight 502

    Breed Characteristics 502

The Nova Scotia Duck Tolling Retriever 503

    Lifespan 505

    Height and Weight 505

    Breed Characteristics 505

O 507

The Old English Sheepdog 508

    Lifespan 510

    Height and Weight 510

    Breed Characteristics 510

The Otterhound 512

    Lifespan 513

    Height and Weight 513

    Breed Characteristics 514

P 515

The Papillon 516

    Lifespan 517

    Height and Weight 517

    Breed Characteristics 517

The Peekapoo 519

    Lifespan 520

    Height and Weight 520

    Breed Characteristics 521

The Pekingese 522
    Lifespan 523
    Height and Weight 524
    Breed Characteristics 524

The Pembroke Welsh Corgi 525
    Lifespan 527
    Height and Weight 527
    Breed Characteristics 527

The Petit Basset Griffon Vendeen 529
    Lifespan 530
    Height and Weight 531
    Breed Characteristics 531

The Pharaoh Hound 533
    Lifespan 535
    Height and Weight 535
    Breed Characteristics 535

The Plott 537

Lifespan 538

Height and Weight 538

Breed Characteristics 539

The Pocket Beagle 540

Lifespan 541

Height and Weight 541

Breed Characteristics 542

The Pointer 543

Lifespan 544

Height and Weight 545

Breed Characteristics 545

The Polish Lowland Sheepdog 546

Lifespan 547

Height and Weight 547

Breed Characteristics 548

The Pomeranian 549

Lifespan 549

Height and Weight 550

Coat 550

Breed Characteristics 550

The Poodle 552

Size Variants 552

Height 553

Weight 553

Lifespan 553

Breed Characteristics 553

The Portuguese Water Dog 555

Lifespan 556

Height and Weight 556

Breed Characteristics 557

The Pug 558

Lifespan 558

Height and Weight 558

Company 559

- Obesity 559
- Eye Prolapse 559
- Breed Characteristics 560
- The Puggle 561
  - Lifespan 562
  - Height and Weight 562
  - Breed Characteristics 563
- The Puli 564
  - Lifespan 565
  - Height and Weight 566
  - Breed Characteristics 566
- The Pyrenean Shepherd 567
  - Lifespan 569
  - Height and Weight 569
  - Breed Characteristics 569
- R 571
- The Rat Terrier 572

- Lifespan 573
- Height and Weight 573
- Breed Characteristics 574

The Redbone Coonhound 575
- Lifespan 576
- Height and Weight 576
- Breed Characteristics 577

The Rhodesian Ridgeback 578
- Lifespan 579
- Height and Weight 580
- Breed Characteristics 580

The Rottweiler 582
- Lifespan 582
- Size 582
- Children 583
- Introducing New Animals and Dogs 583
- Breed Characteristics 584

S 585

The Saint Bernard 586

    Lifespan 588

    Height and Weight 588

    Breed Characteristics 588

The Saluki 590

    Lifespan 591

    Height and Weight 592

    Breed Characteristics 592

The Samoyed 593

    Lifespan 594

    Height and Weight 594

    Breed Characteristics 595

The Schipperke 596

    Lifespan 598

    Height and Weight 598

    Breed Characteristics 598

The Schnoodle 600

    Lifespan 601

    Height and Weight 601

    Breed Characteristics 602

The Scottish Deerhound 603

    Lifespan 605

    Height and Weight 605

    Breed Characteristics 605

The Scottish Terrier 607

    Lifespan 609

    Height and Weight 609

    Breed Characteristics 609

The Sealyham Terrier 611

    Lifespan 612

    Height and Weight 613

    Breed Characteristics 613

The Shetland Sheepdog 614

- Lifespan 615
- Height and Weight 616
- Breed Characteristics 616

The Shiba Inu 618
- Lifespan 619
- Height and Weight 620
- Breed Characteristics 620

The Shih Tzu 621
- Lifespan 621
- Height and Weight 622
- The Tea Cup and Imperial Shih Tzu 622
- Breed Characteristics 622

The Siberian Husky 624
- Lifespan 624
- Height and Weight 624
- Coat 625
- Behavior 625

Breed Characteristics 626

The Silky Terrier 628

Lifespan 629

Height and Weight 629

Breed Characteristics 630

The Skye Terrier 631

Lifespan 632

Height and Weight 633

Breed Characteristics 633

The Sloughi 634

Lifespan 635

Height and Weight 636

Breed Characteristics 636

The Small Munsterlander Pointer 637

Lifespan 639

Height and Weight 639

Breed Characteristics 639

The Soft Coated Wheaten Terrier 641

    Lifespan 643

    Height and Weight 643

    Breed Characteristics 644

The Stabyhoun 645

    Lifespan 646

    Height and Weight 647

    Breed Characteristics 647

The Staffordshire Bull Terrier 648

    Lifespan 648

    Height and Weight 649

    Socialization 649

    Breed Characteristics 649

The Standard Schnauzer 651

    Lifespan 653

    Height and Weight 653

    Breed Characteristics 653

The Sussex Spaniel 655

    Lifespan 657

    Height and Weight 657

    Breed Characteristics 657

The Swedish Vallhund 659

    Lifespan 661

    Height and Weight 661

    Breed Characteristics 661

T 663

The Tibetan Mastiff 664

    Lifespan 666

    Height and Weight 666

    Breed Characteristics 666

The Tibetan Spaniel 668

    Lifespan 670

    Height and Weight 670

    Breed Characteristics 670

The Tibetan Terrier 672

    Lifespan 673

    Height and Weight 673

    Breed Characteristics 674

The Toy Fox Terrier 675

    Lifespan 676

    Height and Weight 676

    Breed Characteristics 677

The Treeing Tennessee Brindle 678

    Lifespan 679

    Height and Weight 680

    Breed Characteristics 680

The Treeing Walker Coonhound 681

    Lifespan 683

    Height and Weight 683

    Breed Characteristics 683

V 685

The Vizsla 686

    Lifespan 687

    Height and Weight 688

    Breed Characteristics 688

W 689

The Weimaraner 690

    Lifespan 692

    Height and Weight 692

    Breed Characteristics 692

The Welsh Springer Spaniel 694

    Lifespan 695

    Height and Weight 696

    Breed Characteristics 696

The Welsh Terrier 697

    Lifespan 698

    Height and Weight 698

    Breed Characteristics 699

The Whippet 700

    Lifespan 701

    Height and Weight 702

    Breed Characteristics 702

The West Highland White Terrier 703

    Lifespan 705

    Height and Weight 705

    Breed Characteristics 705

The Wirehaired Pointing Griffon 707

    Lifespan 708

    Height and Weight 709

    Breed Characteristics 709

X 710

The Xoloitzcuintli 711

    Lifespan 712

    Height and Weight 712

    Breed Characteristics 713

Y 714

The Yorkshire Terrier 715

    Lifespan 715

    Size 716

    Hypoallergenic Coat 716

    Yorkie Clubs 716

    Breed Characteristics 717

ABOUT THE AUTHOR 718

Other Popular Books by Dog Care Professionals 719

INTRODUCTION

Before purchasing any pet it is important to understand that as a pet owner you are responsible for the care and wellbeing of your pet. It is important to try and learn as much as you can about the animal you are considering to keep as a pet to make sure that your lifestyle, household and financial status are suited to provide your pet with the best possible care. This encyclopedic guide has been designed to provide you with both precise and concise information about over 200 breeds, cross breeds and breed variations of dog. This encyclopedia aims to give you an in-depth description of each dog breed, including its lifespan, height and weight, breed characteristics and any other important facts to allow you to choose a breed that best suits you.

WHY SHOULD YOU PURCHASE A DOG?

In the United States of America it is estimated that there are between 70 and 80 million pet dogs owned and over 40% of the county's households own a dog! As the statistic shows dogs are incredibly popular pets – but why? Any dog owner will happily tell you all the benefits and joys of owning a dog! The following section will outline 5 key benefits of owning a dog:

Companionship

Dogs are incredibly loyal and loving animals and make a great addition to any household. If you build a strong relationship with your pet they can transcend just being a pet and become a friend, or ever a member of your family! However your dog brings you companionship in other ways. You are more likely to interact with strangers while walking your dog than if you were walking alone. Owning a dog also allows you to go to dog parks and converse with other dog owners. If you walk your dog around your neighborhood on a regular basis, you may also develop a friendly relationship with your neighbors who own dogs as you are likely to pass each other several times a day.

Exercise

Owning a dog increases your chance of exercising due to the fact that you will need to play with and walk your dog. Taking your pet for frequent walks will decrease your chance of becoming over weight. A recent study in Australia found that children with a pet dog are 50% less likely to be overweight! Exercising on a regular basis has a plethora of other health benefits such as reducing the chance of heart disease, strokes and high blood pressure. A dog can be a great exercise companion as well as being a great motivation due to the fact that it is cruel to not provide your dog with adequate exercise.

Watchdog

Dogs are very territorial, loyal and aware as a species. Even from as early as puppyhood, a dog is able to detect potential burglars and dangers. Your dog will bark at anything suspicious or out of the ordinary which will alert you to any potential trouble. Most criminals are instantly put off by the barking of a watchdog.

Nurturing

The majority of humans have a deep desire to nurture. This desire used to be fulfilled by caring for, and raising, a baby or caring for younger siblings. Across the Western World the average family size is decreasing which makes pets the perfect outlet for people's nurturing desires. In families with no children, or one child, dogs are fulfilling the role of being substitute children and siblings! Dogs are intelligent beings and respond well to being nurtured which makes it a positive and rewarding experiences for both the owner and the pet. Dogs also seem to nurture children. Children who own a dog tend to have a high self-esteem and are more popular with their classmates!

Empathy

Dogs are incredibly empathetic animals! They will sense the mood of their owner and either attempt to provide comfort, through physical contact, or a distraction through a humorous playful act. It is not uncommon for dogs to bring their distressed owners their favorite toy as an attempt to cheer them up. Dogs have also saved their owners from countless dangers – such as house fires and burglaries.

Encyclopedia of Dog Breeds

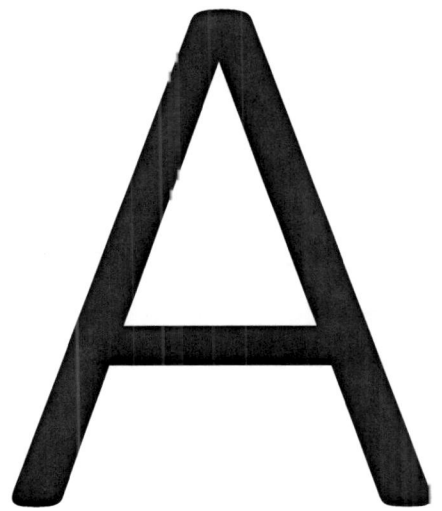

THE AFFENPINSCHER

The Affenpinscher is a small 'toy breed' of terrier like dog. Despite their appearance being similar to terriers, the Affenpinscher is actually part of the 'Pinscher-Schnauzer' grouping of dogs. The breed originates from Germany and is thought to have been developed during the 17th century. The Affenpinscher is also commonly known as the 'Monkey Terrier,' due to the fact that the name is derived from the German word *'Affe'* which means 'ape' or 'monkey.' The breed was created for the purpose of hunting rats and other small rodents in kitchens, stables and granaries. The breed as a whole is active, adventurous, curious, playful and loyal. Affenpinschers relish spending time with their family unit and get along very well with children and other animals. It is important to note that due to their small size, the Affenpinscher may not be a suitable pet for families with small children due to the fact that they may drop, or accidentally injury, the dog.

Lifespan

An Affenpinscher will normally live to be between 10 and 12 years old. However it is not uncommon for an Affenpinscher to live to be as old as 14, providing that they do not develop any serious health issues.

Height and Weight

A fully grown Affenpinscher will normally stand between 9 to 11 inches (23 to 28cm) tall at the shoulder. A healthy adult Affenpinscher will normally weigh between 7 and 9 pounds (3 to 4kg). It is important to note that the weight of a healthy dog depends on how large the dog is – taller dogs should weigh more.

Breed Characteristics

The following section will give you a simplistic overview of the characteristics of a Affenpinscher. Our rating system is from 1 to 10 – with 1 being the lowest score and 10 being the highest.

- **Adaptability:** 6/10
- **Friendliness:** 6/10
- **Health:** 4/10
- **Ease of Grooming:** 6/10
- **Amount of Shedding:** 1/10
- **Trainability:** 8/10
- **Intelligence:** 6/10
- **Exercise Needed:** 8/10
- **Playfulness:** 8/10
- **Family Friendliness:** 8/10

THE AFGHAN HOUND

The Afghan Hound originates from the cold mountains of Afghanistan. The breed has multiple different names such as: Kuchi hound, Balkin Hound, Galanday Hound and the Tāžī Spay (which is what it is known as locally in Afghanistan). The breed is known for its highly distinguishable thick and silky coat and ring curl tail. Traditionally the Afghan Hound has been used as a sighthound during hunting. This means that the breed has a high 'prey drive' and may not get along with small animals or children. Due to this fact it is recommended to not keep an Afghan Hound in the same household as small children, other small pets or dogs. However, the temperament of a typical Afghan Hound is aloof, sensitive, loyal, friendly and dignified. However they are known to be extremely puppy-like and happy while playing. Due to their sensitive nature, it is important to never shout at your Afghan Hound in an aggressive manner.

Lifespan

An Afghan Hound will normally live to be between 10 and 11 years old. However it is not uncommon for an Afghan Hound to live to be as old as 12, providing it does not develop any serious health issues.

Height and Weight

A fully grown Afghan Hound will normally stand between 24 to 28 inches (61 to 71cm) tall at the shoulder. A healthy adult Afghan Hound will normally weigh between 50 to 60 pounds (22.5 to 27kg). It is important to note that the weight of a healthy dog depends on how large the dog is – taller dogs should weigh more.

Grooming

It is important to note that grooming an Afghan Hound is a long and essential process. The Afghan Hound has an extremely thick and long coat. It is important to consider if you are willing to groom your dog, or pay for a professional groomer, on a regular basis and for a long period of time. There will be a more detail section on grooming later in this guidebook.

Low Pain Threshold

The Afghan Hound has been noted to have a relatively low pain threshold. This means that a small, or seemingly minor wound, may bother your Afghan Hound more than another breed. It is important to note that your Afghan Hound is, most likely, not being whiny for no reason and to address the reason of its pain.

Breed Characteristics

The following section will give you a simplistic overview of the characteristics of an Afghan Hound. Our rating system is from 1 to 10 – with 1 being the lowest score and 10 being the highest.

- **Adaptability:** 8/10
- **Friendliness:** 8/10
- **Health:** 4/10
- **Ease of Grooming:** 2/10
- **Amount of Shedding:** 9/10
- **Trainability:** 5/10
- **Intelligence:** 10/10
- **Exercise Needed:** 8/10
- **Playfulness:** 8/10
- **Family Friendliness:** 10/10

THE AIREDALE TERRIER

The Airedale Terrier (often known simply as the 'Airedale) is a dog breed of terrier that originates from the valley of the River Aire, which is located in Yorkshire, England. The breeds name is derived from the the River Aire and the fact that a commonly used word for valley is 'Dale' – hence 'Airedale.' The Airedale is also commonly known as the Bingley Terrier and the Waterside Terrier. In England, the breed is traditionally known as the 'King of Terrier' due to the fact that it is the largest breed within the Terrier grouping. The breed was originally developed to hunt otters but was also commonly used as a war dog and a police dog. In modern times the Airedale Terrier is more commonly found being employed as a guide dog or as a family pet. The breed has a medium-length black and tan coat with a harsh topcoat and a much softer undercoat. The breed is typically energetic, non-aggressive, loyal and friendly which make it perfect for any family with children and other pets.

Lifespan

A Airedale Terrier will normally live to be between 10 and 12 years old. However it is not uncommon for a Airedale Terrier to live to be as old as 13, providing that it does not develop any serious health issues.

Height and Weight

A fully grown Airedale Terrier will normally stand between 21 to 23 inches (53.25 to 58.5 cm) tall at the shoulder. A healthy adult Airedale Terrier will normally weigh between 40 to 65 pounds (18 to 30 kg). It is important to note that the weight of a healthy dog depends on how large the dog is – taller dogs should weigh more.

Breed Characteristics

The following section will give you a simplistic overview of the characteristics of a Airedale Terrier. Our rating system is from 1 to 10 – with 1 being the lowest score and 10 being the highest.

- **Adaptability:** 4/10
- **Friendliness:** 8/10
- **Health:** 6/10
- **Ease of Grooming:** 4/10
- **Amount of Shedding:** 4/10
- **Trainability:** 10/10
- **Intelligence:** 10/10
- **Exercise Needed:** 10/10
- **Playfulness:** 10/10

➢ **Family Friendliness:** 10/10

THE AKITA

The Akita is a large breed of working dog that originates from the mountainous regions of Japan. The breed was originally developed to hunt large prey, such as bears, wild boar and deer. The breed is split into two variant strains: the Japanese strain and the American strain. The Japanese strain is commonly known as 'Akita Inu' ('Inu' meaning 'dog' in Japanese) and the 'Great Japanese dog.' The Japanese strain has a narrow range of coat colorations which are red, fawn, sesame, brindle and pure white. The American strain of Akita comes in a much wider range of colorations – it can basically have any color that is normally found on dogs. The Akita will commonly have a short double coat, in a similar fashion to the Siberian Husky. However it is not uncommon for a Akita to have a long coat due to a recessive gene. The Akita is an independent, powerful and domineering breed. They are commonly aloof with strangers but highly affectionate towards their family unit. As a breed they are generally very hardy and energetic.

Lifespan

An Akita will normally live to be between 10 and 11 years old. However it is not uncommon for an Akita to live to be as old as 12, providing they do not develop any serious health issues.

Height and Weight

A fully grown Akita will normally stand between 24 to 28 inches (61 to 71 cm) tall at the shoulder. A healthy adult Akita will normally weigh between 70 to 130 pounds (32 to 59 kg). It is important to note that the weight of a healthy dog depends on how large the dog is – taller dogs should weigh more.

Children and Other Pets

It is important to note that, as a breed, the Akita is highly independent and domineering. Akita's should not be kept in households with other dogs or pets. This is due to the fact that the Akita has a tendency to be aggressive towards other dogs and unknown animals. It is important to always supervise your children around your dog. An Akita is a perfect playmate for an older child. However it is not recommended to keep an Akita in a household with a small child due to the fact that they may mistreat or distress the animal.

Breed Characteristics

The following section will give you a simplistic overview of the characteristics of a Akita. Our rating system is from 1 to 10 – with 1 being the lowest score

and 10 being the highest.

- ➢ **Adaptability:** 6/10
- ➢ **Friendliness:** 5/10
- ➢ **Health:** 8/10
- ➢ **Ease of Grooming:** 10/10
- ➢ **Amount of Shedding:** 1/10
- ➢ **Trainability:** 6/10
- ➢ **Intelligence:** 6/10
- ➢ **Exercise Needed:** 8/10
- ➢ **Playfulness:** 10/10
- ➢ **Family Friendliness:** 10/10

THE ALASKA MALAMUTE

The Alaskan Malamute is a large breed of domestic dog that is very similar in appearance to other artic breeds, such as the Greenland dog, the Siberian Husky and the Samoyed. As the name suggests, the Alaskan Malamute originates from Alaska. The breed was originally developed to be capable of surviving in cold weathers and to have the strength and endurance to be able to pull heavy freights and sleds. Traditionally, the Alaskan Malamute was also used for hunting purposes and were more than capable of hunting larger prey, such as bears. The Alaskan Malamute was also kept as a domestic dog due to their loving and loyal temperament. The breed has a double coat, similar to a Siberian Husky. The undercoat has an oily texture and is normally about two inches thick. The outer coat is shorter, coarser and stands off the body. The breeds coat allows it to excel in cold climates and snowy conditions due to its, almost, waterproof oily undercoat. The breeds coats come in various shades of gray, white, and black. However red based colors and solid white coats are not uncommon.

Lifespan

An Alaskan Malamute will normally live to be

between 10 and 13 years old. However it is not uncommon for an Alaskan Malamute to live to be as old as 15, providing that it does not develop any serious health issues.

Height and Weight

A fully grown Alaskan Malamute will normally stand between 23 to 25 inches (58.5 to 89cm) tall at the shoulder. A healthy adult Alaskan Malamute will normally weigh between 75 to 100 pounds (34 to 45.5kg). It is important to note that the weight of a healthy dog depends on how large the dog is – taller dogs should weigh more.

Temperament

It is important to note that as a breed developed for hunting purposes, the Alaskan Malamute has a high prey drive. It is therefore considered best practice to not keep an Alaskan Malamute in a household with small children or other small animals. The breed has a long genetic foundation of living in harsh environments and has therefore developed a temperament suited to these environments. The breed is known to be independent, resourceful and highly intelligent. They are also incredibly energetic dogs. The breed is highly loyal and affectionate, making it great for any family with older children.

Breed Characteristics

The following section will give you a simplistic overview of the characteristics of a Alaskan Malamute. Our rating system is from 1 to 10 – with 1 being the lowest score and 10 being the highest.

- **Adaptability:** 4/10
- **Friendliness:** 8/10
- **Health:** 8/10
- **Ease of Grooming:** 4/10
- **Amount of Shedding:** 10/10
- **Trainability:** 8/10
- **Intelligence:** 8/10
- **Exercise Needed:** 10/10
- **Playfulness:** 10/10
- **Family Friendliness:** 10/10

THE AMERICAN ENGLISH COONHOUND

The American English Coonhound, also known simply as the 'Redtick Coonhound' or the 'English Coonhound,' is a breed of coonhound that is typically bred in the Southern United States. The breed is a descendant of the hunting hounds brought to America by the settlers during the 17th and 18th centuries. Unlike other breeds of coonhounds, a variety of coat colorations are accepted to meet the American English Coonhound breed standards. Coat colorations are most commonly redtick, bluetick, tricolored and tricolored with ticking. It is commonly thought that the breed has developed greater levels of intelligence, and an innate ability to hunt, due to the breeders focusing on these aspects of the dog rather than superficial aesthetic aspects – such as coat colorations. The American English Coonhound is a highly energetic breed and will require regular walking and exercise. The American English Coonhound is known to be a highly loyal, loving, strong willed, intelligent and family orientated breed.

Lifespan

An American English Coonhound will normally live to be between 10 and 11 years old. However it is not uncommon for an American English Coonhound to live to be as old as 12, providing that they do not develop any serious health issues.

Height and Weight

A fully grown American English Coonhound will normally stand between 23 to 26 inches (58.5 to 66cm) tall at the shoulder. A healthy adult American English Coonhound will normally weigh between 40 to 66 pounds (18 to 30kg). It is important to note that the weight of a healthy dog depends on how large the dog is – taller dogs should weigh more. It is important to note that females tend to be slightly smaller than males and will also therefore weigh less.

Prey Drive

As previously mentioned, the American English Coonhound has been bred for its intelligence and innate ability to hunt. The breed therefore has a very high prey drive. They are known to hunt small animals unless they are trained not to do so. It is therefore recommended to not keep a American English Coonhound in the same household as other small animals. Despite the breed being family orientated and not known to attack children, it is still considered best practice to also not keep a American English Coonhound in the same household as young children – it isn't worth the risk!

Breed Characteristics

The following section will give you a simplistic overview of the characteristics of a American English Coonhound. Our rating system is from 1 to 10 – with 1 being the lowest score and 10 being the highest.

- **Adaptability:** 6/10
- **Friendliness:** 10/10
- **Health:** 8/10
- **Ease of Grooming:** 10/10
- **Amount of Shedding:** 6/10
- **Trainability:** 10/10
- **Intelligence:** 8/10
- **Exercise Needed:** 10/10
- **Playfulness:** 10/10
- **Family Friendliness:** 10/10

THE AMERICAN ESKIMO DOG

The American Eskimo Dog is a breed of companion dog. Despite having 'Eskimo' present within its name, the breed actually originates from Germany. The breed was originally named the 'German Splitz' but due to anti-German prejudice during the First World War, the breed was renamed to the American Eskimo Dog. The American Eskimo Dog is a member of the Splitz family of dogs. The breed has traditionally been employed as a companion dog or as a watchdog. However during the 1940s the breed became a very popular choice as a circus performer. There are three size varieties of American Eskimo Dog: the toy, the miniature and the standard. It is important to watch your pet's weight. As a whole the American Eskimo Dog breed has a tendency to become overweight and it is therefore important to make sure that your provide your pet with adequate exercise. The breed is known to be affectionate, loving, intelligent and easy to train. They are also excellent around children due to their affectionate nature and willingness to please. They are highly intelligent and inquisitive and will become hyperactive if they are not exercised adequately.

Lifespan

An American Eskimo Dog will normally live to be between 10 and 12 years old. However it is not uncommon for a American Eskimo Dog to live to be as old as 15, providing they do not develop any serious health issues.

Height and Weight (Toy Variety)

A fully grown, Toy Variety, American Eskimo Dog will normally stand between 9 to 12 inches (22 to 30 cm) tall at the shoulder. A healthy adult, Toy Variety, American Eskimo Dog will normally weigh between 6 to 10 pounds (3 to 5kg). It is important to note that the weight of a healthy dog depends on how large the dog is – taller dogs should weigh more.

Height and Weight (Miniature Variety)

A fully grown, Miniature Variety, American Eskimo Dog will normally stand between 12 to 15 inches (30 to 40cm) tall at the shoulder. A healthy adult, Miniature Variety, American Eskimo Dog will normally weigh between 10 to 17 pounds (5 to 8kg). It is important to note that the weight of a healthy dog depends on how large the dog is – taller dogs should weigh more.

Height and Weight (Standard Variety)

A fully grown, Standard Variety, American Eskimo Dog will normally stand between 15 to 20 inches (40 to 50cm) tall at the shoulder. A healthy adult, Standard Variety, American Eskimo Dog will normally weigh between 18 to 35 pounds (8 to 16 kg). It is important to note that the weight of a healthy dog depends on how large the dog is – taller dogs should weigh more.

Breed Characteristics

The following section will give you a simplistic overview of the characteristics of a American Eskimo Dog. Our rating system is from 1 to 10 – with 1 being the lowest score and 10 being the highest.

- **Adaptability:** 8/10
- **Friendliness:** 10/10
- **Health:** 6/10
- **Ease of Grooming:** 6/10
- **Amount of Shedding:** 10/10
- **Trainability:** 8/10
- **Intelligence:** 10/10
- **Exercise Needed:** 8/10
- **Playfulness:** 10/10
- **Family Friendliness:** 10/10

THE AMERICAN FOXHOUND

The American Foxhound is a breed of dog that has a similar ancestral background to the English Foxhound. The breed was developed to be a scent hound with the primary focus of hunting foxes on their scent alone. The breed is known to have originated in the states of Maryland and Virginia, and is still the state dog of Virginia. The breed has a very musical and loud howl that can be heard for miles. The aided in the dogs desirability as a scent hound. However it also means that the American Foxhound is not suited well to city-living due to the fact that its howl is likely to disturb neighbors. The breed has a close, hard hound coat of a medium length. There are no standardized colorations for the American Foxhound as the breed was developed for practical hunting purposes rather than aesthetic purposes. However the most common coat colorations are: white, tan and black. The breed is known to be docile, affectionate and loving. They make perfect pets for households with small children and other small animals. The breed is known to be wary of strangers at first, but will warm up to people quickly. The breed is highly energetic and will need to be exercised properly to avoid them developing any destructive, hyper active, habits due to an abundance of energy.

Lifespan

An American Foxhound will normally live to be between 10 and 12 years old. However it is not uncommon for an American Foxhound to live to be as old as 13, providing that it does not develop any serious health issues.

Height and Weight

A fully grown American Foxhound will normally stand between 21 to 25 inches (53 to 63.5cm) tall at the shoulder. A healthy adult American Foxhound will normally weigh between 40 to 60 pounds (18 to 27kg). It is important to note that the weight of a healthy dog depends on how large the dog is – taller dogs should weigh more.

Breed Characteristics

The following section will give you a simplistic overview of the characteristics of a American Foxhound. Our rating system is from 1 to 10 – with 1 being the lowest score and 10 being the highest.

- **Adaptability:** 5/10
- **Friendliness:** 10/10
- **Health:** 8/10
- **Ease of Grooming:** 10/10

- ➢ **Amount of Shedding:** 6/10
- ➢ **Trainability:** 8/10
- ➢ **Intelligence:** 6/10
- ➢ **Exercise Needed:** 10/10
- ➢ **Playfulness:** 10/10
- ➢ **Family Friendliness:** 10/10

THE AMERICAN PITBULL TERRIER

The American Pitbull Terrier is a medium-sized, solidly built, short-haired breed of dog. The Pitbull Terrier was created by cross breeding Old English Terriers and Old English Bulldogs, to produce a combination of the Terrier's gameness and the strength and athletic ability of the bulldog. The Pitbull Terrier was created in England and was introduced to the United States of America in the 18th century. The American Pitbull Terrier was traditionally used in bloodsports such as bull baiting, bear baiting and dog fighting. After these bloodsports were outlawed in the mid-19th century, the American Pitbull Terrier was employed to catch semi wild cattle, hogs and other ranch animals. Due to the strength and athleticism they were also used to hunt and drive livestock. In modern times, the American Pitbull Terrier is mainly used as a police dog, therapy dog or as a family companion. An average American Pitbull Terrier will be confident, eager to please and greet guests, loving, loyal and obedient.

Lifespan

An American Pitbull Terrier will normally live to be between 12 and 14 years old. However it is not uncommon for a American Pitbull Terrier to live to be as old as 16, providing that it does not develop any serious health issues.

Height and Weight

A fully grown American Pitbull Terrier will normally stand between 17 to 20 inches (43 to 51 cm) tall at the shoulder. A healthy adult American Pitbull Terrier will normally weigh between 30 to 85 pounds (13.5 to 38.5kg). It is important to note that the weight of a healthy American Pitbull Terrier depends on how large the American Pitbull Terrier is – taller American Pitbull Terriers should weigh more.

Children and other Pets

American Pitbull Terrier make perfect companions for children of all ages. They are sturdily built and have an affectionate and patient temperament. However no dog, of any size, should be left unsupervised around small children to eliminate the risk of any potential accidents. It is important to teach your children to respect your pet. American Pitbull Terrier get on well with other small household pets, such as cats. However it is important to note that due to their dog-fighting background, the American Pitbull Terrier has a tendency to be aggressive to strange dogs. It is important to socialize your American Pitbull Terrier from puppyhood.

Breed Characteristics

The following section will give you a simplistic overview of the characteristics of a American Pitbull Terrier. Our rating system is from 1 to 10 – with 1 being the lowest score and 10 being the highest.

- **Adaptability:** 6/10
- **Friendliness:** 8/10
- **Health:** 8/10
- **Ease of Grooming:** 10/10
- **Amount of Shedding:** 8/10
- **Trainability:** 8/10
- **Intelligence:** 8/10
- **Exercise Needed:** 10/10
- **Playfulness:** 10/10
- **Family Friendliness:** 10/10

THE AMERICAN WATER SPANIEL

The American Water Spaniel (often abbreviated to AWS), is a breed of Spaniel that originates from the United States of America. The breed was developed in the state of Wisconsin during the 19th century by cross breeding the Irish and English Water Spaniels. Despite being the state dog of Wisconsin, they are actually a relatively rare breed of dog – there are thought to only be around 3,000 in existence! The American Water Spaniel is a medium-sized dog that has a double layered coat. The breed coat comes in a wide variety of colorations that are based in browns. The breed is an excellent and versatile hunting dog that performs well on land and in water. The breeds double layered coat is also water resistant, which allows the American Water Spaniel to hunt throughout the year. The breed was traditionally used to hunt small game, such as ducks and other birds. However in modern times, the American Water Spaniel is mainly kept as a companion dog that is perfect for apartment living due to their quiet, loyal, affectionate and obedient temperament.

Lifespan

A American Water Spaniel will normally live to be between 10 to 13 years old. However it is not uncommon for a American Water Spaniel to live to be as old as 15, providing that it does not develop any serious health issues.

Height and Weight

A fully grown American Water Spaniel will normally stand between 15 to 21 inches (38 to 53cm) tall at the shoulder. A healthy adult American Water Spaniel will normally weigh between 25 to 45 pounds (11 to 20.5kg). It is important to note that the weight of a healthy American Water Spaniel depends on how large the American Water Spaniel is – taller American Water Spaniels should weigh more.

Roaming

The American Water Spaniel is known to be an independent breed who loves to hunt. If you keep your American Water Spaniel in a garden without a fence, it is likely to go hunting on its own initiative. It is therefore important to make sure that your garden fence is sturdy and goes at least two foot underground.

Breed Characteristics

The following section will give you a simplistic overview of the characteristics of a American Water Spaniel. Our rating system is from 1 to 10 – with 1 being the lowest score and 10 being the highest.

- **Adaptability:** 6/10
- **Friendliness:** 8/10
- **Health:** 8/10
- **Ease of Grooming:** 6/10
- **Amount of Shedding:** 6/10
- **Trainability:** 8/10
- **Intelligence:** 6/10
- **Exercise Needed:** 8/10
- **Playfulness:** 10/10
- **Family Friendliness:** 10/10

THE ANATOLIAN SHEPHERD DOG

The Anatolian Shepherd Dog is a large breed of dog that originates from the Anatolian region located in central Turkey. The breed was developed to guard livestock and has a large, rugged and strong body with incredible hearing and eyesight. The breed is able to guard livestock using its great sense of sight and hearing as well as chase away predators using its large and agile body. The breed is highly intelligent, resourceful and independent due to the fact that they were tasked with guarding livestock without human assistance or direction. However, these traits make the Anatolian Shepherd Dog a potentially challenging pet. It is not recommended to keep a Anatolian Shepherd Dog as a first time dog owner as they need to be socialized and trained properly during their puppyhood. The breed is also known to roam and it is therefore considered best practice to microchip your Anatolian Shepherd Dog. The breed gets along well with small children and other household pets – providing the Anatolian Shepherd Dog has been correctly socialized in its early years.

Lifespan

An Anatolian Shepherd Dog will normally live to be between 10 and 12 years old. However it is not uncommon for an Anatolian Shepherd Dog to live to be as old as 13, providing that it does not develop any serious health issues.

Height and Weight

A fully grown Anatolian Shepherd Dog will normally stand between 27 to 30 inches (68.5 to 76 cm) tall at the shoulder. A healthy adult Anatolian Shepherd Dog will normally weigh between 80 to 150 pounds (27 to 68 kg). It is important to note that the weight of a healthy Anatolian Shepherd Dog depends on how large the Anatolian Shepherd Dog is – taller Anatolian Shepherd Dogs should weigh more.

Appearance

The Anatolian Shepherd Dog is a large muscular breed. They have thick necks, broad heads and strong well-muscled bodies. They have triangular ears and lips that are lie tight to their muzzle. There is no standardized colorations for the Anatolian Shepherd Dog coats. However white, sesame and cream colors are most common. The breed has a thick double coat and very thick fur around their thick necks.

Breed Characteristics

The following section will give you a simplistic

overview of the characteristics of a Anatolian Shepherd Dog. Our rating system is from 1 to 10 – with 1 being the lowest score and 10 being the highest.

- **Adaptability:** 6/10
- **Friendliness:** 4/10
- **Health:** 6/10
- **Ease of Grooming:** 8/10
- **Amount of Shedding:** 4/10
- **Trainability:** 6/10
- **Intelligence:** 8/10
- **Exercise Needed:** 6/10
- **Playfulness:** 10/10
- **Family Friendliness:** 6/10

THE APPENZELLER SENNENHUNDE

The Appenzeller Sennenhunde is a medium-size breed of dog. It is one of the four regional breeds of Sennenhunde-type dogs that originate from the Swiss Alps. The name 'Sennenhunde' comes from the Swiss word 'Senn' which refers to the herders from the Appenzell region in Switzerland. The breed was originally developed to be both a cattle herding dog and a flock guardian. The breed is extremely loyal and has been to known to give their own lives to protect their herd! In modern times they are mainly employed as an all-purpose farm dog or simply kept as a very loving and loyal companion dog. The breed has a heavy and athletic build and a distinctive tri-colored coat. They have small triangular ears which are set high on the face. The breed has a thick, shiny topcoat and a long and thick undercoat. The breed is easy to groom but sheds profusely. It is important to note that while Appenzeller Sennenhunde are very affectionate towards humans, they have been known to nip at small children to 'herd' them. If you plan on keeping a Appenzeller Sennenhunde in a household with small children, or other small pets, it is important to properly socialize your dog and put it through vigorous obedience training.

Lifespan

An Appenzeller Sennenhunde will normally live to be between 9 and 11 years old. However it is not uncommon for an Appenzeller Sennenhunde to live to be as old as 12, providing that it does not develop any serious health issues.

Height and Weight

A fully grown Appenzeller Sennenhunde will normally stand between 19 to 22 inches (48 to 56 cm) tall at the shoulder. A healthy adult Appenzeller Sennenhunde will normally weigh between 48 to 55 pounds (22 to 25 kg). It is important to note that the weight of a healthy Appenzeller Sennenhunde depends on how large the Appenzeller Sennenhunde is – taller Appenzeller Sennenhundes should weigh more.

Breed Characteristics

The following section will give you a simplistic overview of the characteristics of a Appenzeller Sennenhunde. Our rating system is from 1 to 10 – with 1 being the lowest score and 10 being the highest.

- **Adaptability:** 6/10
- **Friendliness:** 8/10
- **Health:** 7/10

- ➢ **Ease of Grooming:** 10/10
- ➢ **Amount of Shedding:** 6/10
- ➢ **Trainability:** 8/10
- ➢ **Intelligence:** 8/10
- ➢ **Exercise Needed:** 10/10
- ➢ **Playfulness:** 8/10
- ➢ **Family Friendliness:** 10/10

THE AUSTRALIAN CATTLE DOG

The Australian Cattle Dog, commonly known as simply the 'Cattle Dog' or by its initialism ADC, is a breed of herding dog. The breed originates from Australia and was developed to be able to drive cattle over long distances of rough terrain. The Australian Cattle Dog is a medium-sized, short-coated dog that occurs in two main colorations. The breed will either have a brown or black hair distributed throughout its white coat. Due to this speckling affect the breed has commonly be known as the 'red Heeler' or the 'blue Heeler' dog – depending if the speckled color is brown or black. The Australian Cattle Dog is known to be highly energetic and intelligent as well as having an independent streak. As a whole, the breed responds well to interesting and challenging structured training. The Australian Cattle Dog is also known to be highly affectionate and loyal. They make fantastic guards dogs and will happily guard places, people and possessions.

Lifespan

An Australian Cattle Dog will normally live to be between 10 and 12 years old. However it is not uncommon for an Australian Cattle Dog to live to be as old as 15, providing that it does not develop any serious

health issues.

Height and Weight

A fully grown Australian Cattle Dog will normally stand between 17 to 20 inches (43 to 51 cm) tall at the shoulder. A healthy adult Australian Cattle Dog will normally weigh between 30 to 50 pounds (13.5 to 22.5 kg). It is important to note that the weight of a healthy Australian Cattle Dog depends on how large the Australian Cattle Dog is – taller Australian Cattle Dogs should weigh more.

Breed Characteristics

The following section will give you a simplistic overview of the characteristics of a Australian Cattle Dog. Our rating system is from 1 to 10 – with 1 being the lowest score and 10 being the highest.

- **Adaptability:** 6/10
- **Friendliness:** 8/10
- **Health:** 10/10
- **Ease of Grooming:** 8/10
- **Amount of Shedding:** 6/10
- **Trainability:** 8/10
- **Intelligence:** 10/10
- **Exercise Needed:** 10/10

- **Playfulness:** 10/10
- **Family Friendliness:** 10/10

THE AUSTRALIAN SHEPHERD

The Australian Shepherd is a medium-sized breed of dog. Interestingly the Australian Shepherd was not actually developed in Australia, but was actually developed on the ranches in the Western United States of America during the 19th century. The breed rose to popularity after World War 2 due to an increase in western riding, horse shows, rodeos and the fact that they were used in Disney movies. The Australian Shepherd has always been a popular choice of working dog due to their versatility, intelligence, obedience and trainability. They are also known to be highly empathetic dogs. They have mainly been used as stock dogs and herding dogs. Like all working breeds of dog, the Australian Shepherd is incredibly energetic as will often rank highly in dog sports, such as agility and Frisbee, at dog shows. The breed is also commonly employed as search and rescue dogs, detection dogs, guide dogs, service dogs and therapy dogs. The breed has a similar aesthetic to the English Shepherd and Border Collie breeds. They have ranked within the top 20 most popular breeds within the United States of American since they rose to popularity.

Lifespan

A Australian Shepherd will normally live to be between 10 and 13 years old. However it is not uncommon for a Australian Shepherd to live to be as old as 15, providing that it does not develop any serious health issues.

Height and Weight

A fully grown Australian Shepherd will normally be between 18 and 23 inches (45.75 to 58.5cm) tall at the shoulder. A healthy adult Australian Shepherd will normally weigh between 40 and 65 pounds (18 to 30kg) – dependent upon their size.

Coat

Australian Shepherds have a medium-length water-resistant coat. Their coats are normally somewhat wavy and curly while being smooth and short on their heads. Australian Shepherds come in several colors: blue merle, red merle, tri color (white, black and tan) and black.

Breed Characteristics

The following section will give you a simplistic overview of the characteristics of a Australian Shepherd. Our rating system is from 1 to 10 – with 1 being the

lowest score and 10 being the highest.

- **Adaptability:** 6/10
- **Friendliness:** 8/10
- **Health:** 4/10
- **Ease of Grooming:** 1/10
- **Amount of Shedding:** 6/10
- **Trainability:** 10/10
- **Intelligence:** 10/10
- **Exercise Needed:** 10/10
- **Playfulness:** 10/10
- **Family Friendliness:** 10/10

THE AUSTRALIAN TERRIER

The Australian Terrier is a small breed of terrier type dog. The breed was developed in Australia, hence the name 'Australian Terrier.' However the breed is descended from the rough coated terriers that originate from Great Britain. The Australian Terrier, like most terrier type dogs, was developed to hunt mice, rats and other small vermin. The breed has small legs and a small compact body structure. They have a long shaggy coat that is not normally trimmed. The Australian Terrier is known to have a mischievous, upbeat and energetic personality and will always have a strong affectionate attachment to their family unit. The breed is known to be highly empathetic and will often match your mood – for example if you are sad your Australian Terrier will be quiet and subdued whereas if you are happy your Australian Terrier will be energetic and playful. It is important to note that the breed does not do well around other small animals. The Australian Terrier was developed to hunt and has a strong prey instinct. Due to this the breed is known to kill rabbits, squirrels and even small cats.

Lifespan

A Australian Terrier will normally live to be

between 10 and 12 years old. However it is not uncommon for a Australian Terrier to live to be as old as 15, providing that it does not develop any serious health issues.

Height and Weight

A fully grown Australian Terrier will normally stand between 10 to 11 inches (25.5 to 28 cm) tall at the shoulder. A healthy adult Australian Terrier will normally weigh between 14 to 16 pounds (6.5 to 7.25 kg). It is important to note that the weight of a healthy Australian Terrier depends on how large the Australian Terrier is – taller Australian Terriers should weigh more.

Coat

Despite having a long shaggy coat, the Australian Terrier barely sheds and is very easy to groom. Most owners choose to keep their pets coat long but it is also not uncommon for the breed's coat to be cut short. The breeds coat is rough to the touch and comes in three colorations: blue and tan, sandy and red.

Breed Characteristics

The following section will give you a simplistic overview of the characteristics of a Australian Terrier. Our rating system is from 1 to 10 – with 1 being the

lowest score and 10 being the highest.

- **Adaptability:** 6/10
- **Friendliness:** 6/10
- **Health:** 10/10
- **Ease of Grooming:** 10/10
- **Amount of Shedding:** 1/10
- **Trainability:** 8/10
- **Intelligence:** 10/10
- **Exercise Needed:** 8/10
- **Playfulness:** 10/10
- **Family Friendliness:** 8/10

THE AZAWAKH

The Azawakh is a breed of sighthound that originates from Africa. The breed was mainly developed by the nomads of the Sahara desert and in the countries Mali, Niger, Burkina Faso and southern Algeria. The Azawakh was originally developed to be a guard dog as well as having the ability to spot and hunt large and fast prey, such as gazelles and desert hares. The Azawakh is highly athletic and energetic due to match its original purpose and can achieve running speeds of up to 40 miles per hour! Unlike most sighthounds, the Azawakh is a pack hunter. They chase their prey as a pack and 'bump' the preys hindquarters until it reaches the point of exhaustion. The breed is also known to guard as a pack. If a single Azawakh senses danger they will bark and alert the rest of the pack, who will group around the alpha dog and either scare off or attack the predator or source of danger. The Azawakh is an incredibly hardy animal: it has incredibly high physical endurance and can happily run in heats of over 100 degrees Fahrenheit (which would kill a greyhound)! However the Azawakh is known to become whiney and unhappy in cold and wet climates, and it is therefore not recommended to own a Azawakh in a country that is not hot for the majority of the year. The breed is known to create a strong bond with their owners but as still able to function independently due to their high levels of intelligence. The Azawakh is also known to be affectionate, loving and loyal. The breed is known to be good around small children as they have traditionally always served the nomads of the Sahara as 'protectors,' when they are not being used to hunt.

Lifespan

A Azawakh will normally live to be between 10 and 12 years old. However it is not uncommon for a Azawakh to live to be as old as 15, providing that it does not develop any serious health issues.

Height and Weight

A fully grown Azawakh will normally stand between 23 to 29 inches (58.5 to 73.5 cm) tall at the shoulder. A healthy adult Azawakh will normally weigh between 33 to 55 pounds (15 to 25 kg). It is important to note that the weight of a healthy Azawakh depends on how large the Azawakh is – taller Azawakhs should weigh more.

Coat

The Azawakh has a short and smooth coat that covers with majority of its body. The breed will normally have a hairless, or nearly hairless, stomach to help them combat high temperatures. The Azawakh's coat comes in a variety of colorations including: clear, sandy, dark red, white, black, blue, gray, brindle and a wide variety of browns.

Breed Characteristics

The following section will give you a simplistic overview of the characteristics of a Azawakh. Our rating system is from 1 to 10 – with 1 being the lowest score and 10 being the highest.

- **Adaptability:** 6/10
- **Friendliness:** 7/10
- **Health:** 7/10
- **Ease of Grooming:** 10/10
- **Amount of Shedding:** 6/10
- **Trainability:** 6/10
- **Intelligence:** 6/10
- **Exercise Needed:** 8/10
- **Playfulness:** 6/10
- **Family Friendliness:** 9/10

THE BARBET

The Barbet is a breed of medium-sized water dog that originates from France. The breeds name, 'Barbet,' comes from the French word *'barbe'* which means 'beard,' which is a reference to the breeds unique coat. Traditionally, the breed has been used as a gun dog, a guard dog and as a sailor's assistant. The Barbet is considered to be a rare breed and can only be officially registered in France, Holland, Germany, Sweden and Canada. However the breed is gaining popularity as a household pet, mainly in Scandinavian countries and North America, due to its flexibility and affectionate personality. The breed comes in a variety of colorations but it is most common for a Barbet's coat to be black, white and black or brown. It is not uncommon for the Barbet to have white paws or a white crest of hair on its chest. The breed has a very unique and characteristic coat. The Barbet's coat is very long and thick and must be groomed on a regular basis to avoid matting. If a Barbet's coat is not groomed on a regular basis it is not uncommon for their coat to shed huge chunks of hair. The Barbet is known to be friendly, obedient, intelligent and affectionate. The Barbet is very family orientated and will want to spend its time in the same room as its family members. The breed is also known to be very gentle which makes it a perfect for families with small children or the elderly.

Lifespan

A Barbet will normally live to be between 10 and 13 years old. However it is not uncommon for a Barbet to live to be as old as 15, providing that it does not develop any serious health issues.

Height and Weight

A fully grown Barbet will normally stand between 20 to 25 inches (51 to 63.5cm) tall at the shoulder. A healthy adult Barbet will normally weigh between 37 to 62 pounds (16.75 to 28kg). It is important to note that the weight of a healthy Barbet depends on how large the Barbet is – taller Barbets should weigh more.

Breed Characteristics

The following section will give you a simplistic overview of the characteristics of a Barbet. Our rating system is from 1 to 10 – with 1 being the lowest score and 10 being the highest.

- **Adaptability:** 6/10
- **Friendliness:** 8/10
- **Health:** 8/10
- **Ease of Grooming:** 1/10

- ➢ **Amount of Shedding:** 4/10
- ➢ **Trainability:** 6/10
- ➢ **Intelligence:** 8/10
- ➢ **Exercise Needed:** 7/10
- ➢ **Playfulness:** 8/10
- ➢ **Family Friendliness:** 10/10

THE BASENJI

The modern Basenji is a breed of hunting dog that originates from Africa. However the Basenji is believed to be a descendant from Chinese and southeast Asian wolves. The Basenji does not have a traditional bark but rather a unique yodeling sound. The yodeling, rather than barking, sound is due to the breeds strangely shaped larynx. This trait has given the Basenji the nickname of the 'soundless dog.' Traditionally the breed was bred for its independent thinking, which makes the Basenji incredibly hard to train. It is possible to train a Basenji to an extent, but it is common for a Basenji to only obey humans when it feels like it. It is important to note that Basenji do not do well in homes with small children or other small animals due to their hunting history. Basenji will commonly chase cats and other small pets around the household – especially if they have not been exercised properly. To minimize the chance of your Basenji 'hunting' your other pets it is important to socialize it with other animals during the Basenji's puppyhood. The breed is highly energetic and is likely to develop destructive behaviors if they are not exercised thoroughly on a regular basis. The breed is highly affectionate and will want to spend its time relaxing with its family unit – the Basenji is prone to following people from room to room.

Lifespan

A Basenji will normally live to be between 10 and 11 years old. However it is not uncommon for a Basenji to live to be as old as 13, providing that it does not develop any serious health issues.

Height and Weight

A fully grown Basenji will normally stand between 16 to 17 inches (40.5 to 43 cm) tall at the shoulder. A healthy adult Basenji will normally weigh between 22 to 24 pounds (10 to 11 kg). It is important to note that the weight of a healthy Basenji depends on how large the Basenji is – taller Basenjis should weigh more.

Coat

The Basenji has a short, fine coat. Their coats come in the following four colorations: chestnut red, black, brindle (black stripes on a chestnut body) and tricolor (black and chestnut). All Basenji will have a white chest, white feet and a white tip at the end of their tail.

BREED CHARACTERISTICS

The following section will give you a simplistic overview of the characteristics of a Basenji. Our rating system is from 1 to 10 – with 1 being the lowest score and 10 being the highest.

- **Adaptability:** 8/10
- **Friendliness:** 10/10
- **Health:** 8/10
- **Ease of Grooming:** 10/10
- **Amount of Shedding:** 1/10
- **Trainability:** 8/10
- **Intelligence:** 8/10
- **Exercise Needed:** 6/10
- **Playfulness:** 3/10
- **Family Friendliness:** 10/10

THE BASSET HOUND

The Basset Hound is a short-legged breed of hound dog. The name 'Basset' is derived from the French word *'bas,'* which translates to 'low,' which is an obvious reference to the breeds low body. The Basset Hound's short legs are due to a form of dwarfism. However their short stature can be deceiving! Due to the length of their body, the Basset Hound is able to reach table tops that a dog of a similar size could never reach. The breed was developed to have an incredible sense of smell and therefore falls under the scent hound family of dog. The Basset Hound was originally developed to hunt hare and other small animals. It is believed that the Basset Hound's sense of smell, for tracking purposes, is second only to the Bloodhound. The breed normally has a bicolored or tricolored coat of standard hound colorations (black, white, tan and off-lemon yellow). The breed has a medium-short coat that has a hard but smooth texture. Despite the short length of their coat, the breed is known to shed frequently. The Basset Hound is known to be a highly intelligent, friendly and outgoing breed. They are also known to be gentle which makes them a perfect breed for any household with small children or other animals.

Lifespan

A Basset Hound will normally live to be around 9 to 11 years old. However it is not uncommon for a Basset Hound to live to be as old as 12, providing that it does not develop any serious health issues.

Height and Weight

A fully grown Basset Hound will normally stand between 10 to 14 inches (25.5 to 35.5 cm) tall at the shoulder. A healthy adult Basset Hound will normally weigh between 50 to 65 pounds (22.5 to 29.5kg). It is important to note that the weight of a healthy Basset Hound depends on how large the Basset Hound is – taller Basset Hounds should weigh more.

General Health

Due to poor breeding practices, and imbreeding, the Basset Hound is prone to certain genetic disease. This does not mean that all Basset Hounds will develop hereditary disease, but they are more likely too. If you are purchasing a puppy it is important to make sure that neither of the puppy's parents have any serious health issues.

Breed Characteristics

The following section will give you a simplistic overview of the characteristics of a Basset Hound. Our rating system is from 1 to 10 – with 1 being the lowest score and 10 being the highest.

- **Adaptability:** 6/10
- **Friendliness:** 10/10
- **Health:** 2/10
- **Ease of Grooming:** 10/10
- **Amount of Shedding:** 8/10
- **Trainability:** 8/10
- **Intelligence:** 8/10
- **Exercise Needed:** 3/10
- **Playfulness:** 4/10
- **Family Friendliness:** 10/10

THE BEAGLE

The Beagle is a small sized breed of scent hound that has been bred for the specific purpose of hunting hare. The Beagle has approximately 220 million scent receptors within its nose – which is over 40 times as many as humans! Due to their incredible sense of smell and ingrained ability to track, the Beagle is often employed as a detection dog within he agriculture and food industries. Breeds similar to the Beagle have existed for the last 2500 years, but the modern day Beagle was developed in the United Kingdom in the early 1800s. Due to its size, good temperament and lack of inherited health issues, the Beagle has become a very popular household pet.

Lifespan

Most Beagles will live to be between 8 and 10 years old. However it is not uncommon for a Beagle to live for as long as 15 years if they do not develop any serious health issues.

Height and Weight

On average an adult Beagle will stand at around 13 to 15 inches tall (33 to 38cm). They also normally weigh between 18 and 30 pounds (8 to 13kg). It is important to remember that males are normally slightly larger and heavier than females.

Children and Other Pets

Beagles are very compassionate dogs and will bond with everyone in your family, especially children. It is important to remember that Beagles are a very playful breed and should be supervised while with children. Beagles tend to use their mouth during play, which can frighten some small children. It is important to teach your children how to approach your Beagle to help keep it calm. Beagles are pack dogs and enjoy the company of other dogs and animals (such as house rabbits and cats).

Breed Characteristics

The following section will give you a simplistic overview of the characteristics of a Beagle. Our rating system is from 1 to 10 – with 1 being the lowest score and 10 being the highest.

- **Adaptability:** 6/10
- **Friendliness:** 10/10
- **Health:** 6/10
- **Ease of Grooming:** 8/10
- **Amount of Shedding:** 6/10
- **Trainability:** 8/10

- ➢ **Intelligence:** 7/10
- ➢ **Exercise Needed:** 10/10
- ➢ **Playfulness:** 10/10
- ➢ **Family Friendliness:** 10/10

THE BEARDED COLLIE

The Bearded Collie (also commonly known as a 'Beardie') is a breed of herding dog. Traditionally the breed was primarily used by Scottish shepherds due to its hardy and reliably nature. The breed also has a thick double coat which allows it to work throughout the harshest weather conditions. The Bearded Collie is also known to be highly intelligent and independent and is more than capable of minding a herd alone. However, the Bearded Collie has become dramatically less common as a working dog over the last few decades and has secured itself as a popular choice for a family companion dog. The Bearded Collie makes an excellent family pet due to friendly, enthusiastic and playful nature. It is recommended for a Bearded Collie to live in an energetic household to match the high level of energy that the Bearded Collie has. It is not uncommon for a Bearded Collie to develop destructive behaviors if they have not been exercised properly. The Bearded Collie needs to be groomed on a regular basis to prevent its long double coat from becoming matted. Some owners choose to keep their Bearded Collie's coat short, in a 'Puppy Cut,' to ease the intensive grooming. The Bearded Collie coat comes in the following colorations: black, brown, blue and fawn. Each coat coloration will either have white or tan markings across the majority of its body.

Lifespan

A Bearded Collie will normally live to be between 10 and 12 years old. However it is not uncommon for a Bearded Collie to live to be as old as 14, providing that it does not develop any serious health issues.

Height and Weight

A fully grown Bearded Collie will normally stand between 20 to 22 inches (50.8 to 56 cm) tall at the shoulder. A healthy adult Bearded Collie will normally weigh between 45 to 55 pounds (20.5 to 25kg). It is important to note that the weight of a healthy Bearded Collie depends on how large the Bearded Collie is – taller Bearded Collies should weigh more.

Breed Characteristics

The following section will give you a simplistic overview of the characteristics of a Bearded Collie. Our rating system is from 1 to 10 – with 1 being the lowest score and 10 being the highest.

- **Adaptability:** 6/10
- **Friendliness:** 10/10
- **Health:** 6/10

- ➢ **Ease of Grooming:** 4/10
- ➢ **Amount of Shedding:** 8/10
- ➢ **Trainability:** 8/10
- ➢ **Intelligence:** 8/10
- ➢ **Exercise Needed:** 8/10
- ➢ **Playfulness:** 10/10
- ➢ **Family Friendliness:** 10/10

THE BEDLINGTON TERRIER

The Bedlington Terrier is a small breed of dog that is named after the small mining town of Bedlington, in Northumberland, in North East England. The Bedlington Terrier is also commonly known as the 'Rothbury Terrier,' the 'Rodbery Terrier' and the 'Rothbury's Lamb.' The breed was originally developed to hunt small vermin in mines. However in recent years the Bedlington Terrier has been used in dog races, dog sports, dog conformation shows, as a companion dog and as a general family pet. The breed is known to be extremely quick, athletic and capable of out swimming many water dog breeds. The breed has a unique coat which gives it a similar aesthetic appearance to a lamb. Their coats normally come in the following four colorations: white, liver, blue or sandy. The Bedlington Terrier is known to be affectionate, playful, friendly and incredibly loyal to their family unit. However, it is important to know that the Bedlington Terrier is a highly jealous breed and is not afraid of 'fighting' or attacking other dogs, or pets, that its owners are showing attention to.

Lifespan

A Bedlington Terrier will normally live to be between 12 and 14 years old. However it is not uncommon for a Bedlington Terrier to live to be as old as 16, providing that they do not develop any serious health issues.

Height and Weight

A fully grown Bedlington Terrier will normally stand between 15 to 16 inches (38 to 40 cm) tall at the shoulder. A healthy adult Bedlington Terrier will normally weigh between 17 to 23 pounds (7.7 to 10.5kg). It is important to note that the weight of a healthy Bedlington Terrier depends on how large the Bedlington Terrier is – taller Bedlington Terriers should weigh more.

BREED CHARACTERISTICS

The following section will give you a simplistic overview of the characteristics of a Bedlington Terrier. Our rating system is from 1 to 10 – with 1 being the lowest score and 10 being the highest.

- **Adaptability:** 8/10
- **Friendliness:** 10/10
- **Health:** 6/10
- **Ease of Grooming:** 1/10
- **Amount of Shedding:** 10/10
- **Trainability:** 8/10

- ➢ **Intelligence:** 10/10
- ➢ **Exercise Needed:** 8/10
- ➢ **Playfulness:** 10/10
- ➢ **Family Friendliness:** 10/10

THE BELGIAN MALINOIS

The Belgian Malinois is a medium-to-large breed of dog. The breed is also commonly referred to as the 'Belgian Shepherd,' due to its similar appearance to the German Shepherd. The name 'Malinois' is derived from the French word 'Malines,' which is the French name for the breed's city of origin. Traditionally the breed has been used as a working dog as has mainly been tasked with odor based detection (such as bomb detection narcotic detection) and in arson investigations. The breed is also commonly used as a general purposes guard dog, police dog and as a search and rescue dog. Due to the breed being developed for its physical traits, and ability for its sense of smell, the Belgian Malinois can vary greatly in appearance. However most pure breed Belgian Malinois will have a short coat, a medium-to-large muscular body and large pointed ears. It is most common for a Belgian Malinois's coat to come in the following colorations: black, fawn, mahogany and tan. The breed has a black mask-like marking over its muzzle in a similar fashion to the German Shepherd. The Belgian Malinois is known to be a highly intelligent, athletic, friendly, loyal and protective breed. They make for perfect family pets as they are very gentle and affectionate towards small children and other small animals. The breed is likewise very easy to train due to the fact that they are very reward orientated.

Lifespan

A Belgian Malinois will normally live to be between 10 and 12 years old. However it is not uncommon for a Belgian Malinois to live to be as old as 15, providing that it does not develop any serious health issues.

Height and Weight

A fully grown Belgian Malinois will normally stand between 22 to 26 inches (56 to 66 cm) tall at the shoulder. A healthy adult Belgian Malinois will normally weigh between 40 to 80 pounds (18 to 36kg). It is important to note that the weight of a healthy Belgian Malinois depends on how large the Belgian Malinois is – taller Belgian Malinois should weigh more.

Breed Characteristics

The following section will give you a simplistic overview of the characteristics of a Belgian Malinois. Our rating system is from 1 to 10 – with 1 being the lowest score and 10 being the highest.

- **Adaptability:** 6/10
- **Friendliness:** 8/10
- **Health:** 8/10

- **Ease of Grooming:** 10/10
- **Amount of Shedding:** 3/10
- **Trainability:** 8/10
- **Intelligence:** 10/10
- **Exercise Needed:** 10/10
- **Playfulness:** 10/10
- **Family Friendliness:** 10/10

THE BELGIAN SHEEPDOG

The Belgian Sheepdog (also commonly known as the Belgian Shepherd) is a breed of medium-to-large-sized herding dog. As the name suggests, the breed originates from Belgium and is similar to other herding dogs from that region such as: the German Shepherd, the Dutch Shepherd and the Briard. There are four different varieties of Belgian Sheepdog: the Groenendael, the Laekenois, the Tervuren and the Malinois. Each variety of Belgian Sheepdog has a different coat coloration and hair texture.

- The Groenendael: The Groenendael has a fairly long haired double coat. This varieties' hair texture is stiff, tight and thick. The Groenendael generally has a solid black coat coloration.
- The Laekenois: The Laekenois has a wiry coat texture of a medium length. This variant normally has a light brown coat coloration and lacks the black ears and face mask present on the other variants.
- The Malinois: The Malinois is a short haired variant. This variant normally comes in a tan brown coloration and will commonly have white markings on its toes and chest.

- <u>The Tervuren</u>: The Tervuen has a similar coat coloration to the Malinois, but tends to be slightly more grey. This variant has long hair and a thick double coat like the Groenendael. Like the Malinois, it occasionally has white markings on its chest and toes.

As a whole the Belgian Sheepdog is known to be highly intelligent, alert, sensitive, affectionate and loyal. They also make great household pets for families with children, due to their playful and fun loving nature. The breed is highly energetic and is likely to develop destructive behaviors, out of boredom, if they are not exercised properly.

Lifespan

A Belgian Sheep dog will normally live to be between 10 and 11 years old. However it is not uncommon for a Belgian Sheepdog to live to be as old as 12, providing they do not develop any serious health issues.

Height and Weight

A fully grown Belgian Sheepdog will normally stand between 22 to 26 inches (56 to 66 cm) tall at the shoulder. A healthy adult Belgian Sheepdog will normally weigh between 60 to 75 pounds (27 to 34kg). It is important to note that the weight of a healthy Belgian Sheepdog depends on how large the Belgian Sheepdog is – taller Belgian Sheepdogs should weigh more.

Breed Characteristics

The following section will give you a simplistic overview of the characteristics of a Belgian Sheepdog. Our rating system is from 1 to 10 – with 1 being the lowest score and 10 being the highest.

- **Adaptability:** 8/10
- **Friendliness:** 10/10
- **Health:** 6/10
- **Ease of Grooming:** 6/10
- **Amount of Shedding:** 10/10
- **Trainability:** 8/10
- **Intelligence:** 10/10
- **Exercise Needed:** 10/10
- **Playfulness:** 10/10
- **Family Friendliness:** 10/10

THE BELGIAN TERVUREN

The Belgian Tervuren, commonly known simply as the 'Tervuren,' is a breed working dog from Belgium. The breed is named after a small village in Belgium. Traditionally, the Belgian Tervuren is a variant of the Belgian Sheepdog. However in 1959 the American Kennel Club recognized the Belgian Tervuren as being a breed in its own right. The Belgian Tervuren is a medium-sized, athletic and muscular herding type of dog. It has a thick double coat that normally comes in a mahogany coloration with hints of black speckled throughout its coat. The breed also has a black mask that covers its muzzle which gives it a similar appearance to the German Shepherd. As a whole the Belgian Tervuren is a highly energetic and intelligent dog. They need constant attention and exercise to keep them occupied. Like most working dogs, the breed is known to develop destructive habits if they are not exercised properly. The Belgian Tervuren is, generally, not recommended for a first time dog owner due to their high maintenance level.

Lifespan

A Belgian Tervuren will normally live to be between 10 and 11 years old. However it is not uncommon for a

Belgian Tervuren to live to be as old as 13, providing that it does not develop any serious health issues.

Height and Weight

A fully grown Belgian Tervuren will normally stand between 21 to 26 inches (53 to 66 cm) tall at the shoulder. A healthy adult Belgian Tervuren will normally weigh between 40 to 70 pounds (18to 31.75kg). It is important to note that the weight of a healthy Belgian Tervuren depends on how large the Belgian Tervuren is – taller Belgian Tervurens should weigh more.

The Other Variants

As previously mentioned the X is one of four Belgian Sheepdog variants. The other three variants are the:

- The Groenendael: The Groenendael has a fairly long haired double coat. This varieties' hair texture is stiff, tight and thick. The Groenendael generally has a solid black coat coloration.
- The Laekenois: The Laekenois has a wiry coat texture of a medium length. This variant normally has a light brown coat coloration and lacks the black ears and face mask

present on the other variants.
- <u>The Malinois</u>: The Malinois is a short haired variant. This variant normally comes in a tan brown coloration and will commonly have white markings on its toes and chest.

Breed Characteristics

The following section will give you a simplistic overview of the characteristics of a Belgian Tervuren. Our rating system is from 1 to 10 – with 1 being the lowest score and 10 being the highest.

- **Adaptability:** 6/10
- **Friendliness:** 6/10
- **Health:** 6/10
- **Ease of Grooming:** 6/10
- **Amount of Shedding:** 8/10
- **Trainability:** 8/10
- **Intelligence:** 10/10
- **Exercise Needed:** 8/10
- **Playfulness:** 10/10
- **Family Friendliness:** 8/10

THE BERGER PICARD

The Berger Picard is a breed of herding dog that originates from France. The breed is named after the Picardie region of France where they were developed. The Berger Picard is also commonly known as the 'Picardy Shepherd,' the 'Picardy Sheepdog,' and simply as the 'Picard.' The breed nearly went extinct during World War 1 and World War 2 and is still considered to be a rare breed of dog. Like most working dogs, the Berger Picard has a well-muscled and medium-sized body. Due to the breed being developed to work, the Berger Picard is a highly energetic breed. It is important to make sure that you provide your Berger Picard with high levels of exercise as an abundance of energy and boredom will lead it to develop destructive behaviors. The breed is known to be highly intelligent and has become an increasingly popular choice for dog sports, obedience and herding competitions. As a whole the Berger Picard is known to be people-orientated, loyal, affectionate, playful and friendly. Due to the breed's herding history it is important to make sure that you properly socialize your Berger Picard to avoid it accidentally 'herding' small children and other household pets.

Lifespan

A Berger Picard will commonly live to be between 12 and 13 years old. However it is not uncommon for a Berger Picard to live to be as old as 14, providing that it does not develop any serious health issues.

Height and Weight

A fully grown Berger Picard will normally stand between 21 to 25 inches (53 to 63.5cm) tall at the shoulder. A healthy adult Berger Picard will normally weigh between 50 to 70 pounds (22.5 to 31.75kg). It is important to note that the weight of a healthy Berger Picard depends on how large the Berger Picard is – taller Berger Picards should weigh more.

Breed Characteristics

The following section will give you a simplistic overview of the characteristics of a Berger Picard. Our rating system is from 1 to 10 – with 1 being the lowest score and 10 being the highest.

- **Adaptability:** 8/10
- **Friendliness:** 8/10
- **Health:** 10/10
- **Ease of Grooming:** 10/10
- **Amount of Shedding:** 8/10

- ➢ **Trainability:** 6/10
- ➢ **Intelligence:** 10/10
- ➢ **Exercise Needed:** 10/10
- ➢ **Playfulness:** 10/10
- ➢ **Family Friendliness:** 10/10

THE BERNESE MOUNTAIN DOG

The Bernese Mountain Dog, also commonly known as the 'Bemer Sennenhund,' is a large-sized breed of dog that originates from the Swiss Alps. The breed was originally used as a mountain dog, an all-purpose farm dog and as a draft dog. The Bernese Mountain Dog is a large muscular breed of dog that has a distinctive tri-colored coat (mainly black and white with rust color marking around its eyes and chest). As a whole the Bernese Mountain Dog is known to be docile, friendly, good natured and self-assured. Like with all big dogs, the Bernese Mountain Dog needs to be properly socialized during its puppyhood. If properly socialized, a Bernese Mountain Dog can make a perfect companion for any small child and will live peacefully with other household pets. Due to the breeds working history, the Bernese Mountain Dog is a highly energetic breed that thrives in the outdoors. It is important to make sure that you properly exercise your Bernese Mountain Dog to avoid it developing any destructive behaviors due to boredom. Despite being a highly energetic breed the Bernese Mountain Dog does not have high levels of endurance, which makes exercising it very easy.

The Other Breeds of Sennenhund

The Bernese Mountain Dog is one of the four breeds within the Sennenhund-type of dog. The other three breeds within this typing are:

- Greater Swiss Mountain Dog
- Appenzeller
- Entlebucher Mountain Dog

Lifespan

A Bernese Mountain Dog will normally live to be around 6 years old. However it is not uncommon for a Bernese Mountain Dog to live to be as old as 8, providing that it does not develop any serious health issues.

Height and Weight

A fully grown Bernese Mountain Dog will normally stand between 23 to 28 inches (58.5 to 71cm) tall at the shoulder. A healthy adult Bernese Mountain Dog will normally weigh between 70 to 115 pounds (154 to 253.5kg). It is important to note that the weight of a healthy Bernese Mountain Dog depends on how large the Bernese Mountain Dog is – taller Bernese Mountain Dogs should weigh more.

Breed Characteristics

The following section will give you a simplistic overview of the characteristics of a Bernese Mountain Dog. Our rating system is from 1 to 10 – with 1 being the lowest score and 10 being the highest.

- **Adaptability:** 4/10
- **Friendliness:** 10/10
- **Health:** 2/10
- **Ease of Grooming:** 10/10
- **Amount of Shedding:** 6/10
- **Trainability:** 8/10
- **Intelligence:** 10/10
- **Exercise Needed:** 8/10
- **Playfulness:** 8/10
- **Family Friendliness:** 10/10

THE BICHON FRISE

The Bichon Frise is a small breed of dog that is part of the 'Bichon' typing. The 'Bichon' typing is believed to have gotten its name from the French word *'Barbichon'* which translates to 'small poodle.' The breed is a member of the 'Non-Sporting Group' of dog breeds in the United States and a member of the 'Toy Dog Group' in the United Kingdom. The Bichon Frise descends from the Barbet, Water Spaniels and the Poodle. The Bichon Frise, like the other dogs within the 'Bichon' typing, originally comes from the Mediterranean and was taken to France in the early 14th century by sailors. The breed quickly became popular with the nobility of Europe: most notably King Francis the 1st of France and King Henry the 3rd of England. As a whole the breed is known to be playful, affectionate, friendly and gentle. They are known to love human company and will often be highly demanding of their owner's attention. The breed is also known to be highly sociable and will easily get along with strangers, small children and other household pets. The Bichon Frise is also known to be highly obedient if they are trained consistently from puppyhood.

Lifespan

A Bichon Frise will normally live to be between 10

and 12 years old. However it is not uncommon for a Bichon Frise to live to be as old as 15, providing that it does not develop any serious health issues.

Height and Weight

A fully grown Bichon Frise will normally stand between 9 to 11 inches (23 to 28cm) tall at the shoulder. A healthy adult Bichon Frise will normally weigh between 7 to 12 pounds (3 to 5.5kg). It is important to note that the weight of a healthy Bichon Frise depends on how large the Bichon Frise is – taller Bichon Frises should weigh more.

Coat

The Bichon Frise has a double-coat that is always white. The breed has a soft and densely packed undercoat and a course outer coat. The coat stands away from the Bichon Frise's body which gives the breed a 'powder puff' appearance. It is common for owner's to trim their Bichon Frise's coat short but some owner's allow their pet's coat to grow longer.

Breed Characteristics

The following section will give you a simplistic overview of the characteristics of a Bichon Frise. Our rating system is from 1 to 10 – with 1 being the lowest score and 10 being the highest.

- ➢ **Adaptability:** 8/10
- ➢ **Friendliness:** 10/10
- ➢ **Health:** 8/10
- ➢ **Ease of Grooming:** 1/10
- ➢ **Amount of Shedding:** 3/10
- ➢ **Trainability:** 6/10
- ➢ **Intelligence:** 10/10
- ➢ **Exercise Needed:** 8/10
- ➢ **Playfulness:** 10/10
- ➢ **Family Friendliness:** 10/10

THE BLACK AND TAN COONHOUND

The Black and Tan Coonhound is a breed of dog that originates in the United States of America. The breed was developed by mixing the Bloodhound and the Black and Tan Virginia Foxhound. The breed was originally developed for the purpose of being a game dog. The Black and Tan Coonhound uses its incredible sense of smell to track its prey, by scent alone, and chase them up a tree. The Black and Tan Coonhound is also known to have a courageous temperament and an athletic build which makes it proficient at hunting larger prey such as deer, wolf, bear and cougar. In 1945 the Black and Tan Coonhound became the first of six varieties of Coonhound to be recognized by the American Kennel Club. The other five varieties where not recognized until 2010 and are the Redbone Coonhound, the Plott Hound, the Bluetick Coonhound, the English Coonhound and the Treeing Walker Coonhound. The Black and Tan Coonhound makes an excellent household pet for an experienced dog owner. The breed is known to have a mellow, affectionate and loyal temperament. Inexperienced dog owners may have trouble controlling the Black and Tan Coonhound's desire to track and hunt prey and it is known to wander if it catches a scent.

Lifespan

A Black and Tan Coonhound will normally live to be between 9 and 11 years old. However it is not uncommon for a Black and Tan Coonhound to live to be as old as 12, providing that it does not develop any serious health issues.

Height and Weight

A fully grown Black and Tan Coonhound will normally stand between 23 to 28 inches (58.5 to 71cm) tall at the shoulder. A healthy adult Black and Tan Coonhound will normally weigh between 75 to 100 pounds (34 to 45.3kg). It is important to note that the weight of a healthy Black and Tan Coonhound depends on how large the Black and Tan Coonhound is – taller Black and Tan Coonhounds should weigh more.

Breed Characteristics

The following section will give you a simplistic overview of the characteristics of a Black and Tan Coonhound. Our rating system is from 1 to 10 – with 1 being the lowest score and 10 being the highest.

- **Adaptability:** 6/10
- **Friendliness:** 10/10
- **Health:** 10/10

- ➢ **Ease of Grooming:** 8/10
- ➢ **Amount of Shedding:** 10/10
- ➢ **Trainability:** 8/10
- ➢ **Intelligence:** 10/10
- ➢ **Exercise Needed:** 10/10
- ➢ **Playfulness:** 10/10
- ➢ **Family Friendliness:** 10/10

THE BLACK RUSSIAN TERRIER

The Black Russian Terrier is a breed of dog that was developed in the USSR, in the Red Star Kennel, during the late 1940s. The breed is commonly known as the 'Tchiorny Terrier' and in its abbreviated form 'BRT.' The Black Russian Terrier was originally developed to be used as a military and working dog. Despite the breeds name including 'Terrier,' the Black Russian Terrier is not actually part of the terrier grouping of dogs. The breed is believed to be a mixture of seventeen different breeds including the Giant Schnauzer, the Rottweiler, The Airedale and the Newfoundland. In modern times the breed is normally employed as a work dog, a guard dog, a sporting dog or simply as a companion dog. The Black Russian Terrier has a double coat with a coarse outercoat and a slightly softer undercoat. The breed's coat is known to have a hard and dense texture. It is typical for owner's to trim their Black Russian Terrier's coat to create a 'beard' and 'eyebrows' on the dog's face – in a similar fashion to Schnauzers. The Black Russian Terrier will always have a predominantly black coat but may have a few grey hair scattered across its body. As a whole the breed is known to be calm, confident, intelligent and protective.

Lifespan

A Black Russian Terrier will normally live to be between 8 and 10 years old. However it is not uncommon for a Black Russian Terrier to live to be as old as 12, providing that it does not develop any serious health issues.

Height and Weight

A fully grown Black Russian Terrier will normally stand between 27 to 31 inches (69 to 78.75cm) tall at the shoulder. A healthy adult Black Russian Terrier will normally weigh between 80 to 140 pounds (36 to 63.5kg). It is important to note that the weight of a healthy Black Russian Terrier depends on how large the Black Russian Terrier is – taller Black Russian Terriers should weigh more.

Breed Characteristics

The following section will give you a simplistic overview of the characteristics of a Black Russian Terrier. Our rating system is from 1 to 10 – with 1 being the lowest score and 10 being the highest.

- **Adaptability:** 6/10
- **Friendliness:** 8/10
- **Health:** 6/10

- ➢ **Ease of Grooming:** 5/10
- ➢ **Amount of Shedding:** 5/10
- ➢ **Trainability:** 8/10
- ➢ **Intelligence:** 8/10
- ➢ **Exercise Needed:** 8/10
- ➢ **Playfulness:** 10/10
- ➢ **Family Friendliness:** 10/10

THE BLOODHOUND

The Bloodhound, also commonly known as the 'Sleuth Hound,' is a large breed of scent hound that was originally developed to be able to hunt deer and wild boar. During the Middle Ages the Bloodhound was also used to track people. The breed has an incredible sense of smell that allows it to discern specific human scents across great distances. The mixture of the breeds innate hunting instinct and sense of smell has lead the Bloodhound to be used by modern day police and law enforcement across the world. The breed primarily is used to track escaped prisoners, lost children, missing people and lost pets. However due to the breeds tireless tracking, when following a scent, they can be difficult to obedience train. The Bloodhound has an affectionate and gentle temperament which has lead the breed to become an ever increasingly popular household pet. The breed has a loose and thin coat that sheds seasonally. The Bloodhound's coat comes in three common colorations: black and tan, liver and tan, and red. It is not uncommon for a Bloodhound to have flecks of white throughout its coat and to have white patches on its feet, chest and tip of its tail.

Lifespan

A Bloodhound will normally live for between 11 and 13 years. However it is not uncommon for a Bloodhound to live to be as old as 15, providing that it does not develop any serious health issues.

Height and Weight

A fully grown Bloodhound will normally stand between 24 to 28 inches (61 to 71cm) tall at the shoulder. A healthy adult Bloodhound will normally weigh between 80 to 110 pounds (36.25 to 50kg). It is important to note that the weight of a healthy Bloodhound depends on how large the Bloodhound is – taller Bloodhounds should weigh more.

Voice

The Bloodhound has an impressively loud voice. When a Bloodhound is tracking alone, or is the only Bloodhound in a household, they tend to be quieter and less likely to bark. However if they are hunting in a pack, or live with multiple other Bloodhounds, they can be excepted to be very vocal. It is important to consider your neighbors if you are thinking about owning multiple Bloodhounds.

Breed Characteristics

The following section will give you a simplistic overview of the characteristics of a Bloodhound. Our rating system is from 1 to 10 – with 1 being the lowest score and 10 being the highest.

- **Adaptability:** 6/10
- **Friendliness:** 10/10
- **Health:** 8/10
- **Ease of Grooming:** 2/10
- **Amount of Shedding:** 8/10
- **Trainability:** 8/10
- **Intelligence:** 8/10
- **Exercise Needed:** 9/10
- **Playfulness:** 10/10
- **Family Friendliness:** 10/10

THE BLUETICK COONHOUND

The Bluetick Coonhound is a breed of Coonhound that originates from the United States of America. The breed was developed in Louisiana by mixing the English Foxhound, the Cur dog, the American Foxhound, the Black and Tan Coonhound and the 'Bleu de Gascogne' hound which originates from southwest France. The Bluetick Coonhound was originally registered as a variant of the English Foxhound and was only recognized as an individual breed in late 1940s. The Bluetick Coonhound gets its 'blue' coloring from black ticking on a white background, which gives the illusion of a navy blue coloration. The breed has a moderate length and glossy coat that will have the unique 'blue' in sporadic patches across its coat. The Bluetick Coonhound was bred to be able to efficiently hunt raccoons and other small prey. Due to their hunting history, the breed is highly hardy, athletic and energetic. The breed is known to be challenging to socialize with other small household animals, such as cats, as the Bluetick Coonhound has a tendency to 'hunt' them. However once trained, the Bluetick Coonhound is known to be a very mindful and affectionate breed that does extremely well in a household environment.

Lifespan

A Bluetick Coonhound will normally live to be between 8 and 10 years old. However it is not uncommon for a Bluetick Coonhound to live to be as old as 12, providing that it does not develop any serious health issues.

Height and Weight

A fully grown Bluetick Coonhound will normally stand between 23 to 30 inches (58.5 to 76.25cm) tall at the shoulder. A healthy adult Bluetick Coonhound will normally weigh between 45 to 100 pounds (20.5 to 45.5kg). It is important to note that the weight of a healthy Bluetick Coonhound depends on how large the Bluetick Coonhound is – taller Bluetick Coonhounds should weigh more.

Breed Characteristics

The following section will give you a simplistic overview of the characteristics of a Bluetick Coonhound. Our rating system is from 1 to 10 – with 1 being the lowest score and 10 being the highest.

- **Adaptability:** 6/10
- **Friendliness:** 8/10
- **Health:** 8/10

- **Ease of Grooming:** 10/10
- **Amount of Shedding:** 4/10
- **Trainability:** 8/10
- **Intelligence:** 8/10
- **Exercise Needed:** 9/10
- **Playfulness:** 10/10
- **Family Friendliness:** 10/10

THE BOLOGNESE

The Bolognese is a small breed of dog that is a part of the Bichon typing. The Bolognese originates from Italy and its name 'Bolognese' is a reference to the central Italian city of Bologna. The breed is part of the Toy Dog grouping and is considered to be a companion dog, as it was nor bred for a working purpose. The Bolognese's exact history is a mystery but it is known that it is closely related to the Maltese – however it is unknown if the Bolognese or the Maltese came first! The breed is small with a compact body and a distinctive white single coat. The Bolognese's distinctive single coat falls in loose open ringlets that cover the entirety of its body while its face is covered in shorter white hairs. The breed's coat is known to not shed often, but it will still require regular grooming to prevent matting. Due to the fact that the breed barely sheds, the Bolognese is considered to be a hypoallergenic breed and perfect for any household that contains someone with a dog hair allergy. The Bolognese is known to be a playful, intelligent, loyal and affectionate breed. They make perfect household pets for families with small children and other household pets due to their easy going nature.

Lifespan

A Bolognese will normally live to be between 10 and 12 years old. However it is not uncommon for a Bolognese to live to be as old as 14, providing that it does not develop any serious health issues.

Height and Weight

A fully grown Bolognese will normally stand between 9 to 12 inches (23 to 30.5cm) tall at the shoulder. A healthy adult Bolognese will normally weigh between 8 to 14 pounds (3.5 to 6.5kg). It is important to note that the weight of a healthy Bolognese depends on how large the Bolognese is – taller Bologneses should weigh more.

Breed Characteristics

The following section will give you a simplistic overview of the characteristics of a Bolognese. Our rating system is from 1 to 10 – with 1 being the lowest score and 10 being the highest.

- **Adaptability:** 6/10
- **Friendliness:** 10/10
- **Health:** 8/10
- **Ease of Grooming:** 1/10
- **Amount of Shedding:** 1/10

- ➢ **Trainability:** 8/10
- ➢ **Intelligence:** 8/10
- ➢ **Exercise Needed:** 5/10
- ➢ **Playfulness:** 5/10
- ➢ **Family Friendliness:** 10/10

THE BORDER COLLIE

The Border Collie is a breed of working and herding dog that was developed in the Anglo-Scottish border region. The breed being developed on the border between England and Scotland is thought to be the origin of the breeds name – the 'Border' Collie! Likewise, the term 'Collie' is thought to have been derived from the Celtic word for 'useful.' The breed was originally developed to be capable of herding livestock, especially sheep, and to be highly intelligent and obedient. The Border Collie is a descends from the Landrace collies that originate from the British Isles. The Border Collie has a double coat, soft dark eyes, a well-defined stop and a athletically built body. The breeds double coat can come in two texture variations: smooth and rough. The rough coat variation is of a medium to long length and has feathering on the dog's legs, chest and belly. The smooth coat variation is short all over and has minimal feathering. The breed will most commonly have a black coat with white patches on its face, neck, feet, legs and tail. However it is not uncommon to find Border Collies with bicolored, tricolored, merle or solid coat colorations. As a whole, the Border Collie is known to be a intelligent, loyal and affectionate breed. Due to the breed's working background, the Border Collie is also a highly energetic breed and thrives in an active household. It is important to make sure that you provide your Border Collie with adequate levels of exercise as they tend to develop destructive behaviors due to boredom or having an abundance of energy.

Lifespan

A Border Collie will normally live to be between 10 and 12 years old. However it is not uncommon for a Border Collie to live to be as old as 15, providing that it does not develop any serious health issues.

Height and Weight

A fully grown Border Collie will normally stand between 18 to 22 inches (45.75 to 56cm) tall at the shoulder. A healthy adult Border Collie will normally weigh between 30 to 45 pounds (13.5 to 20.5kg). It is important to note that the weight of a healthy Border Collie depends on how large the Border Collie is – taller Border Collies should weigh more.

Breed Characteristics

The following section will give you a simplistic overview of the characteristics of a Border Collie. Our rating system is from 1 to 10 – with 1 being the lowest score and 10 being the highest.

- **Adaptability:** 8/10
- **Friendliness:** 8/10
- **Health:** 5/10
- **Ease of Grooming:** 6/10
- **Amount of Shedding:** 6/10
- **Trainability:** 7/10
- **Intelligence:** 10/10
- **Exercise Needed:** 10/10
- **Playfulness:** 10/10
- **Family Friendliness:** 10/10

THE BORDER TERRIER

The Border Terrier is a small breed of dog that is a member of the terrier grouping. The breed is a descends from the Bedlington Terrier and the Dandie Dinmot Terrier. The Border Terrier was originally developed to be able to hunt both small vermin, like mice and rats, and foxes. The breed therefore has a small compact body and large legs. The Border Terrier's large legs allowed it to keep up with horses and other foxhounds during a hunt while its small body allowed it to crawl down fox burrows to chase the fox into the open. The Border Terrier has a very unique shaped head with a broad skull and a short muzzle with a scissor bite. The breed also has v-shaped ears on the side of its skull that fall towards its cheeks. The Border Terrier has a rough coat that normally comes in grizzle-and-tan, blue-and-tan, red or wheaten colorations. As a whole the Border Terrier is known to be a friendly, intelligent and loyal breed. It is important to note that due to their high levels of intelligence the Border Terrier has a tendency to be strong willed and stubborn: which can lead it to be hard to train. The Border Terrier is known to be extremely child friendly but is known to chase other small animals and pets due to its high prey instinct.

Lifespan

A Border Terrier will normally live to be between 10 and 12 years old. However it is not uncommon for a Border Terrier to live to be as old as 15, providing that it does not develop any serious health issues.

Height and Weight

A fully grown Border Terrier will normally stand between 10 to 11 inches (25.4 to 28cm) tall at the shoulder. A healthy adult Border Terrier will normally weigh between 11 to 15 pounds (5 to 6.8kg). It is important to note that the weight of a healthy Border Terrier depends on how large the Border Terrier is – taller Border Terriers should weigh more.

Breed Characteristics

The following section will give you a simplistic overview of the characteristics of a Border Terrier. Our rating system is from 1 to 10 – with 1 being the lowest score and 10 being the highest.

- **Adaptability:** 6/10
- **Friendliness:** 8/10
- **Health:** 8/10
- **Ease of Grooming:** 4/10
- **Amount of Shedding:** 6/10

- ➢ **Trainability:** 8/10
- ➢ **Intelligence:** 10/10
- ➢ **Exercise Needed:** 10/10
- ➢ **Playfulness:** 10/10
- ➢ **Family Friendliness:** 10/10

THE BORZOI

The Borzoi is a breed of domestic dog that originates from Russia. The breed is also commonly known as the Russian Wolfhound and the Russian Hunting Sighthound. In Russian the breeds name, 'Borzoi,' literally translates to 'fast.' As the name suggests the Borzoi is an especially fast moving and athletic breed which is built in a similar shape to the Greyhound. The Borzoi was originally developed to be a sighthound capable of chasing down foxes, hares and other small game and keeping up with horse-mounted hunters. However the breed was quickly used to hunt wolves. Hunters would release two or three Borzoi to pursue a wolf. The dogs would pursue the wolf and attack it from multiple angels. If the Borzoi were successful they would hold the wolf by the neck until the hunter arrived. However, in modern times the Borzoi is mainly found as a domestic household pet. The Borzoi makes a perfect household pet due to its intelligence, loyalty and lack of territorial instinct – which makes the breed very accepting of other animals and strangers. The breed is also known to be very quiet and hardly ever bark. The Borzoi has a long top coat and a shorter, thicker under coat. The breed's coat can come in virtually any coloration.

Lifespan

A Borzoi will normally live to be between 8 and 10 years old. However it is not uncommon for a Borzoi to live to be as old as 12, providing that it does not develop any serious health issues.

Height and Weight

A fully grown Borzoi will normally stand between 26 to 32 inches (66 to 81.25cm) tall at the shoulder. A healthy adult Borzoi will normally weigh between 55 to 105 pounds (25 to 47.6kg). It is important to note that the weight of a healthy Borzoi depends on how large the Borzoi is – taller Borzois should weigh more.

Breed Characteristics

The following section will give you a simplistic overview of the characteristics of a Borzoi. Our rating system is from 1 to 10 – with 1 being the lowest score and 10 being the highest.

- **Adaptability:** 8/10
- **Friendliness:** 8/10
- **Health:** 8/10
- **Ease of Grooming:** 8/10
- **Amount of Shedding:** 10/10
- **Trainability:** 8/10

- **Intelligence:** 10/10
- **Exercise Needed:** 4/10
- **Playfulness:** 5/10
- **Family Friendliness:** 8/10

THE BOSTON TERRIER

The Boston Terrier is a breed of dog that originates from the United States of America. The breed is also commonly known as the 'American Gentleman,' the 'Boston Bull,' the 'Boxwood' and the 'Boston Bull Terrier.' The Boston Terrier has characteristic markings: a white coat with large amounts of black, brindle or seal (dark brown) colored markings across its body. The breed's characteristic 'tuxedo' appearance lead to the nickname the 'American Gentleman.' Any other coat colorations are not accepted by the American Kennel Club, as they are usually obtained by crossbreeding. The Boston Terrier has a compactly-built, muscled and well-proportioned body with a square-shaped head, erect ears and a slightly arched neck. The breed generally has a short and unwrinkled muzzle. The Boston Terrier is known to be a gentle, happy, friendly and loyal breed of dog. They are incredibly eager to please their owners and are therefore easy to train. The breed is known to be extremely territorial and protective and is therefore not recommended to be kept in a household with other small pets.

Lifespan

A Boston Terrier will normally live to be between 10

and 13 years old. However it is not uncommon for a Boston Terrier to live to be as old as 15, providing that it does not develop any serious health issues.

Height and Weight

A fully grown Boston Terrier will normally stand between 12 to 15 inches (30.5 to 38cm) tall at the shoulder. A healthy adult Boston Terrier will normally weigh between 10 to 25 pounds (4.5 to 11.5kg). It is important to note that the weight of a healthy Boston Terrier depends on how large the Boston Terrier is – taller Boston Terriers should weigh more. The American Kennel Club divides the breed into three classes: under 15 pounds, 15 pounds and under 20 pounds, and 20 pounds and not exceeding 25 pounds.

Breed Characteristics

The following section will give you a simplistic overview of the characteristics of a Boston Terrier. Our rating system is from 1 to 10 – with 1 being the lowest score and 10 being the highest.

- **Adaptability:** 8/10
- **Friendliness:** 10/10
- **Health:** 8/10
- **Ease of Grooming:** 10/10

- ➢ **Amount of Shedding:** 4/10
- ➢ **Trainability:** 6/10
- ➢ **Intelligence:** 8/10
- ➢ **Exercise Needed:** 8/10
- ➢ **Playfulness:** 10/10
- ➢ **Family Friendliness:** 10/10

THE BOUVIER DES FLANDRES

The Bouvier des Flandres is a breed of herding dog that originates from Flanders, in Belgium. The breed is also commonly known as the 'Flanders Cattle Dog' as well as being known by the breed's literal French translation of 'Cow Herder of Flanders.' The breed was traditionally used for general farm work including cattle herding, sheep herding, cart pulling and animal droving. Traditionally the Bouvier des Flandres had its tail docked and its ears cropped. It is believed that the owner's would have done this to indicate that the Bouvier des Flandres is a working dog, rather than a pet, which means that it would not be subject to pet taxations. It is also thought that the ear cropping and tail docking was an attempt to avoid the dog injuring itself while it works. The breed nearly went extinct during World War 1 due to the devastation that occurred across the region of Flanders. A male trained trench dog, named Nic, who served during World War 1 was awarded a multiple titles at dog shows after the war and is considered the founder of the Bouvier des Flandres breed. In modern times the Bouvier des Flandres is mainly employed as a guard dog, a police dog or a domestic household pet. The breed is known to be gentle, loyal, protective and loving by nature. They make excellent household pets due to their high levels of obedience and intelligence.

Lifespan

A Bouvier des Flandres will normally live to be between 10 and 12 years old. However it is not uncommon for a Bouvier des Flandres to live to be as old as 13, providing that it does not develop any serious health issues.

Height and Weight

A fully grown Bouvier des Flandres will normally stand between 23 to 28 inches (58.5 to 71cm) tall at the shoulder. A healthy adult Bouvier des Flandres will normally weigh between 70 to 100 pounds (31.75 to 45.5kg). It is important to note that the weight of a healthy Bouvier des Flandres depends on how large the Bouvier des Flandres is – taller Bouvier des Flandres should weigh more.

Coat

The Bouvier des Flandres has a thick weather-resistant double coat. The breed's outer coat is coarse and long. While the breed's inner coat is fine and dense. The breeds coat come in the following colorations: black, salt and pepper, fawn, brined and sometimes black with white flecks on its chest.

Breed Characteristics

The following section will give you a simplistic overview of the characteristics of a Bouvier des Flandres. Our rating system is from 1 to 10 – with 1 being the lowest score and 10 being the highest.

- **Adaptability:** 6/10
- **Friendliness:** 8/10
- **Health:** 6/10
- **Ease of Grooming:** 3/10
- **Amount of Shedding:** 1/10
- **Trainability:** 6/10
- **Intelligence:** 8/10
- **Exercise Needed:** 8/10
- **Playfulness:** 8/10
- **Family Friendliness:** 10/10

THE BOXER

The Boxer is a medium-sized breed of dog that originates from Germany. The Boxer is a cross between the Old English Bulldog and the now extinct Bullenbeisser. The purpose of the cross breeding was to eliminate the likelihood of having an all-white coat. The boxer has a smooth short-haired coat in the following three colorations: fawn, brindle and white. The breed has broad muscular shoulders, a relatively small short skull and a short muzzle. The Boxer has a large under bite and a strong jaw which makes it incredibly adept at holding onto prey. Its powerful jaw and sturdy body has lead the Boxer to be primarily used for herding and hunting purposes.

Lifespan

Boxers will normally live for between 9 and 11 years. However it is not uncommon for a Boxer to live to be over 12 years old, providing they do not develop any serious health issues.

Height and Weight

An adult Boxer is normally between 21 and 25 (53 to 63cm) inches tall at the shoulder. A full grown Boxer will generally weigh between 60 and 70 pounds (27 to

32kg). It is important to note that male Boxers generally have larger bodies and weigh more.

Temperament

Boxers an intelligent and energetic breed due to their history as working dogs. However in recent years, the Boxer has secured its place as a popular family pet. The breed is both extremely playful and patient – which makes it a perfect dog for families with children. They are also very protective and affectionate towards their family unit. The Boxer does not have an aggressive nature, however it is important to provide your Boxer with adequate exercise or it is likely to develop destructive behaviors through boredom.

Breed Characteristics

The following section will give you a simplistic overview of the characteristics of a Boxer. Our rating system is from 1 to 10 – with 1 being the lowest score and 10 being the highest.

- **Adaptability:** 6/10
- **Friendliness:** 8/10
- **Health:** 8/10
- **Ease of Grooming:** 10/10
- **Amount of Shedding:** 8/10

- ➢ **Trainability:** 7/10
- ➢ **Intelligence:** 7/10
- ➢ **Exercise Needed:** 10/10
- ➢ **Playfulness:** 10/10
- ➢ **Family Friendliness:** 10/10

THE BOYKIN SPANIEL

The Boykin Spaniel is a medium-sized breed of dog that is a member of the Spaniel grouping. The breed is also commonly known as the 'Swamp Poodle,' the 'LBD' (Little Brown Dog) and simply as the 'Boykin.' The Boykin Spaniel originates from the United States of America. The breed was originally developed for the purpose of hunting turkeys and ducks in the Wateree River Swamp located in South Carolina. However due to their stamina in hot weather and eagerness to hunt, the Boykin Spaniel was quickly used for dove hunts and to hunt pheasants and other larger game. The Boykin Spaniel is actually the state dog of South Carolina. The Boykin Spaniel is slightly larger than the English Cocker Spaniel but has a much heavier body. The breed has no standard coat type or coloration due to the breed recent background. It is not uncommon for the Boykin Spaniel's coat to be curly in a similar style to the American Water Spaniel's coat, fine and straight like a Field Spaniel's coat and shorter and straighter like a Labrador Retriever's coat. As a whole, the Boykin Spaniel is known to be a friendly, sociable and loyal breed that makes it a perfect family pet. It is important to note that the Boykin Spaniel is a highly energetic breed. If it is not exercised properly it is highly likely that a Boykin Spaniel will develop destructive behaviors, due to boredom and having an abundance of excess energy.

Lifespan

A Boykin Spaniel will normally live to be between 10 and 12 years old. However it is not uncommon for a Boykin Spaniel to live to be as old as 13, providing that it does not develop any serious health issues.

Height and Weight

A fully grown Boykin Spaniel will normally stand between 14 to 18 inches (35.5 to 45.75cm) tall at the shoulder. A healthy adult Boykin Spaniel will normally weigh between 25 to 40 pounds (11.25 to 18kg). It is important to note that the weight of a healthy Boykin Spaniel depends on how large the Boykin Spaniel is – taller Boykin Spaniel should weigh more.

Breed Characteristics

The following section will give you a simplistic overview of the characteristics of a Boykin Spaniel. Our rating system is from 1 to 10 – with 1 being the lowest score and 10 being the highest.

- **Adaptability:** 6/10
- **Friendliness:** 8/10
- **Health:** 4/10

- ➢ **Ease of Grooming:** 1/10
- ➢ **Amount of Shedding:** 8/10
- ➢ **Trainability:** 8/10
- ➢ **Intelligence:** 8/10
- ➢ **Exercise Needed:** 10/10
- ➢ **Playfulness:** 8/10
- ➢ **Family Friendliness:** 10/10

THE BRACCO ITALIANO

The Bracco Italiano is a breed of versatile gun dog that was bred and developed in Italy. The breed has a tendency to 'point' in the direction of prey and has therefore been given the nicknames of the 'Italian Pointer' and the 'Italian Pointer Dog.' It is believed that the breed was first developed sometime between the 4th and 5th century – making it one of the oldest breeds in existence. The Bracco Italiano is considered to be a mix of both the Segugio Italiano (a coursing hound) and the Asiatic Mastiff. There are two variations of the Bracco Italiano: the Pledmontese Pointer and the Lombard Pointer. The first variation, the Pledmontese Pointer, originated from Pledmont and has a lighter build and coat. The second variation, the Lombard Pointer, originated from Lombardy and has a more athletic build to allow it to combat the mountainous terrain of Lombardy. Traditionally, the Bracco Italiano was originally employed as a hunting hound by the Italian aristocracy. However in modern times, the Bracco Italiano is mainly found as a domestic family dog due to its people-loving temperament. The Bracco Italiano is also known to be a particularly friendly to children and other household pets, if it has been socialized properly.

Lifespan

A Bracco Italiano will normally live to be between 10 and 12 years old. However it is not uncommon for a Bracco Italiano to live to be as old as 13, providing that it does not develop any serious health issues.

Height and Weight

A fully grown Bracco Italiano will normally stand between 21 to 26 inches (53 to 66cm) tall at the shoulder. A healthy adult Bracco Italiano will normally weigh between 33 to 88 pounds (15 to 40kg). It is important to note that the weight of a healthy Bracco Italiano depends on how large the Bracco Italiano is – taller Bracco Italiano should weigh more.

Coat

The Bracco Italiano has dense, short and shiny coat. The breed will normally have a white coat with some form of marking across its entire body. These markings normally come in the following colorations: dark amber, orange and chestnut.

Breed Characteristics

The following section will give you a simplistic overview of the characteristics of a Bracco Italiano. Our

rating system is from 1 to 10 – with 1 being the lowest score and 10 being the highest.

- ➤ **Adaptability:** 6/10
- ➤ **Friendliness:** 8/10
- ➤ **Health:** 5/10
- ➤ **Ease of Grooming:** 6/10
- ➤ **Amount of Shedding:** 6/10
- ➤ **Trainability:** 6/10
- ➤ **Intelligence:** 8/10
- ➤ **Exercise Needed:** 8/10
- ➤ **Playfulness:** 6/10
- ➤ **Family Friendliness:** 10/10

THE BRIARD

The Briard is a breed of herding dog that originates from France. The breed is thought to be a mixture of the Barbet and the Beauceron. The Briard was only standardized after a dog show, in Paris, in the late 1800s. Traditionally the Briard was bred and developed to both guard and herd flocks of sheep without the presence of the farmer. Most sheepdogs either herd or guard flocks. Breeds that herd normally have small, compact and agile builds to allow them to efficiently, and quickly, herd sheep. Guard dogs normally have larger, heavier and more athletic builds to allow them to adequately defend the flocks of sheep. The Briard is a mixture of both a herding and guarding dog: it has a compact and athletic body while not being small. The Briard is also known to be highly intelligent and was more than capable of minding a flock of sheep alone. The French military employed the Briard was a sentry, messenger and a search and rescue dog during World War 1. The Briard was actually used to such an extent that the breed nearly went extinct! In modern times the Briard is still used as a military dog, a police dog, a search and rescue dog and as a domesticated companion dog. The Briard has a characteristic coarse, long and shaggy overcoat and fine and dense undercoat that sits tightly to the dog's stomach. As a whole, the breed is known to be extremely intelligent, empathetic, loyal and loving. They have been a popular choice for family pets and therapy dogs due to their kind natures.

Lifespan

A Briard will normally live to be between 10 and 12 years old. However it is not uncommon for a Briard to live to be as old as 13, providing that it does not develop any serious health issues.

Height and Weight

A fully grown Briard will normally stand between 22 to 27 inches (56 to 69cm) tall at the shoulder. A healthy adult Briard will normally weigh between 70 to 100 pounds (31.75 to 45.3kg). It is important to note that the weight of a healthy Briard depends on how large the Briard is – taller Briard should weigh more.

Breed Characteristics

The following section will give you a simplistic overview of the characteristics of a Briard. Our rating system is from 1 to 10 – with 1 being the lowest score and 10 being the highest.

- **Adaptability:** 6/10
- **Friendliness:** 8/10

- ➢ **Health:** 6/10
- ➢ **Ease of Grooming:** 1/10
- ➢ **Amount of Shedding:** 1/10
- ➢ **Trainability:** 8/10
- ➢ **Intelligence:** 8/10
- ➢ **Exercise Needed:** 8/10
- ➢ **Playfulness:** 8/10
- ➢ **Family Friendliness:** 10/10

THE BRITTANY

The Brittany is a breed of gun dog that was bred and developed in the Brittany province of France. The breed was originally developed to be a gun dog that was designed to hunt birds. The Brittany breed is believed to have been developed during the 17th century, as this is when they were first depicted on French tapestries. However despite being an old breed, the Brittany was not recognized as a breed until 1907 when an orange and white male was registered in France. The breed is commonly nicknamed the 'Brittany Spaniel.' However despite the common reference to Spaniels, the Brittany's working characteristics are more similar to that of a pointer or setter. As a whole the breed typically has a compact, athletic and solidly built body but without being heavy. They have large floppy ears that hang low on the sides of their heads. The Brittany is also known to have a very intelligent and alert expression. Due to its history as a hunting dog, the Brittany is known to be intelligent, obedient, easy to train, loyal and sweet-natured. It is important to note that the Brittany is more sensitive to human correction than most other breeds – do not use a harsh tone while training it as it will become upset. The Brittany make a perfect household pet as they are energetic, playful and sociable with children and other small animals. It is important to note that if you do not provide your Brittany with adequate exercise it is likely to develop destructive behaviors due to boredom and having an abundance of energy!

Lifespan

A Brittany will normally live to be between 10 and 12 years old. However it is not uncommon for a Brittany to live to be as old as 13, providing that it does not develop any serious health issues.

Height and Weight

A fully grown Brittany will normally stand between 17 to 20 inches (43 to 51cm) tall at the shoulder. A healthy adult Brittany will normally weigh between 30 to 40 pounds (13.5 to 18kg). It is important to note that the weight of a healthy Brittany depends on how large the Brittany is – taller Brittany should weigh more.

Breed Characteristics

The following section will give you a simplistic overview of the characteristics of a Brittany. Our rating system is from 1 to 10 – with 1 being the lowest score and 10 being the highest.

➢ **Adaptability: 6/10**

- **Friendliness:** 10/10
- **Health:** 8/10
- **Ease of Grooming:** 6/10
- **Amount of Shedding:** 6/10
- **Trainability:** 8/10
- **Intelligence:** 10/10
- **Exercise Needed:** 10/10
- **Playfulness:** 10/10
- **Family Friendliness:** 10/10

THE BRUSSELS GRIFFON

The Brussels Griffon, also commonly known as the Griffon Bruxellois, is a breed of toy dog that was named after its city of origin Brussels, Belgium. The breed descends from an ancient dog type names the 'Smousje.' The 'Smousje' was a small, rough coated terrier-like dog that was kept in stables to catch and kill rodents. In the 19th the Brussels Griffon was bred with other toy dog breeds that were imported from around the world. The modern Brussels Griffon's appearance is mainly due to it being crossbred with the Pug and King Charles Spaniel. The Brussels Griffon nearly went extinct during the first and second World Wars. But thanks to a small dedicated group of breeders (mainly located in the United Kingdom), the Brussels Griffon managed to survive. As a whole, the Brussels Griffon is known to be highly affectionate and loyal towards their owner. However the breed is somewhat dismissive of strangers, children and other pets as they would rather spend their time in the company of their owner. The breed is known to be highly sensitive and emotional and it is therefore every important to socialize your Brussels Griffon at a young age.

Lifespan

A Brussels Griffon will normally live to be between 12 and 13 years old. However it is not uncommon for a Brussels Griffon to live to be as old as 15, providing that it does not develop any serious health issues.

Height and Weight

A fully grown Brussels Griffon will normally stand between 7 to 8 inches (17.75 to 20.25cm) tall at the shoulder. A healthy adult Brussels Griffon will normally weigh between 7 to 12 pounds (3.1 to 5.5kg). It is important to note that the weight of a healthy Brussels Griffon depends on how large the Brussels Griffon is – taller Brussels Griffon should weigh more.

Variants

The Brussels Griffon is one of three variants. The other two variants are called the 'Belgian Griffon' and the 'Petit Brabançon.' All three variants are separated by their different coats and coat colorations. The **Brussels Griffon has a rough and dense coat and normally comes in the following colorations: red, black and tan, beige and black.**

Breed Characteristics

The following section will give you a simplistic overview of the characteristics of a Brussels Griffon. Our rating system is from 1 to 10 – with 1 being the lowest score and 10 being the highest.

- **Adaptability:** 6/10
- **Friendliness:** 6/10
- **Health:** 6/10
- **Ease of Grooming:** 6/10
- **Amount of Shedding:** 5/10
- **Trainability:** 6/10
- **Intelligence:** 8/10
- **Exercise Needed:** 8/10
- **Playfulness:** 10/10
- **Family Friendliness:** 10/10

THE BULL TERRIER

The Bull Terrier is a breed that is a part of the 'Terrier' family of dogs. The breed was first registered to the American Kennel Club (AKC) in 1885 and is thought to have originated in around 1850. The Bull Terrier is thought to be a cross with the Bulldog and a now-extinct white breed of English Terrier. The breed was later cross with the Spanish Pointer to increase its size. There is a smaller version of the Bull Terrier known as the 'Miniature Bull Terrier.' The Bull Terrier has a distinctly 'egg-shaped' head and a black nose that has well developed nostrils. The Bull terrier is the only breed of dog that has triangular shaped eyes. The breed has a strong muscular body with a horizontally carrier tail. The Bull Terrier has a short coat that comes in the following colorations: white, black, brindle, red, fawn, or a combination of these colors.

Lifespan

The Bull Terrier normally lives to be between 10 and 12 years old. However it is not uncommon for a Bull Terrier to live to be as old as 14, providing it does not develop any serious health issues.

Size and Weight

An adult Bull Terrier will normally be between 20 and 22 inches (51 to 55cm) tall at the shoulder. Males tend to weigh more than females and will normally weigh between 40 and 75 pounds (18 to 34kg). Female Bull Terriers will normally weigh between 35 and 65 pounds (16 to 29.5kg).

Temperament

Bull Terriers are known to be both independent and stubborn and due to this are not recommended for novice dog owners. However despite being stubborn they are still very affectionate and loyal pets. The Bull Terrier is a good choice for families with older children but are not a good choice for families with babies or toddlers due to their rough and rambunctiously playful nature.

Banned

The Bull Terrier is a restricted, or banned, breed in some states, provinces and cities. It is highly important to research your local areas ruling on the Bull Terrier before purchasing one. If you are caught with a restricted, or banned, breed you are likely to receive and fine and the dog will most likely be put down!!

Breed Characteristics

The following section will give you a simplistic overview of the characteristics of a Bull Terrier. Our rating system is from 1 to 10 – with 1 being the lowest score and 10 being the highest.

- **Adaptability:** 6/10
- **Friendliness:** 10/10
- **Health:** 6/10
- **Ease of Grooming:** 10/10
- **Amount of Shedding:** 6/10
- **Trainability:** 8/10
- **Intelligence:** 10/10
- **Exercise Needed:** 10/10
- **Playfulness:** 10/10
- **Family Friendliness:** 10/10

THE BULLDOG

The Bulldog is a medium-sized, muscular and short haired breed of dog. They are characterized by having wrinkled faces and pushed-in noses. The breed is commonly known as the '*English Bulldog*' or the '*British Bulldog,*' due to the fact that it is native to the United Kingdom. Originally the breed was used for bull baiting and dog fighting until these activities were outlawed in Britain in the 1500s. The Bulldog emigrated to America and was used to round up bulls. Due to the breeds intelligence and loving nature they have ranked in the top 5 most popular breeds in the USA and UK for the last 100 years! The Bulldog makes a great family pet as they are very gentle and protective around small children.

Lifespan

Bulldogs will normally live for between 6 and 8 years. However, it is not uncommon for a Bulldog to live to be around 10 years old if they do not develop any serious health issues.

Size

Both males and females normally stand at around 12 to 16 inches (31 to 41cm). Males tend to have a more muscular body and normally weigh more than females.

The average healthy weight for a male Bulldog is between 53 and 55 pounds (24 to 25kg). Females normally weigh around 48 to 50 pounds (22 to 23kg).

Appearance

The Bulldog has a wide head and shoulders and a pronounced under bite with an upturned jaw. They generally have thick wrinkled skin surrounding their eyes and jaw. These characteristic folds are called 'ropes.' Their coats come in multiple different colorations: white, black, fawn, red and brindle to name a few. The Bulldog has a naturally short tail due to the breeds history in dog fighting and bull herding.

Intelligence

Bulldogs are known to be an intelligent, but stubborn, breed. Their stubbornness means that they are not easy dogs to train. The Bulldog is also a highly empathetic breed and therefore responds well to voice commands. It is important to never use a negative tone or shout at your Bulldog as this is likely to upset them. Negative tones will also lead your Bulldog to start ignoring you.

Breed Characteristics

The following section will give you a simplistic

overview of the characteristics of a Bulldog. Our rating system is from 1 to 10 – with 1 being the lowest score and 10 being the highest.

- **Adaptability:** 6/10
- **Friendliness:** 8/10
- **Health:** 6/10
- **Ease of Grooming:** 6/10
- **Amount of Shedding:** 3/10
- **Trainability:** 7/10
- **Intelligence:** 8/10
- **Exercise Needed:** 6/10
- **Playfulness:** 10/10
- **Family Friendliness:** 8/10

THE BULLMASTIFF

The Bullmastiff is a large-sized breed of domestic dog. During the 19th century, the Bullmastiff was developed by gamekeepers and guards for the purpose of guarding large estates. The Bullmastiff was developed by interbreeding the English Mastiff and the Old English Bulldog. The Bullmastiff is solidly built and has the perfect mix of the Old English Bulldog's strength and speed and the English Mastiff's less aggressive temperament. The breed is commonly known as the 'Gamekeeper's Night Dog' due to the fact that the breed rarely barks which makes it ideal for night time security According the breed standards of the American Kennel Club, a Bullmastiff's coat can only come in the following colorations: fawn (ranging from light brown to a slight reddish brown), red (ranging from a light fawn-red to a dark, rich red) or brindle (stripes over either a fawn or red base). Gamekeeper's would normally favor brindle coat colorations as it provides the Bullmastiff with effective camouflage at night. Bullmastiff are very popular household pets due to their intelligence, loyalty and trainability. As a whole the breed gets along well with children and other household pets, providing that the dog has been socialized properly from an early age.

Lifespan

A Bullmastiff will normally live to be between 7 and 9 years old. However it is not uncommon for a Bullmastiff to live to be as old as 10, providing that it does not develop any serious health issues.

Height and Weight

A fully grown Bullmastiff will normally stand between 24 to 27 inches (61 to 68.5cm) tall at the shoulder. A healthy adult Bullmastiff will normally weigh between 100 to 130 pounds (45.3 to 59kg). It is important to note that the weight of a healthy Bullmastiff depends on how large the Bullmastiff is – taller Bullmastiff should weigh more.

Breed Characteristics

The following section will give you a simplistic overview of the characteristics of a Bullmastiff. Our rating system is from 1 to 10 – with 1 being the lowest score and 10 being the highest.

- **Adaptability:** 6/10
- **Friendliness:** 8/10
- **Health:** 6/10
- **Ease of Grooming:** 10/10
- **Amount of Shedding:** 1/10

- ➢ **Trainability:** 6/10
- ➢ **Intelligence:** 5/10
- ➢ **Exercise Needed:** 8/10
- ➢ **Playfulness:** 10/10
- ➢ **Family Friendliness:** 10/10

Encyclopedia of Dog Breeds

THE CAIRN TERRIER

The Cairn Terrier is one of the oldest breeds of terrier and originates from the Scottish Highlands. The Cairn Terrier is one of Scotland's earliest recorded breeds of working dog. The breed's name is derived from its working purpose: to hunt and chase rodents found between the cairns located in the Scottish Highlands. Unusually the breed tends to be left-pawed, which is a trait that commonly correlates to a superior sense of smell and performance in scent related tasks and hunting. The Cairn Terrier has an abundant, coarse and shaggy outer coat and a dramatically softer undercoat. Despite having a dense and relatively long coat, the Cairn Terrier tends to shed very little. The breed's coat comes in five common colorations which are: black, cream, brindle, deep red and light gray. Despite being a relatively small breed, the Cairn Terrier is a highly playful and energetic dog! It is important to make sure that you properly exercise your Cairn Terrier as, due to its working history, it is likely to develop destructive behaviors if it is bored or has an abundance of energy. As a whole the Cairn Terrier is a known to be an extremely friendly, affectionate and playful breed who generally enjoys meeting new people. It is important to remember that Cairn Terriers are terrier: which means that they are independent, tough, alert and have a high prey drive which may lead to it chasing other small household pets. If you own a Cairn Terrier it is important to train and socialize it thoroughly to minimize the chances of it developing any antisocial behaviors.

Lifespan

A Cairn Terrier will normally live to be between 10 and 12 years old. However it is not uncommon for a Cairn Terrier to live to be as old as 15, providing that it does not develop any serious health issues.

Height and Weight

A fully grown Cairn Terrier will normally stand between 9 to 10 inches (23 to 25.5cm) tall at the shoulder. A healthy adult Cairn Terrier will normally weigh between 12 to 14 pounds (5.5 to 6.5kg). It is important to note that the weight of a healthy Cairn Terrier depends on how large the Cairn Terrier is – taller Cairn Terrier should weigh more.

Breed Characteristics

The following section will give you a simplistic overview of the characteristics of a Cairn Terrier. Our rating system is from 1 to 10 – with 1 being the lowest score and 10 being the highest.

- **Adaptability:** 8/10
- **Friendliness:** 10/10
- **Health:** 8/10
- **Ease of Grooming:** 10/10
- **Amount of Shedding:** 5/10
- **Trainability:** 8/10
- **Intelligence:** 10/10
- **Exercise Needed:** 10/10
- **Playfulness:** 10/10
- **Family Friendliness:** 10/10

THE CANAAN DOG

The Canaan Dog is a breed of pariah dog that has been in existence for thousands of years and is the national dog of Israel. A 'pariah dog' refers to a breeds of free-ranging dogs that survive by scavenging food waste from human settlements. The breed became domesticated in the 1930s by Dr. Rudolphina Menzel. Menzel captured a small selection of semi-wild Canaan Dogs and tamed, trained and bred them. Menzel found that the breed was incredibly adaptable, trainable and relatively easy to completely domesticate. By the early 1950s Menzel had successfully trained Canaan Dog to work as guard dogs, guide dogs and fully domesticated family pets. Sadly there are not many wild Canaan Dogs left in Israel as the government destroyed most of them to combat an outbreak of rabies. The Canaan Dog has the appearance typical to primitive pariah dogs. The breed has a medium-sized square build with erect and low set ears on its wedge-shaped head. The breed has a dense, coarse, harsh and straight outer coat of a short to medium-short length. The Canaan Dog has a close undercoat that is either short and sparse or short to medium length and dense dependent on the season. The Canaan Dog's coat will normally come in black, white or tan colorations. However it is not uncommon to find a Canaan Dog with a reddish or brownish coat. As a whole the breed has a strong survival instinct which leads them to be generally very wary of strangers. They make excellent watchdogs as they are highly alert and prone to bark at unknown sounds, scents and events. Despite being highly defensive, the Canaan Dog is not an aggressive breed. They get along very well with children and other household pets. The Canaan Dog is also known to be an extremely intelligent and adaptable breed.

Lifespan

A Canaan Dog will normally live to be between 12 and 13 years old. However it is not uncommon for a Canaan Dog to live to be as old as 15, providing that it does not develop any serious health issues.

Height and Weight

A fully grown Canaan Dog will normally stand between 19 to 24 inches (48.25 to 61cm) tall at the shoulder. A healthy adult Canaan Dog will normally weigh between 35 to 55 pounds (16 to 25kg). It is important to note that the weight of a healthy Canaan Dog depends on how large the Canaan Dog is – taller Canaan Dog should weigh more.

Breed Characteristics

The following section will give you a simplistic overview of the characteristics of a Canaan Dog. Our rating system is from 1 to 10 – with 1 being the lowest score and 10 being the highest.

- **Adaptability:** 8/10
- **Friendliness:** 7/10
- **Health:** 6/10
- **Ease of Grooming:** 10/10
- **Amount of Shedding:** 1/10
- **Trainability:** 6/10
- **Intelligence:** 8/10
- **Exercise Needed:** 8/10
- **Playfulness:** 8/10
- **Family Friendliness:** 9/10

THE CANE CORSO

The Cane Corso is a breed of companion, hunting, catch and guard dog from Italy. The breed's name translates from the Italian words Cane, meaning 'dog, and Corso, meaning 'courtyard or guard.' The breed is also commonly referred to as the 'Italian Mastiff' and the 'Italian Corso.' The Cane Corso is a distant descendant of the Canis Pugnax, which was a breed used by the Romans as attack dogs during war time. Traditionally the Cane Corso was used to hunt and catch large prey such as boar, deer and bears as well as used by farmers to guard cattle. The breed was quickly employed as night watchdogs, keepers and bodyguards due to their high levels of intelligence, trainability and loyalty. In modern times the breed is mainly kept as a domesticated companion dog but also is still used for its original farming purposes. The Cane Corso has a similar appearance to the Italian Molosser, but has a much large build. The Cane Corso is muscly but is less bulky than other breeds within the Mastiff typing. It is important to note that the Cane Corso is not a breed recommended for novice dog owners! As previously mentioned the Cane Corso is both loyal, trainable and intelligent but it is also incredibly head strong. A Cane Corso puppy needs strong leadership and consistent training to ensure that it is a well behaved dog. It is also important to socialize your Cane Corso at an early age to encourage a more relaxed nature. Although not an aggressive breed, the Cane Corso is known to become highly protective over their family unit during serious threats.

Lifespan

A Cane Corso will normally live to be between 8 and 10 years old. However it is not uncommon for a Cane Corso to live to be as old as 12, providing that it does not develop any serious health issues.

Height and Weight

A fully grown Cane Corso will normally stand between 23 to 27 inches (? to ?cm) tall at the shoulder. A healthy adult Cane Corso will normally weigh between 90 to 120 pounds (? to ?kg). It is important to note that the weight of a healthy Cane Corso depends on how large the Cane Corso is – taller Cane Corso should weigh more.

Breed Characteristics

The following section will give you a simplistic overview of the characteristics of a Cane Corso. Our rating system is from 1 to 10 – with 1 being the lowest score and 10 being the highest.

- **Adaptability:** 3/10
- **Friendliness:** 6/10
- **Health:** 6/10
- **Ease of Grooming:** 10/10
- **Amount of Shedding:** 5/10
- **Trainability:** 6810
- **Intelligence:** 10/10
- **Exercise Needed:** 8/10
- **Playfulness:** 4/10
- **Family Friendliness:** 8/10

THE CARDIGAN WELSH CORGI

The Cardigan Welsh Corgi, commonly known as simply the 'Cardigan' or 'Cardi,' is one of the oldest herding breeds that originated from Whales, in the United Kingdom. The breed is believed to be well over 3,000 years old! The Cardigan Welsh Corgi is believed to be descended from the Teckel family of dogs, which also produced the Dachshund breed. The breed is one of two separate breeds that are known as 'Welsh Corgis,' the other breed is the 'Pembroke Welsh Corgi.' Originally the Cardigan Welsh Corgi was used as a farm guardian but eventually developed the traits of a cattle drovers and herders. In modern times the Cardigan Welsh Corgi is mainly kept as a domesticated companion dog but is also still employed on farms primarily in herding based activities. As previously mentioned the Cardigan Welsh Corgi shares a similar origin to the Dachshund - the Cardigan Welsh Corgi is similarly a long and low bodies breed of dog with a long thin tail. The Cardigan Welsh Corgi is often double coated and can come in the following standardized colorations: red, sable, black, tan, brindle and blue merle. The breed will normally have characteristic white feet and a white chest. The Cardigan Welsh Corgi has proven to be an excellent household pet due to its loving nature, intelligence, affectionate nature and relatively sturdiness for a small breed of dog.

Lifespan

A Cardigan Welsh Corgi will normally live to be between 10 and 12 years old. However it is not uncommon for a Cardigan Welsh Corgi to live to be as old as 15, providing that it does not develop any serious health issues.

Height and Weight

A fully grown Cardigan Welsh Corgi will normally stand between 10 to 12 inches (25.4 to 30.5cm) tall at the shoulder. A healthy adult Cardigan Welsh Corgi will normally weigh between 25 to 38 pounds (11.3 to 17.25kg). It is important to note that the weight of a healthy Cardigan Welsh Corgi depends on how large the Cardigan Welsh Corgi is – taller Cardigan Welsh Corgi should weigh more.

Breed Characteristics

The following section will give you a simplistic overview of the characteristics of a Cardigan Welsh Corgi. Our rating system is from 1 to 10 – with 1 being the lowest score and 10 being the highest.

- **Adaptability:** 8/10
- **Friendliness:** 8/10
- **Health:** 8/10

- **Ease of Grooming:** 6/10
- **Amount of Shedding:** 7/10
- **Trainability:** 6/10
- **Intelligence:** 10/10
- **Exercise Needed:** 5/10
- **Playfulness:** 8/10
- **Family Friendliness:** 10/10

THE CATAHOULA CUR

The Catahoula Cur is a medium-large breed of dog that originates from the United States of America as is named after Catahoula Parish, Louisiana. The Catahoula Cur was made the state dog of Louisiana in 1979 to recognize the breeds importance in the history of the region. The Catahoula Cur is an outstanding hunters and trackers and have been used to hunt feral pigs, deer, hogs, black bears and even mountain lions! The Catahoula Cur tracks its prey silently but will bay (howl) when it has closed in on its prey. The breed is known to be able to lock its prey in place with only the use of posture, eye contact and lateral shifts! Due to the fact that the Catahoula Cur does not touch its prey during hunts, the breed was quickly employed in cattle herding. During cattle herding, the Catahoula Cur uses the same technique to hold the cattle in place. The breed is commonly called the 'Catahoula Hound' despite not actually being a true hound type but rather a cur. The breed is also often nicknamed the 'Catahoula Hog Dog,' due to its historical use in hog hunts, and the 'Catahoula Leopard Dog,' due to its leopardesque spotted coat. The Catahoula Cur is believed to have been developed by crossbreeding molossers, greyhounds and dogs used by Native Americans. As a whole the Catahoula Cur is known to be a highly intelligent, energetic and empathetic breed. They make perfect family pets and are very protective over small children. It is important to note that the breed has a tendency to have an assertive nature which means that owners will need to have a strong willed temperament to be able to handle a Catahoula Cur.

Lifespan

A Catahoula Cur will normally live to be between 10 and 12 years old. However it is not uncommon for a Catahoula Cur to live to be as old as 15, providing that it does not develop any serious health issues.

Height and Weight

A fully grown Catahoula Cur will normally stand between 20 to 26 inches (51 to 66cm) tall at the shoulder. A healthy adult Catahoula Cur will normally weigh between 50 to 90 pounds (22.5 to 41kg). It is important to note that the weight of a healthy Catahoula Cur depends on how large the Catahoula Cur is – taller Catahoula Cur should weigh more.

Coat

The Catahoula Cur is known to have a very uniquely spotted coat. The spots are always a contrasting color to the rest of the coat. The most common colorations are brindle, blue-grey, black and browns. The Catahoula Cur is known to have three different coat types: slick, coarse and wooly. The following sections will give a brief description of each coat type:

- Slick Coat: This coat type is the most common and is made up of short hairs that lie very close the dog's body. The slick coat will dry incredibly quickly which makes it the easiest coat type to clean and groom.
- Coarse Coat: This coat type is of a medium length but does not require complicated maintenance. This coat type has a 'fluffy' appearance.
- Wooly Coat: This is the longest coat type that the Catahoula Cur has. Most Catahoula Cur will have a wooly coat during puppyhood but shed it to have a coarse coat. However it is not uncommon for a Catahoula Cur's hair to keep growing in to a wooly coat.

Breed Characteristics

The following section will give you a simplistic overview of the characteristics of a Catahoula Cur. Our rating system is from 1 to 10 – with 1 being the lowest score and 10 being the highest.

- **Adaptability:** 5/10
- **Friendliness:** 6/10

- **Health:** 6/10
- **Ease of Grooming:** 10/10
- **Amount of Shedding:** 6/10
- **Trainability:** 6/10
- **Intelligence:** 7/10
- **Exercise Needed:** 8/10
- **Playfulness:** 5/10
- **Family Friendliness:** 10/10

THE CAVALIER KING CHARLES SPANIEL

The Cavalier King Charles Spaniel is a small breed of spaniel. It is classified as a 'toy dog' breed by the American Kennel Club. The Cavalier King Charles Spaniel originates from the United Kingdom and is not one of the most popular dog breeds worldwide. The Cavalier King Charles Spaniel rose to popularity in the United States during the early 2000s and is now ranked 18th most popular dog breed. The breed is known for their silky coat and smooth undocked tail. The coat of the Cavalier King Charles Spaniel is recognized as having four different colors: Blenheim (chestnut and white), Ruby, black and tan, and Tricolor (a mixture of black, white and tan). The breed was mixed with other small 'lap dog' breeds to create its small stature. An adult Cavalier King Charles Spaniel is normally a similar size to an adolescent in any other spaniel breed.

Lifespan

Most Cavalier King Charles Spaniel will live to be between 9 and 12 years old. However it not uncommon for a Cavalier King Charles Spaniel to live to be as old as 14, providing that they do not develop any serious health issues.

Height and Weight

A fully grown Cavalier King Charles Spaniel will normally stand at around 12 to 13 inches (30 to 33cm) tall at the shoulder. Due to the breed being classified as a 'toy dog' it is dramatically uncommon for a Cavalier King Charles Spaniel to be taller than this. A healthy adult Cavalier King Charles Spaniel will normally weigh 13 and 18 pounds (6 to 8kg). It is important to note that, as a breed, the Cavalier King Charles Spaniel are highly susceptible to becoming overweight.

Breed Characteristics

The following section will give you a simplistic overview of the characteristics of a Cavalier King Charles Spaniel. Our rating system is from 1 to 10 – with 1 being the lowest score and 10 being the highest.

- **Adaptability:** 8/10
- **Friendliness:** 10/10
- **Health:** 8/10
- **Ease of Grooming:** 8/10
- **Amount of Shedding:** 6/10
- **Trainability:** 6/10
- **Intelligence:** 8/10
- **Exercise Needed:** 8/10
- **Playfulness:** 10/10

- **Family Friendliness:** 10/10

THE CESKY TERRIER

The Cesky Terrier is a small breed of terrier type dog that originates from Czechoslovakia. The breed is also commonly referred to as the 'Bohemian Terrier' as this is a literal translation of its Czech name. The breed was developed during the late 1940's by cross breeding the Sealyham Terrier and the Scottish Terrier. The aim of the breeds development was to produce a breed capable of easily hunting in the forests of Bohemia. Despite the breed becoming somewhat popular in the early 50s, the Cesky Terrier is now one of the six rarest breeds of dogs worldwide! The Cesky Terrier was imported to the United States of America in the 1980s by a small group of enthusiasts. These enthusiasts later formed the Cesky Terrier Club and the breed is now recognized by all the major English speaking kennel clubs and is eligible to compete KC competitions around the world. The Cesky Terrier has a small well-muscled body with short legs – the breed is actually longer than it is tall! Due to its rarity little is known about the breeds temperament but the breed standard in America calls for a calm, non-aggressive, quiet and less active dog.

Lifespan

A Cesky Terrier will normally live to be between 10

and 13 years old. However it is not uncommon for a Cesky Terrier to live to be as old as 15, providing that it does not develop any serious health issues.

Height and Weight

A fully grown Cesky Terrier will normally stand between 10 to 13 inches (25.5 to 33cm) tall at the shoulder. A healthy adult Cesky Terrier will normally weigh between 13 to 30 pounds (6 to 13.5kg). It is important to note that the weight of a healthy Cesky Terrier depends on how large the Cesky Terrier is – taller Cesky Terrier should weigh more.

Coat

The Cesky Terrier has a long soft coat. The breed is not stripped (dead hair pulled out with fingers or a specialized knife) like other terriers, but rather is clippered or groomed with scissors. Most owners trim the top half of their Cesky Terrier's coat to a short length and leave the underside long. Interestingly all Cesky Terrier puppies have black coats that slowly lighten into a blue-grey coloration as they age.

Breed Characteristics

The following section will give you a simplistic overview of the characteristics of a Cesky Terrier. Our

rating system is from 1 to 10 – with 1 being the lowest score and 10 being the highest.

- **Adaptability:** 6/10
- **Friendliness:** 7/10
- **Health:** 6/10
- **Ease of Grooming:** 8/10
- **Amount of Shedding:** 1/10
- **Trainability:** 6/10
- **Intelligence:** 5/10
- **Exercise Needed:** 4/10
- **Playfulness:** 10/10
- **Family Friendliness:** 10/10

THE CHESAPEAKE BAY RETRIEVER

The Chesapeake Bay Retriever is a large-sized breed of dog that is a member of the Retriever, Gundog and Sporting breed groupings. The breed is also commonly known as the 'Chessie,' 'Chesapeake' and by its initials as simply the 'CBR.' As the breeds name suggests, the Chesapeake Bay Retriever was developed in the Chesapeake Bay area located in the United States of America. The breed was historically used to hunt waterfowl and other small prey. The breed is especially adept at hunting water-based prey due to its love of water and ability to swim. However in recent years the breed has established itself as a commonplace household pet. The Chesapeake Bay Retriever has a very similar appearance to the Labrador Retriever. The main aesthetic difference between the two breeds is the fact that the Chesapeake Bay Retriever has a wavy coat and the Labrador Retriever has a straight haired and smooth coat. The Chesapeake Bay Retriever is known to have beautiful, expressive and clear eyes of either a yellowish or amber hue. As a whole the Chesapeake Bay Retriever is known to be a happy, energetic intelligent and affection breed with a protective and family orientated nature.

Lifespan

A Chesapeake Bay Retriever will normally live to be between 10 and 12 years old. However it is not uncommon for a Chesapeake Bay Retriever to live to be as old as 14, providing that it does not develop any serious health issues.

Height and Weight

A fully grown Chesapeake Bay Retriever will normally stand between 21 to 26 inches (53.5 to 66cm) tall at the shoulder. A healthy adult Chesapeake Bay Retriever will normally weigh between 55 to 80 pounds (25 to 36.25kg). It is important to note that the weight of a healthy Chesapeake Bay Retriever depends on how large the Chesapeake Bay Retriever is – taller Chesapeake Bay Retriever should weigh more.

Breed Characteristics

The following section will give you a simplistic overview of the characteristics of a Chesapeake Bay Retriever. Our rating system is from 1 to 10 – with 1 being the lowest score and 10 being the highest.

- **Adaptability:** 6/10
- **Friendliness:** 6/10
- **Health:** 8/10

- ➢ **Ease of Grooming:** 10/10
- ➢ **Amount of Shedding:** 10/10
- ➢ **Trainability:** 6/10
- ➢ **Intelligence:** 8/10
- ➢ **Exercise Needed:** 10/10
- ➢ **Playfulness:** 8/10
- ➢ **Family Friendliness:** 10/10

THE CHIHUAHUA

The Chihuahua is the smallest breed of dog and is named after the Mexican state of 'Chihuahua.' Despite being the smallest overall breed of dog, Chihuahuas come in a wide variety of sizes and have multiple different head shapes, coat lengths and colorations. There are two varieties of Chihuahua: the 'Smooth Coat' (short haired) and the 'Long Coat' (long haired). Both varieties are equally affectionate and easy to keep well-groomed and cleaned. Both varieties can have either an 'apple head' or a 'deer head.' 'Apple heads' have rounded skulls, closely set eyes and shorter ears and legs than 'deer heads.' 'Deer heads' have flat topped skulls and more slender bodies. Chihuahuas are prone to shivering when they are cold, scared or excited. You should provide your Chihuahua with a small sweater or coat during the cold months of the year to avoid shivering.

Lifespan

Despite being the smallest breed of dog, the Chihuahua lives for a relatively long time. Chihuahuas regularly live for between 12 and 16 years. However it is not uncommon for a Chihuahua to live for as long as 18 years, providing they do not develop any serious health issues.

Size

The Chihuahua comes in a wide variety of weights and sizes. An adult Chihuaha will normally be between 6 and 9 inches (15 to 23cm) tall at the shoulder and weigh between 3 and 6 pounds (1.5 to 3kg).

Personality

The Chihuahua has a bold and confident personality and will not back down from a larger dog or animal in a conflict. They are often described as having a temperament similar to a Terrier. Chihuahua are small in size but still make excellent watch dogs due to their alert nature and tendency to bark at strangers. Chihuahuas are prone to bonding with a single person but are normally willing to make friends with new people and animals as long as they are introduced properly. It is important to make sure you purchase a Chihuahua that has been properly socialized during its puppyhood to make introductions easier. Socialization will help to ensure that your Chihuahua grows up to be a well-rounded adult dog.

Children

Most breeders will not sell a Chihuahua to a family

that has a child under the age of 8. Due to their small size and relatively fragile stature, Chihuahuas are easily injured. Young children, and toddlers, are prone to dropping small dogs or squeezing them too tightly both of which can have a serious effect on your Chihuahuas health.

Breed Characteristics

The following section will give you a simplistic overview of the characteristics of a Chihuahua. Our rating system is from 1 to 10 – with 1 being the lowest score and 10 being the highest.

- **Adaptability:** 6/10
- **Friendliness:** 8/10
- **Health:** 4/10
- **Ease of Grooming:** 10/10
- **Amount of Shedding:** 4/10
- **Trainability:** 5/10
- **Intelligence:** 8/10
- **Exercise Needed:** 6/10
- **Playfulness:** 8/10
- **Family Friendliness:** 8/10

THE CHINESE CRESTED

The Chinese Crested is a relatively small breed of hairless dog. Despite the name suggest that the breed originates from China this is not actually correct. The Chinese Crested is believed to have originated in Africa or Mexico. The breed got the name 'Chinese Crested' due to the fact that the breed was widely used on Chinese ships as a ratter. Apart from their history as ratters, the breed is believed to have been bred to be companions for invalids as they are able to stay healthy will relatively small amount of exercise. Despite the breed being considered hairless, there are two varieties of Chinese Crested: one with fur (the 'Powder Puff') and one without (the 'Hairless'). Both 'Powder Puff' and 'Hairless' Chinese Crested can occur in the same litter of puppies. The 'Hairless' gene is a dominant trait and the 'Powder Puff' trait is recessive. If a zygote receives two hairless genes it will never develop into a puppy and will die prenatally – this therefore means that all Chinese Crested carry the 'Powder Puff' gene (even the 'Hairless' variants). As a whole the Chinese Crested is an affectionate, happy and intelligent breed. They enjoy spending time with their owners and doting them with affection. However, the Chinese Crested will be incredibly wary of strangers and will take a long time to get used to new people.

Lifespan

A Chinese Crested will normally live to be between 10 and 12 years old. However it is not uncommon for a Chinese Crested to live to be as old as 14, providing that it does not develop any serious health issues.

Height and Weight

A fully grown Chinese Crested will normally stand between 11 to 13 inches (28 to 33cm) tall at the shoulder. A healthy adult Chinese Crested will normally weigh between 8 to 12 pounds (3.5 to 5.5kg). It is important to note that the weight of a healthy Chinese Crested depends on how large the Chinese Crested is – taller Chinese Crested should weigh more.

Breed Characteristics

The following section will give you a simplistic overview of the characteristics of a Chinese Crested. Our rating system is from 1 to 10 – with 1 being the lowest score and 10 being the highest.

- **Adaptability:** 6/10
- **Friendliness:** 8/10
- **Health:** 10/10
- **Ease of Grooming:** 5/10
- **Amount of Shedding:** 4/10

- ➢ **Trainability:** 6/10
- ➢ **Intelligence:** 8/10
- ➢ **Exercise Needed:** 3/10
- ➢ **Playfulness:** 6/10
- ➢ **Family Friendliness:** 8/10

THE CHINESE SHAR-PEI

The Chinese Shar-Pei is an ancient breed of dog that originates from China. The breed is known for its distinctive wrinkled skin and strangely colored blue-black tongue. Due to the breed originating in China, the breed's name is believed to be derived from the English spelling of the Cantonese equivalent *'sā pèih,'* which translates to 'Sanc Skin.' The name 'Sand Skin' is a clear reference to the breeds short, rough coat and wrinkled features. The **Shar-Pei has dramatically more wrinkles during its puppyhood as it 'grows' into its excess skin.** Despite their ancient history, the Shar-Pei was named one of the world's rarest breeds by 'Time' magazine and the 'Guinness Book of World Records' in the late 1970s. The breed's prickly skin was originally developed to help defend the dog against wild boar, as the Shar-Pei was originally used for hunting purposes. The breed was then used in dog fighting which is where its large amount of excess skin developed. The Shar-Pei's excess skin made it hard for other dogs to grab onto, and if they did manage to grab ahold on the Shar-Pei it still had room to maneuver inside its own skin! Shar-Pei's were known to completely twist around in their own skin to bite assailants back! In modern times the Shar-Pei has mainly been used as a guard dog and a companion dog. As a whole the breed makes very good family pets providing that they are properly socialized with children, strangers and other animals to combat their innate protective, territorial and potentially aggressive nature. However if the breed is properly socialized they are known to be incredibly loyal, fairly affectionate and occasionally playful.

Lifespan

A Chinese Shar-Pei will normally live to be between 8 and 10 years old. However it is not uncommon for a Chinese Shar-Pei to live to be as old as 12, providing that it does not develop any serious health issues.

Height and Weight

A fully grown Chinese Shar-Pei will normally stand between 18 to 20 inches (45.75 to 51cm) tall at the shoulder. A healthy adult Chinese Shar-Pei will normally weigh between 40 to 55 pounds (18 to 25kg). It is important to note that the weight of a healthy Chinese Shar-Pei depends on how large the Chinese Shar-Pei is – taller Chinese Shar-Pei should weigh more.

Breed Characteristics

The following section will give you a simplistic overview of the characteristics of a Chinese Shar-Pei. Our rating system is from 1 to 10 – with 1 being the

lowest score and 10 being the highest.

- **Adaptability:** 6/10
- **Friendliness:** 3/10
- **Health:** 3/10
- **Ease of Grooming:** 8/10
- **Amount of Shedding:** 10/10
- **Trainability:** 6/10
- **Intelligence:** 5/10
- **Exercise Needed:** 4/10
- **Playfulness:** 3/10
- **Family Friendliness:** 5/10

THE CHINOOK

The Chinook is a rare breed of sled dog that originates from the United States of America. The breed was developed in the state of New Hampshire in the early 20th century and is not the official state dog. The breed was developed by a single man named Arthur Treadwell Walden in 1917 and the entire breed's lineage can be traced to a single male dog named 'Chinook' – hence the breed's name. The breed's father, 'Chinook,' was a mix of a husky and a tawny Mastiff-like male which lead him to have a large broad Mastiff-like head with dropped ears and the athletic build of a husky. 'Chinook' was bred with Belgian Shepherd dogs, Canadian Eskimo dogs and German Shepherds to create the Chinook breed. The breeding pool for Chinooks dwindled during the second World War and was as small as 11 by the mid-1980s but due to groups of enthusiasts the breed managed to survive. The breed was traditionally used as a working sled dog but is now more commonly found as a house hold family pet. As a whole the breed is incredibly affectionate and playful especially towards children. It is also an intelligent breed that is eager to learn and please its owners. Despite the breed not being known to show aggression it is still important to make sure that you Chinook is properly socialized with children, strangers and other animals during its puppyhood.

Lifespan

A Chinook will normally live to be between 10 and 13 years old. However it is not uncommon for a Chinook to live to be as old as 15, providing that it does not develop any serious health issues.

Height and Weight

A fully grown Chinook will normally stand between 21 to 27 inches (53.5 to 68.5cm) tall at the shoulder. A healthy adult Chinook will normally weigh between 55 to 70 pounds (25 to 31.75kg). It is important to note that the weight of a healthy Chinook depends on how large the Chinook is – taller Chinook should weigh more.

Breed Characteristics

The following section will give you a simplistic overview of the characteristics of a Chinook. Our rating system is from 1 to 10 – with 1 being the lowest score and 10 being the highest.

- **Adaptability:** 6/10
- **Friendliness:** 8/10
- **Health:** 6/10
- **Ease of Grooming:** 3/10

- **Amount of Shedding:** 1/10
- **Trainability:** 6/10
- **Intelligence:** 8/10
- **Exercise Needed:** 8/10
- **Playfulness:** 8/10
- **Family Friendliness:** 10/10

THE CHOW CHOW

The Chow Chow is an ancient breed of dog that originates from northern China. The Chow Chow is thought to be one of the oldest recognizable dog breeds in the world! It is believed that the Chow Chow breed is the forefather to modern breeds such as the Pomeranian, Norwegian Elkhound, Keeshond and Samoyed. The breed's name in Chinese is 'Songshi Quan' which translates to 'Puffy-lion dog.' It is believed that the Chow Chow is one of the native dogs used as inspiration for the Foo dog, the traditional stone guardians found throughout China in front of palaces, Buddhist temples and places of importance. The Chow Chow was originally bred as a general purpose working dog and would have been commonly used for herding, hunting, guarding and cart pulling purposes. Some historians believe that the Chow Chow is described in ancient texts to have accompanied the Mongolian armies as they invaded southward into China – which would suggest that the Chow Chow has also been used for war purposes. Due to its working history the Chow Chow has a sturdily built square shaped body. The breed has two unique aesthetic features: its thick double coat and its uncommon blue-black tongue. The breed's coat comes in both a smooth and rough variation and comes in the following colorations: red, black, blue, fawn and cream. In modern times the breed is commonly found as a household pet. The breed as a whole is known to be incredibly loyal and affectionate towards their owners but wary of strangers. Due to their history as guard dogs they are also known to be fiercely protective over their family unit and families property. To avoid the potential for a fierce nature it is important that Chow Chow owners prioritize their dog's socialization with strangers and other dogs.

Lifespan

A Chow Chow will normally live to be between 10 and 12 years old. However it is not uncommon for a Chow Chow to live to be as old as 15, providing that it does not develop any serious health issues.

Height and Weight

A fully grown Chow Chow will normally stand between 17 to 20 inches (43 to 51cm) tall at the shoulder. A healthy adult Chow Chow will normally weigh between 40 to 70 pounds (18 to 32kg). It is important to note that the weight of a healthy Chow Chow depends on how large the Chow Chow is – taller Chow Chow should weigh more.

Breed Characteristics

The following section will give you a simplistic overview of the characteristics of a Chow Chow. Our rating system is from 1 to 10 – with 1 being the lowest score and 10 being the highest.

- **Adaptability:** 6/10
- **Friendliness:** 4/10
- **Health:** 6/10
- **Ease of Grooming:** 2/10
- **Amount of Shedding:** 1/10
- **Trainability:** 5/10
- **Intelligence:** 8/10
- **Exercise Needed:** 4/10
- **Playfulness:** 3/10
- **Family Friendliness:** 7/10

THE CLUMBER SPANIEL

The Clumber Spaniel is a breed of dog, within the spaniel typing, that originates from the United Kingdom. The breed's name is derived from 'Clumber Park' which is located in Nottinghamshire and is where the breed was first developed. The Clumber Spaniel is actually the largest breed of dog within the spaniel typing. The breed was originally developed as a gundog that specializes in hunting in areas of heavy coverage. There are two different theories about the breed heritage. The first theory suggests that the Clumber Spaniel was developed by breeding the now extinct Alpine Spaniel with Basset Hounds and Pyrenean Mountain dogs. The second theory suggests that the Clumber Spaniel was developed by breeding King Charles Spaniels with other gundog breeds – the King Charles Spaniel was originally much larger than it is in modern times. The breed was originally restricted to being bred by nobility, but during World War 1 the Clumber Spaniel's numbers dwindle which lead to kennels taking an interest in preserving the breed. Despite the efforts to increase the breed's numbers, the Clumber Spaniel is still considered a vulnerable breed in the UK – which means that under 300 new Clumber Spaniel are registered each year. The Clumber Spaniel has a large heavy bone structure, a large head, large vine-leaf shaped ears and a freckled muzzle. The breed predominantly has a white, lemon, orange or brown coat colorations and there are normally spots of other common coat colorations around their muzzle and body. The Clumber Spaniel has a dense coat with the top half being short and the bottom half being a lot longer. As a whole the Clumber Spaniel is known to be a gentle, loyal and affectionate breed. They are also known to be a very 'sleepy' breed and spend a lot of time relaxing, eating or sleeping.

Lifespan

A Clumber Spaniel will normally live to be between 10 and 12 years old. However it is not uncommon for a Clumber Spaniel to live to be as old as 13, providing that it does not develop any serious health issues.

Height and Weight

A fully grown Clumber Spaniel will normally stand between 17 to 20 inches (43 to 51cm) tall at the shoulder. A healthy adult Clumber Spaniel will normally weigh between 55 to 85 pounds (25 to 38.5kg). It is important to note that the weight of a healthy Clumber Spaniel depends on how large the Clumber Spaniel is – taller Clumber Spaniel should weigh more.

Breed Characteristics

The following section will give you a simplistic overview of the characteristics of a Clumber Spaniel. Our rating system is from 1 to 10 – with 1 being the lowest score and 10 being the highest.

- **Adaptability:** 8/10
- **Friendliness:** 8/10
- **Health:** 8/10
- **Ease of Grooming:** 3/10
- **Amount of Shedding:** 10/10
- **Trainability:** 8/10
- **Intelligence:** 6/10
- **Exercise Needed:** 6/10
- **Playfulness:** 10/10
- **Family Friendliness:** 10/10

THE COCKAPOO

The Cockapoo is a popular mixed-breed of dog that is a cross between a Poodle (most commonly either miniature or toy poodle) and a Cocker Spaniel (either an American Cocker Spaniel or an English Cocker Spaniel). The breed has been known as a 'Cockerpoo' in American since the 1950's. However, Purebred breed associations (such as 'The Kennel Club,' the 'American Kennel Club,' the 'Canadian Kennel Club' and the 'United Kennel Club') do not recognize the Cockapoo as a breed in its own right. Due to their popularity and fashionable status, the Cockapoo is the most likely breeds to be bred in puppy farms or by uninformed and inexperienced amateur breeders looking for a quick profit. If you are looking to purchase a Cockapoo it is important to do careful research on who is breeding the puppies and where they have been bred as it is important to not support business that hold poor breeding conditions. The Cockapoo has become very popular due to the fact that it combines the fun-loving, outgoing and affectionate personality of the Cocker Spaniel with the low-shedding, low-dander qualities of the Poodle. Like a Spaniel, the Cockapoo is an excellent hunting dog and is capable of retrieving game easily. However the Cockapoo has a very needy personality and it is therefore recommended to be owned by families with children.

Lifespan

A Cockapoo will normally live to be between 10 and 12 years old. However it is not uncommon for a Cockapoo to live to be as old as 15, providing that it does not develop any serious health issues.

Height and Weight

A fully grown Cockapoo will normally stand between 15 to 18 inches (38 to 45.75cm) tall at the shoulder. A healthy adult Cockapoo will normally weigh between 19 to 30 pounds (6.5 to 13.55kg). It is important to note that the weight of a healthy Cockapoo depends on how large the Cockapoo is – taller Cockapoo should weigh more.

Coat

The Cockapoo's coat is different from Cockapoo to Cockapoo. However, most will have a coat texture that is somewhere between a Cocker Spaniel and a Poodle. However it is not uncommon for puppies in the same litter to have completely different coats: some having the sleeker coat of the Cocker Spaniel and others having the curly coat of a Poodle. The breed's coat can come in a wide range of colorations but will most commonly be black, white, tan, merle or brindle.

Breed Characteristics

The following section will give you a simplistic overview of the characteristics of a Cockapoo. Our rating system is from 1 to 10 – with 1 being the lowest score and 10 being the highest.

- **Adaptability:** 6/10
- **Friendliness:** 10/10
- **Health:** 5/10
- **Ease of Grooming:** 5/10
- **Amount of Shedding:** 1/10
- **Trainability:** 6/10
- **Intelligence:** 8/10
- **Exercise Needed:** 7/10
- **Playfulness:** 10/10
- **Family Friendliness:** 10/10

THE COCKER SPANIEL

The name 'Cocker Spaniel' belongs to two breeds of spaniel type dogs: the 'American Cocker Spaniel' and the 'English Cocker Spaniel,' both of which are commonly simply called the Cocker Spaniel in their respective countries of origin. The Cocker Spaniel was originally developed to be a hunting dog in the United Kingdom and the 'Cocker' portion of their name is in reference to the Eurasian woodcock which was their main prey. The breed was then transported to the United States of America were the breed went through development to enable it to hunt American woodcocks more efficiently. There are now multiple physical differences between the 'American Cocker Spaniel' and the 'English Cocker Spaniel.' Both types of Cocker Spaniel use their sense of smell to allow them to hunt and flush out their prey for their handlers to shoot. Once the bird is downed the Cocker Spaniel will retrieve it in its mouth, which has been developed to be soft for the purpose of not damaging the prey. The breed's coat comes in multiple different potential colorations but it will most commonly come in black, liver, red or solid golden. As a whole the Cocker Spaniel is known to be a very affectionate and sweet natured breed. They are perfectly suited to life as a household pet as they are playful, gentle and enjoy spending time exercising with their family unit. The breed is known to be 'soft' natured which means that they do not come well with harsh treatment. It is therefore imperative to treat your Cocker Spaniel with a gentle and calm tone at all times during its training.

Lifespan

A Cocker Spaniel will normally live to be between 12 and 13 years old. However it is not uncommon for a Cocker Spaniel to live to be as old as 15, providing that it does not develop any serious health issues.

Height and Weight

A fully grown Cocker Spaniel will normally stand between 14 to 15 inches (35.5 to 38cm) tall at the shoulder. A healthy adult Cocker Spaniel will normally weigh between 24 to 28 pounds (11 to 12.7kg). It is important to note that the weight of a healthy Cocker Spaniel depends on how large the Cocker Spaniel is – taller Cocker Spaniel should weigh more.

The English Cocker Spaniel

The English Cocker Spaniel is the large of the two breeds. The English Cocker Spaniel is split into two strain: working dogs and show dogs. The working of English Cocker Spaniel tends to have a slightly large and more well-muscled body as well as having a short, less feathered and finer coat than the show variety. The working strain also is notably more energetic. The Cocker Spaniel has a wavy medium-length coat with a silky texture.

The American Cocker Spaniel

The American Cocker Spaniel is the smaller of the two Cocker Spaniel types. The reason that the American type is smaller is due to the fact that it was developed to hunt American woodcocks which are smaller than Eurasian woodcocks. The breed appearance is also slightly different: the American Cocker Spaniel has a much thicker and longer coat than their English counterpart. Their coat is short on the head and back but long everywhere else which give the American Cocker Spaniel a regal appearance.

Breed Characteristics

The following section will give you a simplistic overview of the characteristics of a Cocker Spaniel. Our rating system is from 1 to 10 – with 1 being the lowest score and 10 being the highest.

- **Adaptability:** 8/10
- **Friendliness:** 8/10
- **Health:** 8/10

- **Ease of Grooming:** 2/10
- **Amount of Shedding:** 6/10
- **Trainability:** 8/10
- **Intelligence:** 8/10
- **Exercise Needed:** 6/10
- **Playfulness:** 8/10
- **Family Friendliness:** 10/10

THE COLLIE

The Collie is a breed of dog that originates from Scotland, primarily from the Highland regions. The breed's name has two potential points of origin. Some historians believe that the name 'Collie' is based upon the Anglo-Saxon word 'coll' which means black. Other historians believe that the breeds name is based upon the Scottish black-faced sheep named 'Colley,' as the Collie was used to guard these sheep on a regular basis. However most historians agree that the Collie is probably descended from breeds of dog introduced to the United Kingdom by Roman conquerors almost two thousand years ago! Traditionally the Collie was predominately black coated and was much closer in size and shape to today's Border Collie. The breed traditionally had no standardized appearance due to it being bred for intelligence, herding and working ability rather than looks. The breed was widely employed as a herding dog and was known to herd, and guard, cattle, pigs, sheep and goats on a regular basis. In the 1860's Queen Victoria of England fell in love with the good natured temperament and appearance of the Collie and introduced them into English culture, where the breed was known as the 'Scottish Sheep-Dog.' The Collie comes in two potential coat variants: rough and smooth. The rough coated variant has a long, abundant and straight outer coat that is rough to the touch and a soft, thick and furry undercoat. The smooth coat variant has a shorter, dense and flat outercoat and a thick undercoat. The breed's coat comes in four colors: tricolor (black with white and tan markings), white, blue merle (silvery blue and black) and sable (which is commonly known as the 'Lassie' coat coloration). As a whole the breed is known to be incredibly good natured, affectionate and gentle. The Collie thrives in a household environment and enjoys spending time with its family unit. The Collie is also incredibly good around children as they are both protective and playful. The Collie is highly intelligent and is known to be willing to risk its own wellbeing to protect members of its family.

Lifespan

A Collie will normally live to be between 10 and 14 years old. However it is not uncommon for a Collie to live to be as old as 15, providing that it does not develop any serious health issues.

Height and Weight

A fully grown Collie will normally stand between 20 to 26 inches (50.8 to 66cm) tall at the shoulder. A healthy adult Collie will normally weigh between 50 to 70 pounds (22.5 to 31.75kg). It is important to note that the weight of a healthy Collie depends on how large the Collie is – taller Collie should weigh more.

Breed Characteristics

The following section will give you a simplistic overview of the characteristics of a Collie. Our rating system is from 1 to 10 – with 1 being the lowest score and 10 being the highest.

- **Adaptability:** 8/10
- **Friendliness:** 10/10
- **Health:** 6/10
- **Ease of Grooming:** 5/10
- **Amount of Shedding:** 10/10
- **Trainability:** 7/10
- **Intelligence:** 8/10
- **Exercise Needed:** 6/10
- **Playfulness:** 10/10
- **Family Friendliness:** 10/10

THE COTON DE TULEAR

The Coton de Tulear is a small breed of dog that originates from Madagascar, as is actually the island's nation dog. The breed is named after the city of Tuléar, which is located in Madagascar, and for its cotton-like coat texture. The breed is believed to be a descendant of the Tenerife dog that has been mated with a breed native to Madagascar during the 16th century. The Coton de Tulear is a member of the Bichon typing and is still closely related to the Bichon Tenerife and the Tenerife Terrier. The Coton de Tulear has always been a companion dog and has never been feral. Unlike most other breeds of dog developed in Madagascar, the Coton de Tulear has never been used to hunt wild boar or alligators, as its size and strength prove. The Coton de Tulear also has a nonexistent prey drive which further suggests that the breed has always been a companion dog. The breed's cotton-like coat is believed to be a result of a single gene mutation. The Coton de Tulear has a medium-to-long coat that is considered to be hair rather than fur. Despite having long hair the breed is considered to be hypoallergenic as it barely ever sheds once it is full grown – however, like the Poodle and Havanese, the Coton de Tulear will shed its puppy coat. The breed's coat comes in three standardize colorations: white, black and white, and tricolor (which is a mixture of black, white and tan). As a whole the Coton de Tulear is known to be a highly affectionate, intelligent and playful breed. They fit perfectly well into a family household environment. Despite their small size, it is recommended to keep a Coton de Tulear in a house, rather than an apartment, as they are very vocal and will grunt, bark and whine often while playing.

Lifespan

A Coton de Tulear will normally live to be between 12 and 14 years old. However it is not uncommon for a Coton de Tulear to live to be as old as 16, providing that it does not develop any serious health issues.

Height and Weight

A fully grown Coton de Tulear will normally stand between 8 to 12 inches (20.3 to 30.5cm) tall at the shoulder. A healthy adult Coton de Tulear will normally weigh between 8 to 13 pounds (3.5 to 6kg). It is important to note that the weight of a healthy Coton de Tulear depends on how large the Coton de Tulear is – taller Coton de Tulear should weigh more.

Breed Characteristics

The following section will give you a simplistic overview of the characteristics of a Coton de Tulear. Our

rating system is from 1 to 10 – with 1 being the lowest score and 10 being the highest.

- **Adaptability:** 8/10
- **Friendliness:** 10/10
- **Health:** 10/10
- **Ease of Grooming:** 5/10
- **Amount of Shedding:** 1/10
- **Trainability:** 6/10
- **Intelligence:** 8/10
- **Exercise Needed:** 6/10
- **Playfulness:** 10/10
- **Family Friendliness:** 10/10

THE CURLY-COATED RETRIEVER

The Curly-Coated Retriever, commonly referred to as simply a 'Curly,' is a breed of dog that originates from England and was originally developed to hunt upland birds and waterfowl. The Curly-Coated Retriever is the tallest of the retriever typing and is very easily distinguished due to its very unique mass of tight curls that covers the dog's body. Despite the large amount of curled hair, the Curly-Coated Retriever is actually a single coated breed and the small tight curls of a show-standard dog are actually very easy to maintain. Due to the fact that they a single coated breed, the Curly-Coated Retriever does not shed as much as most breeds. The Curly-Coated Retriever's curly coat actually repels water which allowed it to easily hunt waterfowl throughout the coldest seasons of the year. As previously mentioned the breed was developed to hunt birds but in recent years is more commonly found as a household pet or as a show dog. The only accepted coat colorations for a show standard Curly-Coated Retriever are solid black and solid liver. As a whole the Curly-Coated Retriever is a affectionate, intelligent and fun loving breed. They are known to be somewhat aloof with strangers but incredibly loyal towards their family unit.

Lifespan

A Curly-Coated Retriever will normally live to be between 9 and 11 years old. However it is not uncommon for a Curly-Coated Retriever to live to be as old as 12, providing that it does not develop any serious health issues.

Height and Weight

A fully grown Curly-Coated Retriever will normally stand between 23 to 27 inches (58.5 to 68.5cm) tall at the shoulder. A healthy adult Curly-Coated Retriever will normally weigh between 65 to 100 pounds (29.5 to 45.5kg). It is important to note that the weight of a healthy Curly-Coated Retriever depends on how large the Curly-Coated Retriever is – taller Curly-Coated Retriever should weigh more.

Exercise

The Curly-Coated Retriever was bred for its endurance, intelligence and athleticism. It is very important to make sure that your Curly-Coated Retriever receives enough exercise on a daily basis as it is likely to develop destructive behaviors if it has an abundance of energy or is overly bored. The Curly-Coated Retriever love the outdoors and enjoys playing retrieving based games such as fetch and Frisbee. If a Curly-Coated Retriever has been exercised thoroughly it will be calm and laid back in a quiet home environment.

Breed Characteristics

The following section will give you a simplistic overview of the characteristics of a Curly-Coated Retriever. Our rating system is from 1 to 10 – with 1 being the lowest score and 10 being the highest.

- **Adaptability:** 6/10
- **Friendliness:** 8/10
- **Health:** 5/10
- **Ease of Grooming:** 6/10
- **Amount of Shedding:** 6/10
- **Trainability:** 8/10
- **Intelligence:** 10/10
- **Exercise Needed:** 8/10
- **Playfulness:** 10/10
- **Family Friendliness:** 10/10

Encyclopedia of Dog Breeds

THE DACHSHUND

The Dachshund (colloquially known as *'The Sausage Dog'*) is a breed of short-legged and long-bodied hound dog. The standard size Dachshund was bred to flush out badgers, and other burrow dwelling animals. In fact the word *'Dachs,'* in German, means 'Badger.' The miniature Dachshund was bred to hunt smaller animals such as rabbits and prairie dogs. Standard sized Dachshunds weigh between 16 and 32 pounds (7 to 14kg) when fully grown. Miniature Dachshunds weigh 11 pounds (5kg) and under. If a Dachshund weighs between 11 and 16 pounds (5 to 7kg), it is referred to as a Tweenie. The breed has three different types of coat: shorthaired, wirehaired and longhaired. Due to their small size, interesting appearance and lively disposition, the Dachshund has become one of the most popular household dog breeds.

Lifespan

Dachshunds commonly live to be between 12 and 14 years old. However it is not uncommon for a Dachshund to live for as long as 15 years, providing they do not develop any serious health issues.

Appearance

A typical Dachshund has a long muscular body and short, stubby legs. The front two paws are normally wide and paddle-shaped to assist with digging. The Dachshund has a deep chest that provides it with increased lung capacity which allows the breed to have increased stamina while hunting prey underground. They have an increased nose area on their snout to allows them to greatly absorb odors, which again assists the breed in hunting underground. Dachshund coats have a wide variety of colors: chocolate, tan, black, cream and red – to name but a few.

Popularity

The Dachshund is a very popular apartment dog due to its small size. They are ranked among the top ten most popular dog breeds in 76 of 190 major US cities! Due to their popularity it will be very easy for you to join an organized local Dachshund club. This will allow you to meet other owners and introduce your dog to other dogs within its breed.

Breed Characteristics

The following section will give you a simplistic overview of the characteristics of a Dachshund. Our

rating system is from 1 to 10 – with 1 being the lowest score and 10 being the highest.

- **Adaptability:** 6/10
- **Friendliness:** 6/10
- **Health:** 6/10
- **Ease of Grooming:** 7/10
- **Amount of Shedding:** 6/10
- **Trainability:** 8/10
- **Intelligence:** 8/10
- **Exercise Needed:** 6/10
- **Playfulness:** 8/10
- **Family Friendliness:** 10/10

THE DALMATIAN

The Dalmatian is a large breed of dog that originates from Croatia. The breed is most noted for its highly unique black, or liver, spotted coat which has earned the breed the nicknames of 'Plum Pudding Dog' and the 'Leopard Carriage Dog.' Despite the breed originating from Croatia, the Dalmatian was mainly developed and cultivated in the United Kingdom. In 1890 the United Kingdom was the first country to actually have an official Dalmatian club and breed standard. The Dalmatian were originally used for a plethora of different tasks: as dogs of war, as guard dogs and as companion dogs. The modern day Dalmatian still has a high instinct to guard its owners and will be friendly and loyal to people it knows but often aloof with strangers and unknown dogs. In the early 1900s, the Dalmatian started to be used in sporting hunts as was used as a bird dog, trail hound, a retriever and in packs to hunt wild boar or stags. It was discovered that Dalmatians and horses are very compatible, and the Dalmatian soon was used to run in front of horse drawn carriages to clear a path for the horses. As the breed's large amount of working roles suggests, the Dalmatian is a highly adaptable and intelligent breed that is capable of being trained to do nearly any job. The Dalmatian is born with a solid white coat and they slowly develop their characteristic spots at around 3 to 4 weeks old - after about a month or two they have developed most of their spots. Most Dalmatian are born with a smooth short coat that sheds continuously throughout the year. However it is not uncommon for a Dalmatian to be born with a long haired coat – interestingly the long haired Dalmatians shed considerably less than their short haired counterparts. As a whole the Dalmatian is a highly intelligent and affectionate breed that thrives both in working environments and household environments. It is important to well socialize your Dalmatian during its puppyhood to make it less suspicious and aloof with strangers and unknown dogs.

Lifespan

A Dalmatian will normally live to be between 12 and 14 years old. However it is not uncommon for a Dalmatian to live to be as old as 16, providing that it does not develop any serious health issues.

Height and Weight

A fully grown Dalmatian will normally stand between 19 to 24 inches (48.25 to 61cm) tall at the shoulder. A healthy adult Dalmatian will normally weigh between 48 to 55 pounds (21.75 to 25kg). It is important to note that the weight of a healthy Dalmatian depends on how large the Dalmatian is – taller Dalmatian should weigh more.

Breed Characteristics

The following section will give you a simplistic overview of the characteristics of a Dalmatian. Our rating system is from 1 to 10 – with 1 being the lowest score and 10 being the highest.

- **Adaptability:** 6/10
- **Friendliness:** 8/10
- **Health:** 8/10
- **Ease of Grooming:** 10/10
- **Amount of Shedding:** 10/10
- **Trainability:** 6/10
- **Intelligence:** 8/10
- **Exercise Needed:** 10/10
- **Playfulness:** 8/10
- **Family Friendliness:** 10/10

THE DANDIE DINMONT TERRIER

The Dandie Dinmont Terrier is a small breed of dog that belongs to the terrier family and originates from Scotland. The breed has relatively short legs and a long body – giving it a similar body structure to a Dachshund. The Dandie Dinmont Terrier was originally developed to hunt otters and badgers along the board of Scotland and England during the early 1600s. The breed was relatively unknown until the Dandie Dinmont Terrier Club (DDTC) was formed in 1875 and a breed standard was created. The breed became internationally recognized in 1888 when the Dandie Dinmont Terrier was registered with the American Kennel Club. Despite the breed gaining popularity in the late 1800s for hunting purposes, the Dandie Dinmont Terrier was officially considered the rarest breed of dog that is native to the British Isles in 2006. Due to its dwindling numbers the Dandie Dinmont Terrier is now a part of the United Kingdom's list of 'Vulnerable Native Breeds.' The Dandie Dinmont Terrier has a very unique appearance. They have a silky coat that forms a 'topknot' on the top of the dog's head. The breed's coat comes in two potential color ranges: either 'pepper' or 'mustard.' 'Pepper' coats range from a dark blueish black to a very light silvery grey colorations. 'Mustard' coats range from reddish brown to light fawn colorations – it is also not uncommon for 'mustard' colored Dandie Dinmont Terrier to have white heads. As a whole the breed is known to be loyal, affectionate and tough which makes it a perfect pet for a household with older children. Due to the breed's elongated body structure it is not recommend to be kept in a household with small children, as an unlucky drop from a short height could severely injury a Dandie Dinmont Terrier spine. The Dandie Dinmont Terrier is known to make a perfect guard dog, but is considered to be the most docile and undemanding of the terrier family. It is important to socialize your Dandie Dinmont Terrier at a young age due to the fact that they are 'very game' – which means that the Dandie Dinmont Terrier is willing to fight other animals (dogs, foxes, cats etc) for their territory.

Lifespan

A Dandie Dinmont Terrier will normally live to be between 12 and 14 years old. However it is not uncommon for a Dandie Dinmont Terrier to live to be as old as 15, providing that it does not develop any serious health issues.

Height and Weight

A fully grown Dandie Dinmont Terrier will normally stand between 8 to 11 inches (20.5 to 28cm) tall at the shoulder. A healthy adult Dandie Dinmont Terrier will normally weigh between 18 to 24 pounds (8 to 11kg). It is important to note that the weight of a healthy Dandie Dinmont Terrier depends on how large the Dandie Dinmont Terrier is – taller Dandie Dinmont Terrier should weigh more.

Breed Characteristics

The following section will give you a simplistic overview of the characteristics of a Dandie Dinmont Terrier. Our rating system is from 1 to 10 – with 1 being the lowest score and 10 being the highest.

- **Adaptability:** 6/10
- **Friendliness:** 8/10
- **Health:** 6/10
- **Ease of Grooming:** 4/10
- **Amount of Shedding:** 6/10
- **Trainability:** 6/10
- **Intelligence:** 6/10
- **Exercise Needed:** 6/10
- **Playfulness:** 8/10
- **Family Friendliness:** 10/10

THE DOBERMAN PINSCHER

The Doberman Pinscher (also commonly known as either 'Dobermann' or simply 'Doberman') is a medium-large breed of dog that was originally developed in Germany. The breed was initially developed to assist with tax collection in the late 1800s but is now a domesticated family pet. The Doberman Pinscher has a long muzzle which allows it to have an extremely strong bite. The breed stands on the toes of its feet rather than the foot pads. This gives the Doberman Pinscher a light footed and graceful gait. Traditionally, the breed has cropped and posted ears and a docked tail – however in some countries it is considered illegal animal abuse to inflict these. A pure breed will always have distinct markings on its chest, paws, legs, muzzle, underneath its tail and above its eyes. As a whole the breed is known to be intelligent, physically strong, occasionally stubborn, alert and incredibly loyal. The Doberman Pinscher makes an excellent guard dog due to their incredible loyalty to their family unit. Like with all breeds, the personality of a Doberman Pinscher varies from dog to dog – however a properly trained Doberman will tend to always be a loving and devoted companion. With proper training a Doberman Pinscher can also be a great pet to have around small children.

Lifespan

A Doberman Pinscher will normally live to be between 10 and 12 years old. However it is possible for a Doberman Pinscher to live to be as old as 13, providing they do not develop any serious health issues.

Height and Weight

A fully grown Doberman Pinscher will normally be between 24 inches to 28 inches (61 to 71cm) tall at the shoulder. A healthy adult will also normally weigh between 60 and 80 pounds (27 to 36kg).

Hierarchy

As a breed, the Doberman Pinscher is very concerned with 'Pack Hierarchy.' A Doberman Pinscher will always be looking to understand its position within the family unit. It is important to make sure that your Doberman understands that it is not the Alpha of your family unit. It is important to remember that Doberman Pinschers are not an innately aggressive breed despite having a somewhat bad reputation. Once your dog understand that you are the alpha of the pack it will be very eager to please. Dobermans enjoy taking direct cues from their leaders as they value the attention of the 'Alpha.'

Von Willebrand's Disease

'Von Willebrand's Disease' is a blood disorder that is inherited. The disease interferes with the dog's ability to form blood clots. Symptoms include: excessive bleeding after any cut, nose bleeds, bleeding gums and bleeding stomach or intestines. There is no known cure for this disease and the only way to combat it is with a blood transfer from a dog without the disease. It is important to get you Doberman Pinscher tested by a vet to make sure it does not have this disease. When purchasing a puppy from a breeder you should ask for proof that neither of your puppy's parents have 'Von Willebrand's Disease.'

Breed Characteristics

The following section will give you a simplistic overview of the characteristics of a Doberman Pinscher. Our rating system is from 1 to 10 – with 1 being the lowest score and 10 being the highest.

- **Adaptability:** 6/10
- **Friendliness:** 6/10
- **Health:** 8/10
- **Ease of Grooming:** 10/10
- **Amount of Shedding:** 8/10
- **Trainability:** 6/10

- ➤ **Intelligence:** 10/10
- ➤ **Exercise Needed:** 8/10
- ➤ **Playfulness:** 10/10
- ➤ **Family Friendliness:** 10/10

THE DOGUE DE BORDEAUX

The Dogue de Bordeaux is a breed of dog that is a part of the Mastiff breed one of the most ancient breeds of dog that originates from France. The Dogue de Bordeaux is commonly also known as the 'Bordeaux Mastiff' and the 'French Mastiff.' The breed was originally bred and developed in the south of France around the city of Bordeaux and the city lent its name to the breed. The French placed an emphasis on keeping their ancient breeds 'pure' and a Dogue de Bordeaux with a 'black mask' on its muzzle is considered to have been bred with the English Mastiff. A 'pure' Dogue de Bordeaux will have a light pink nose, light colored eyes and a red mask. The Dogue de Bordeaux was originally split into two separate typings: the Douge and the Dougin. The Douge was the larger of the two typings and is what the modern Dogue de Bordeaux is based upon. The smaller Dougin typing is no longer in existence. The breed has a well-balanced, muscular and large powerful build. However despite the breed's large build, the Dogue de Bordeaux is set somewhat low to the ground and is not as tall as many of the other breed's within the Mastiff family. The breed has a short, fine and soft coat that comes in a variety of colorations. However, the breed's coat will commonly come in either a light fawn or a darker mahogany coloration. As a whole the Dogue de Bordeaux is known to be a highly loyal and affectionate breed. They make great household pets as they thrive in a busy household environment.

Lifespan

A Dogue de Bordeaux will normally live to be between 8 and 12 years old. However it is not uncommon for a Dogue de Bordeaux to live to be as old as 13, providing that it does not develop any serious health issues.

Height and Weight

A fully grown Dogue de Bordeaux will normally stand between 23 to 27 inches (58.5 to 68.5cm) tall at the shoulder. A healthy adult Dogue de Bordeaux will normally weigh between 100 to 150 pounds (45.3 to 68kg). It is important to note that the weight of a healthy Dogue de Bordeaux depends on how large the Dogue de Bordeaux is – taller Dogue de Bordeaux should weigh more.

Breed Characteristics

The following section will give you a simplistic overview of the characteristics of a Dogue de Bordeaux. Our rating system is from 1 to 10 – with 1 being the lowest score and 10 being the highest.

- ➤ **Adaptability:** 6/10
- ➤ **Friendliness:** 7/10
- ➤ **Health:** 5/10
- ➤ **Ease of Grooming:** 10/10
- ➤ **Amount of Shedding:** 6/10
- ➤ **Trainability:** 6/10
- ➤ **Intelligence:** 6/10
- ➤ **Exercise Needed:** 6/10
- ➤ **Playfulness:** 7/10
- ➤ **Family Friendliness:** 10/10

Dog Care Professionals

THE ENGLISH COCKER SPANIEL

The English Cocker Spaniel is a breed of gun dog that was developed in England in the mid-19th century. However Spaniel-type dogs have been present within English art and literature for over 500 years. Traditionally the English Cocker Spaniel was not used to retrieve game, during a hunt, but would rather chase the game towards the guns. The English Cocker Spaniel is a sturdy, compact and well-balanced dog. It has a characteristic expression that makes the breed appear intelligent and alert at all times. The breed has dark eyes and large lobular ears that reach past the tip of the dog's nose when pulled forward. The English Cocker Spaniel is very similar to the English Springer Spaniel and at first glance there seems to be no differences – other than the English Springer Spaniel being larger in size. However the English Cocker Spaniel tends to have longer ears and the English Springer Spaniel tends to have a longer muzzle and a less abundant coat.

Lifespan

An English Cocker Spaniel will normally live to be between 10 and 12 years old. However it is not uncommon for a English Cocker Spaniel to live to be as old as 12 or 14, providing they do not develop any serious health issues.

Height and Weight

A fully grown English Cocker Spaniel will normally be between 15 and 17 inches (38 to 43cm) tall at the shoulder. A healthy adult English Cocker Spaniel will normally weigh between 26 and 34 pounds (11.8 to 15.5kg).

Temperament

English Cocker Spaniel are known to be compassionate, determined, kind, athletic, alert and loving animals. Their temperament traits make them a great addition to any family. The breed is known to be exceptionally happy and have a constantly wagging tail, which has led to the breed being nicknamed the 'Merry Cocker.' It is important to note that the English Cocker Spaniel does not like to be left alone and will create an extremely strong bond to a single member of a family unit – normally the person who feed it!

Breed Characteristics

The following section will give you a simplistic overview of the characteristics of a English Cocker Spaniel. Our rating system is from 1 to 10 – with 1 being the lowest score and 10 being the highest.

- ➢ **Adaptability:** 8/10
- ➢ **Friendliness:** 10/10
- ➢ **Health:** 6/10
- ➢ **Ease of Grooming:** 6/10
- ➢ **Amount of Shedding:** 6/10
- ➢ **Trainability:** 8/10
- ➢ **Intelligence:** 10/10
- ➢ **Exercise Needed:** 8/10
- ➢ **Playfulness:** 10/10
- ➢ **Family Friendliness:** 10/10

THE ENGLISH FOXHOUND

The English Foxhound is one of the four foxhound breeds of dog that were specifically developed to be able to hunt foxes by their scent alone. The breed was created in the latter half of the 16th century as a result of the depletion of deer in England. Traditionally the English royalty and nobility hunted deer throughout the country for both sport and food. During these deer hunts the nobility and royalty used both Deerhounds and Staghounds. During the reign of Henry VIII, there was a common consensus that a new prey was needed – and the fox was selected. Hence, the development of the English Foxhound began. The English Foxhound was developed by carefully mixing the Greyhound, the Fox Terrier and the Bulldog. The Greyhound gave the breed speed, the Fox Terrier gave the breed a strong hunting instinct and the Bulldog gave the breed a tenacious nature. English Foxhounds have always been used to hunt foxes over Greyhounds, as the English Foxhound it is believed that it provides a more sporting chase and hunt. When purchasing an English Foxhound it is important to remember that it is a pack hound and therefore enjoys the company of other dogs and humans. The English Foxhound also gets along with large household pets, horses and children as it is an incredibly playful, social, gentle and affectionate breed. The

English Foxhound is a highly energetic breed and thrives in a busy household environment. They make excellent running partners as they have the stamina to run for long periods of time without taking a break.

Lifespan

A English Foxhound will normally live to be between 10 and 12 years old. However it is not uncommon for a English Foxhound to live to be as old as 13, providing that it does not develop any serious health issues.

Height and Weight

A fully grown English Foxhound will normally stand between 25 to 27 inches (63.5 to 68.5cm) tall at the shoulder. A healthy adult English Foxhound will normally weigh between 55 to 75 pounds (25 to 34kg). It is important to note that the weight of a healthy English Foxhound depends on how large the English Foxhound is – taller English Foxhound should weigh more.

Breed Characteristics

The following section will give you a simplistic overview of the characteristics of a English Foxhound. Our rating system is from 1 to 10 – with 1 being the lowest score and 10 being the highest.

- ➢ **Adaptability:** 6/10
- ➢ **Friendliness:** 8/10
- ➢ **Health:** 8/10
- ➢ **Ease of Grooming:** 10/10
- ➢ **Amount of Shedding:** 6/10
- ➢ **Trainability:** 8/10
- ➢ **Intelligence:** 6/10
- ➢ **Exercise Needed:** 8/10
- ➢ **Playfulness:** 10/10
- ➢ **Family Friendliness:** 8/10

THE ENGLISH SETTER

The English Setter is a breed of medium-size dog that is a member of the Setter family. The Setter family also includes the red Irish Setter, the Irish Red and White Setter and the black-and-tan Gordon Setter. The English Setter has a mainly white body coat of a medium length but has longer silky fringes of hair on the back of its legs, under its belly and on its tail. The breed's coat normally has flecks of color scattered all over it. The English Setter was developed for the purpose of hunting birds. The breed would 'set' or 'point' the prey in the direction of the hunters. The English Setter is believed to be about 400 years old and is believed to be a mixture of the Water Spaniel, the English Springer Spaniel and the Spanish Pointer. Its breeding and development was focused around making the English Setter as proficient as possible when it comes to pointing game in the open English countryside. The English Setter hunts by systematically ranging over large distances silently seeking out game by its scent alone. When the English Setter locates its prey, the English Setter will freeze in place – this freezing is known as 'setting.' The English Setter will then wait for its owner to give a command to chase the prey and flush it into the air. Traditionally the hunters would release hawks to kill and retrieve the English Setter flushed out prey but in modern times they use guns. The English Setter's main prey would normally be quail, woodcocks and pigeons. There are two different types of English Setter: the field type and the show type. The field type often has a much smaller body and a less feathered coat with more distinctive spotting – both of these traits are desirable in the field for a working English Setter. A less feathered coat allows for burs and muck to be easily cleaned and a more distinctively spotted coat allows the English Setter to be easily seen and identified by its owner. The English Setter is classified as a 'gundog' in completions held within the United Kingdom and as a 'sporting' dog in the United States of America and Canada.

Lifespan

A English Setter will normally live to be between 11 and 12 years old. However it is not uncommon for a English Setter to live to be as old as 15, providing that it does not develop any serious health issues.

Height and Weight

A fully grown English Setter will normally stand between 23 to 27 inches (58.5 to 68.5cm) tall at the shoulder. A healthy adult English Setter will normally weigh between 45 to 80 pounds (20.5 to 34kg). It is important to note that the weight of a healthy English

Setter depends on how large the English Setter is – taller English Setter should weigh more.

BREED CHARACTERISTICS

The following section will give you a simplistic overview of the characteristics of a English Setter. Our rating system is from 1 to 10 – with 1 being the lowest score and 10 being the highest.

- **Adaptability:** 6/10
- **Friendliness:** 10/10
- **Health:** 6/10
- **Ease of Grooming:** 6/10
- **Amount of Shedding:** 6/10
- **Trainability:** 8/10
- **Intelligence:** 10/10
- **Exercise Needed:** 8/10
- **Playfulness:** 10/10
- **Family Friendliness:** 10/10

THE ENGLISH SPRINGER SPANIEL

The English Springer Spaniel is a breed of gun dog that was developed in England in the mid-19th century. However Spaniel-type dogs have been present within English art and literature for over 500 years. Traditionally the English Springer Spaniel was not used to retrieve game, during a hunt, but would rather flush the game out of their hiding spots and chase them towards the guns. The breeds role during hunts lead to it being called the 'Springer' due to the fact that it would 'spring' prey into flight. The English Springer Spaniel is very similar to the English Cocker Spaniel and at first glance there seems to be no differences – other than the English Springer Spaniel being larger in size. However the English Cocker Spaniel tends to have longer ears and the English Springer Spaniel tends to have a longer muzzle and a less abundant coat. The English Springer Spaniel is now commonly used as a sniffer dog throughout the world.

Lifespan

The English Springer Spaniel will normally live to be between 9 and 12 years old. However it is not uncommon for a English Springer Spaniel to live to be as old as 15, providing that it does not develop any serious

health issues.

Height and Weight

A fully grown English Springer Spaniel will normally be between 18 and 22 inches (46 to 56cm) tall at the shoulder. A healthy adult English Springer Spaniel will normally weigh between 45 and 55 pounds (20.5 to 25kg), depending on its size.

Coat

The English Springer Spaniel comes in two types: Field-bred dogs and Show-bred dogs. The Field-bred dogs have a shorter and more coarse coats than the Show-bred dogs. Both types of English Springer Spaniel will normally only shed in the Spring and Summer months. Their coats normally come in black or liver (dark brown) and will have distinctive white markings.

Temperament

A typical English Springer Spaniel is friendly, intelligent, quick to learn, eager to please and willing to obey which is why they are so commonly used as working dogs. If they are socialized and raised in a happy and friendly household they can also make excellent family pets. It is not uncommon for a English Springer Spaniel to develop a close relationship to a single member of a family unit – normally the person who feed it! It is a sociable breed that enjoys the company of children and other animals.

Breed Characteristics

The following section will give you a simplistic overview of the characteristics of a English Springer Spaniel. Our rating system is from 1 to 10 – with 1 being the lowest score and 10 being the highest.

- **Adaptability:** 6/10
- **Friendliness:** 10/10
- **Health:** 6/10
- **Ease of Grooming:** 4/10
- **Amount of Shedding:** 6/10
- **Trainability:** 8/10
- **Intelligence:** 10/10
- **Exercise Needed:** 10/10
- **Playfulness:** 10/10
- **Family Friendliness:** 10/10

THE ENGLISH TOY SPANIEL

The English Toy Spaniel has existed for centuries and has always been highly favored by both the English and Scottish royal courts. Most notably Mary, Queen of Scots, Charles I and Charles II were known to be incredibly fanatical about the English Toy Spaniel breed – in fact the breed's nickname of 'Charles' is actually in reference to both Charles I and Charles II! It is recorded within history that both Charles I and Mary, Queen of Scots were actually accompanied to their executions by their English Toy Spaniel. Historically the English Toy Spaniel of a few centuries ago looks dramatically different to the English Toy Spaniels of today – traditionally the English Toy Spaniel had a much more pointed muzzle and head. The breed was crossed and mixed with the Japanese Chin and the Pug during the 18th and 19th centuries which resulted in the English Toy Spaniel having a much shorter muzzle and a rounder apple-like head. The English Toy Spaniel was mixed and selectively bred to the point where the original pointed muzzle and head variety of the English Toy Spaniel no longer exists! The main reason that the English Toy Spaniel was so highly favored by royalty through history is the fact that they have a very sweet, loyal and loving nature and are a true example of a companion dog. The breed is also known to be a quiet, happy and devoted breed that enjoys nothing more than spending time with its owners. The English Toy Spaniel also requires relatively little exercise which makes it a perfect lapdog. Another aspects that increases the breed's popularity is the fact that it is incredibly friendly towards strangers, children and other animals, providing that it has been properly socialized during its puppyhood.

Lifespan

A English Toy Spaniel will normally live to be between 10 and 12 years old. However it is not uncommon for a English Toy Spaniel to live to be as old as 13, providing that it does not develop any serious health issues.

Height and Weight

A fully grown English Toy Spaniel will normally stand between 10 to 11 inches (25.5 to 28cm) tall at the shoulder. A healthy adult English Toy Spaniel will normally weigh between 8 to 14 pounds (3.5 to 6.5kg). It is important to note that the weight of a healthy English Toy Spaniel depends on how large the English Toy Spaniel is – taller English Toy Spaniel should weigh more.

Breed Characteristics

The following section will give you a simplistic

overview of the characteristics of a English Toy Spaniel. Our rating system is from 1 to 10 – with 1 being the lowest score and 10 being the highest.

- ➤ **Adaptability:** 6/10
- ➤ **Friendliness:** 8/10
- ➤ **Health:** 5/10
- ➤ **Ease of Grooming:** 8/10
- ➤ **Amount of Shedding:** 10/10
- ➤ **Trainability:** 6/10
- ➤ **Intelligence:** 6/10
- ➤ **Exercise Needed:** 5/10
- ➤ **Playfulness:** 8/10
- ➤ **Family Friendliness:** 10/10

THE ENTLEBUCHER MOUNTAIN DOG

The Entlebucher Mountain Dog, also commonly known as the Entlebucher Mountain Sennenhund or the Entlebucher Cattle Dog, is a medium-sized breed of herding dog. The Entlebucher Mountain Dog is one of the four regional breeds of Sennenhunde-type dogs that originate from the Swiss Alps. The name 'Sennenhunde' comes from the Swiss word 'Senn' which refers to the herders from the Appenzell region in Switzerland. The breed was originally developed to be both a cattle herding dog and a flock guardian. There is a physical difference between the males and females of the Entlebucher Mountain Dog breed: females have a square body shape while males tend to be longer and less square shaped. The breed as a whole has a sturdily built frame, small triangular ears and relatively small brown eyes. The breed standard states that the Entlebucher Mountain Dog is 'good-natured and devoted towards people familiar to him' while being 'slightly suspicious of strangers.' However it is important to remember that the temperament of an individual dog may vary from the breed standard. Due to their size and strength it is important to make sure that your Entlebucher Mountain Dog is well socialized with both adults, children and other animals. The Entlebucher Mountain Dog in modern times is normally found as a family companion dog due to their loving and loyal nature.

Four Breeds of Sennenhund

As previously mentioned, the Entlebucher Mountain Dog is a member of the Sennenhund typing. The breed shares many of the characteristics with the other 3 breeds within the typing. The following section will state the four breeds, within the Sennenhund typing, most popular names.

- Appenzeller Sennenhund, Appenzeller
- Berner Sennenhund, Bernese Mountain Dog
- Entlebucher Sennenhund, Entlebucher Mountain Dog
- Grosser Schweizer Sennenhund, Greater Swiss Mountain Dog

Lifespan

A Entlebucher Mountain Dog will normally live to be between 10 and 12 years old. However it is not uncommon for a Entlebucher Mountain Dog to live to be as old as 13, providing that it does not develop any serious health issues.

Height and Weight

A fully grown Entlebucher Mountain Dog will normally stand between 16 to 20 inches (40.5 to 51cm) tall at the shoulder. A healthy adult Entlebucher Mountain Dog will normally weigh between 45 to 65 pounds (20.5 to 29.5kg). It is important to note that the weight of a healthy Entlebucher Mountain Dog depends on how large the Entlebucher Mountain Dog is – taller Entlebucher Mountain Dog should weigh more.

Coat

The Entlebucher Mountain Dog has a short, thick, dense and tricolored coat. The main color present, within their tricoloration, is a shiny black. The breed normally has white markings on their chest, feet and the tip of their tail. The areas between the white and black are normally a rusty-brown color. The Entlebucher Mountain Dog has a thick undercoat and top coat but only sheds an average amount.

Breed Characteristics

The following section will give you a simplistic overview of the characteristics of a Entlebucher Mountain Dog. Our rating system is from 1 to 10 – with 1 being the lowest score and 10 being the highest.

- **Adaptability:** 6/10
- **Friendliness:** 8/10
- **Health:** 6/10
- **Ease of Grooming:** 10/10
- **Amount of Shedding:** 5/10
- **Trainability:** 9/10
- **Intelligence:** 9/10
- **Exercise Needed:** 10/10
- **Playfulness:** 10/10
- **Family Friendliness:** 10/10

THE FIELD SPANIEL

The Field Spaniel is a medium-sized breed of dog that is a member of the Spaniel typing. During the early 19th century the Field Spaniel was originally developed to be a show breed by competitors who were attempting to create an all-black Spaniel. The breed's original coloration and shape made them incredibly unpopular with sportsmen due to the fact that the Field Spaniel's dark coat made it hard to spot during hunting conditions. The Field Spaniel's elongated shape and small legs also made the breed inadequate at traversing through cover and forests. During the mid-20th century the Field Spaniel was redeveloped as a longer-legged dog that was much more suitable for working purposes – most specifically field work. The newly developed Field Spaniel is considered to be the father of the modern and extremely popular English Cocker Spaniel and American Cocker Spaniel. However, despite being the forefather of two of the most popular breeds worldwide, the Field Spaniel is a rare breed of dog that is actually considered to be a 'vulnerable breed' in the United Kingdom due to their dwindling numbers. The Field Spaniel has the darkest coat of all the breeds within the Spaniel typing. The Field Spaniel also has no undercoat unlike most of the other working type of Spaniels. The Field Spaniel's coat most commonly comes in solid colors but it is not uncommon for there to be occasional markings on the breed's chest. In modern times the Field Spaniel is mainly found as a household family pet. Due to their working and show history, the Field Spaniel can become bored very easily and without some form of purpose it is not uncommon for a Field Spaniel to develop destructive behaviors due to boredom. They make perfect family pets due to their docile, friendly and loving nature. The Field Spaniel is also very good around strangers, small children and other animals, providing that it has been properly socialized during its puppyhood. The Field Spaniel is also known to be highly less excitable than the English Cocker Spaniel and the American Cocker Spaniel, which makes it a better choice for families with small children.

Lifespan

A Field Spaniel will normally live to be between 10 and 12 years old. However it is not uncommon for a Field Spaniel to live to be as old as 13, providing that it does not develop any serious health issues.

Height and Weight

A fully grown Field Spaniel will normally stand between 16 to 19 inches (40.5 to 48.25cm) tall at the shoulder. A healthy adult Field Spaniel will normally weigh between 35 to 45 pounds (16 to 20.5kg). It is important to note that the weight of a healthy Field Spaniel depends on how large the Field Spaniel is – taller Field Spaniel should weigh more.

Breed Characteristics

The following section will give you a simplistic overview of the characteristics of a Field Spaniel. Our rating system is from 1 to 10 – with 1 being the lowest score and 10 being the highest.

- **Adaptability:** 6/10
- **Friendliness:** 10/10
- **Health:** 6/10
- **Ease of Grooming:** 8/10
- **Amount of Shedding:** 6/10
- **Trainability:** 8/10
- **Intelligence:** 10/10
- **Exercise Needed:** 10/10
- **Playfulness:** 10/10
- **Family Friendliness:** 10/10

THE FINNISH LAPPHUND

The Finnish Lapphund is a medium-sized breed of dog that is a member of the Spitz typing. The breed is also commonly known as the 'Lapinkoira Suomenlapinkoira' in its native country of Finland. Despite being an incredibly popular breed within Finland and other Nordic countries, the Finnish Lapphund is relatively rare in the other countries of the world. The Finnish Lapphund lineage is that of a female wolf-male dog hybridization that occurred post-domestication around 3000 years ago. The breed was originally developed to be a reindeer herder for the Sami people. The Sami are an indigenous people who reside in areas that are now classified as Finland, Sweden, Norway and Russia. The Sami have used dogs to herd reindeer for centuries and have always prioritized breeds with long bodies of a rectangular shape, long haired coats and long straight tail that has the ability to curl over the dog's back. The Finnish Lapphund is the most similar modern breed to that of the long haired reindeer herders developed by the Sami people. The Finnish Lapphund is a compactly built muscular breed with large, pricked and highly mobile ears. The breed also has a profuse double coat with a short, fluffy undercoat and a longer top coat. The breed;s double coat allows them to be virtually waterproof and have a high resistence to extreme cold. The breed also has a large amount of hair around its neck which gives the impression of a lion's mane. Due to their history and background in herding, the Finnish Lapphund is a highly energetic breed that excels in dog agility trials, mushing, carting and herding events at dog shows. The Finnish Lapphund is also incredibly intelligent and obedient which makes training the breed relatively easy. The breed is also known to be incredibly friendly, good natured, gentle, alert and loyal. However they do have a tendency to bark at strangers, unknown dogs and unfamiliar things. The Finnish Lapphund is a perfect choice for families with children as they are incredibly adaptable and responsive.

Lifespan

A Finnish Lapphund will normally live to be between 12 and 13 years old. However it is not uncommon for a Finnish Lapphund to live to be as old as 15, providing that it does not develop any serious health issues.

Height and Weight

A fully grown Finnish Lapphund will normally stand between 17 to 20 inches (43 to 50.8cm) tall at the shoulder. A healthy adult Finnish Lapphund will normally weigh between 33 to 53 pounds (15 to 24kg). It is important to note that the weight of a healthy Finnish Lapphund depends on how large the Finnish Lapphund is – taller Finnish Lapphund should weigh more.

Breed Characteristics

The following section will give you a simplistic overview of the characteristics of a Finnish Lapphund. Our rating system is from 1 to 10 – with 1 being the lowest score and 10 being the highest.

- **Adaptability:** 6/10
- **Friendliness:** 8/10
- **Health:** 6/10
- **Ease of Grooming:** 3/10
- **Amount of Shedding:** 1/10
- **Trainability:** 6/10
- **Intelligence:** 8/10
- **Exercise Needed:** 8/10
- **Playfulness:** 8/10
- **Family Friendliness:** 10/10

THE FINNISH SPITZ

The Finnish Spitz is a breed of dog that is a member of the Spitz typing. The breed is also commonly known as the 'Finnish Hunting Dog,' the 'Finnish Spets' and the 'Finsk Spets.' The Finnish Spitz was developed through the selective breeding of Spitz-type dogs that inhabited central Russia thousands of years ago. The main group that developed the Finnish Spitz were known as the Finno-Ugrian. The Finno-Ugrian were tribes of people who relied on dogs to help them hunt for food which helped to produce the breed known as the Finnish Spitz. During the late 1800s, transportation began to bring different people from a plethora of diverse communities together and the Finnish Spitz began to be bred with multiple other types of dogs. In 1880 a man named Hugo Roos observed that the number of Finnish Spitz was beginning to dwindle, due to interbreeding, and decided to try and revive the breed to preserve its unique characteristics and innate hunting ability. The Finnish Spitz has a square shaped build, a soft dense double coat and a plumed tail. The breed's double coat consists of a dense undercoat made up of long and harsh guard hairs that can measure up two inches (5cm) in length! The breed's outer coat is generally much softer but will feel stiff around the dog's neck, back, tail and back of its legs. Finnish Spitz puppies are normally born with a darker coat coloration that will normally include black, brown, dark grey or fawn, which gives them a similar look to that of a red fox cub. By the time the Finnish Spitz reaches adulthood its coat will change color to be more of a pale honey or golden-red. The Finnish Spitz is known to be an incredibly active, alert and lively breed. It is important to make sure that you walk your Finnish Spitz at least twice a day to make sure that it is properly exercised. Finnish Spitz that are bored or have an abundance of energy will normally develop destructive behaviors. It is important to remember that the Finnish Spitz is a breed developed for its innate hunting instinct which means that the Finnish Spitz is a not a breed that is recommended to live in a household with other small animals. However, the Finnish Spitz is a friendly and loving breed when it comes to its own family unit and is generally fine with strangers and unknown dogs (providing that it has been properly socialized).

Lifespan

A Finnish Spitz will normally live to be between 12 and 13 years old. However it is not uncommon for a Finnish Spitz to live to be as old as 15, providing that it does not develop any serious health issues.

Height and Weight

A fully grown Finnish Spitz will normally stand between 15 to 20 inches (38 to 51cm) tall at the shoulder. A healthy adult Finnish Spitz will normally weigh between 20 to 35 pounds (9 to 16kg). It is important to note that the weight of a healthy Finnish Spitz depends on how large the Finnish Spitz is – taller Finnish Spitz should weigh more.

Breed Characteristics

The following section will give you a simplistic overview of the characteristics of a Finnish Spitz. Our rating system is from 1 to 10 – with 1 being the lowest score and 10 being the highest.

- **Adaptability:** 6/10
- **Friendliness:** 8/10
- **Health:** 6/10
- **Ease of Grooming:** 3/10
- **Amount of Shedding:** 1/10
- **Trainability:** 6/10
- **Intelligence:** 8/10
- **Exercise Needed:** 8/10
- **Playfulness:** 8/10
- **Family Friendliness:** 10/10

THE FLAT-COATED RETRIEVER

Flat-Coated Retriever is a breed of gun-dog that originates from, and was developed in, the United Kingdom. The breed was developed in the mid-19th century to be a retriever that is capable of retrieving prey both on land and in the water. The Flat-Coated Retriever is believed to be a descendant of the now extinct St. John's Water Dog which originated from North America. However it is also believed that the Flat-Coated Retriever is also related to the Canadian Newfoundland (a Collie-type dog) and the Setter. The Newfoundland blood was used to give the Flat-Coated Retriever an increased level of trainability whereas the Setter blood was used to give the Flat-Coated Retriever an enhanced ability to scent prey. The Flat-Coated Retriever has a strong muscular jaw and a relatively long muzzle which makes it extremely capable of carrying birds and upland game. The Flat-Coated Retriever has a unique head which is described as being 'of one piece,' which means that its back-skull is a similar length to its muzzle. The Flat-Coated Retriever has dark brown, almond shaped eyes which give the breed an intelligent and friendly expression. The breed has relatively small ears that hang close the dog's head in a pendant shape. The Flat-Coated Retriever has a light body build than most other Retrievers which aids in the breed's ability to be lighter on its feet, racier and have a more elegant appearance. The Flat-Coated Retriever's coat comes in a solid black or a solid liver (brownish-red) coloration. The breed's coat is straight, moderately long and dense which allows the Flat-Coated Retriever to be protected from all types of weather conditions, water and ground cover. The breed has a lot of feather across its ears, chest, front, backs of its forelegs, underside and tail which aids in the coat's protective function. Due to the fact that it is a Retriever, the Flat-Coated Retriever is a highly intelligent and energetic breed. It is therefore important to make sure that you properly exercise your Flat-Coated Retriever (both physically and mentally) as it is likely to develop destructive behaviors due to boredom or having an abundance of energy. However the Flat-Coated Retriever is also a highly trainable and eager to please breed that excels in obedience related activities. Due to the fact that the Flat-Coated Retriever is incredibly loyal, friendly and trainable, it makes a perfect household pet as it is very easy to socialize with children, strangers and other household pets.

Lifespan

A Flat-Coated Retriever will normally live to be between 10 and 12 years old. However it is not uncommon for a Flat-Coated Retriever to live to be as old as 13, providing that it does not develop any serious

health issues.

Height and Weight

A fully grown Flat-Coated Retriever will normally stand between 22 to 24 inches (55.8 to 61cm) tall at the shoulder. A healthy adult Flat-Coated Retriever will normally weigh between 55 to 70 pounds (25 to 31.75kg). It is important to note that the weight of a healthy Flat-Coated Retriever depends on how large the Flat-Coated Retriever is – taller Flat-Coated Retriever should weigh more.

Breed Characteristics

The following section will give you a simplistic overview of the characteristics of a Flat-Coated Retriever. Our rating system is from 1 to 10 – with 1 being the lowest score and 10 being the highest.

- **Adaptability:** 6/10
- **Friendliness:** 10/10
- **Health:** 8/10
- **Ease of Grooming:** 8/10
- **Amount of Shedding:** 6/10
- **Trainability:** 8/10
- **Intelligence:** 8/10
- **Exercise Needed:** 10/10

- **Playfulness:** 10/10
- **Family Friendliness:** 10/10

THE FOX TERRIER

The name 'Fox Terrier' refers to two different breeds of terrier type dog: the Smooth Fox Terrier and the Wire Fox Terrier. Both of these breeds originated in the 19th century from a handful of British Terriers and are related to the modern white terrier breeds. Both types of Fox Terrier have a mostly white coat with different colored markings – the breed's coat colorations and coat texture is the main difference that separates both the Smooth Fox Terrier and the Wire Fox Terrier. The Fox Terrier was originally kept with packs of English Foxhounds and were bred and developed specifically for the purpose of flushing foxes out of their dens during hunts. The Fox Terrier originally had relatively small legs, but as the general pace of the hunt became faster the Fox Terrier began to be bred with longer legs which allowed them to keep up during the hunt. However it got to the point where the Fox Terrier became too large to be used for its original purpose, and its use in hunts began to decline.

Lifespan

Both types of Fox Terrier have a similar lifespan and life expectancy. A Fox Terrier will normally live to be between ? and ? years old. However it is not uncommon for a Fox Terrier to live to be as old as ?, providing that it does not develop any serious health issues.

The Smooth Fox Terrier

The Smooth Fox Terrier has been identified as a Vulnerable Native breed within the United Kingdom due to its dwindling numbers. The Smooth Fox Terrier has a short, hard coat which will come in a predominantly white coloration. The breed also has a long and wedge shaped body, with small, dark eyes and v-shaped ears.

Height and Weight of a Smooth Fox Terrier

A fully grown Smooth Fox Terrier will normally stand between 14 to 15.5 inches (35.5 to 39.5cm) tall at the shoulder. A healthy adult Smooth Fox Terrier will normally weigh between 15 to 19 pounds (6.8 to 8.6kg). It is important to note that the weight of a healthy Smooth Fox Terrier depends on how large the Smooth Fox Terrier is – taller Smooth Fox Terrier should weigh more.

The Wire Fox Terrier

The Wire Fox Terrier has a hard, wiry and crisp double coat which has an incredibly coarse texture underneath that provides the Wire Fox Terrier with good protection from the cold. The breed's coat should be so dense that it is not possible to see or feel its skin. The Wire Fox Terrier's coat hairs should twist but never curl. The Wire Fox Terrier is smaller than the Smooth Fox Terrier but has similar features: small dark eyes, v-shaped ears. The Wire Fox Terrier's body is actually shorter than it is tall.

Height and Weight of a Wire Fox Terrier

A fully grown Wire Fox Terrier will normally stand between 14 to 15 inches (35.5 to 38cm) tall at the shoulder. A healthy adult Wire Fox Terrier will normally weigh between 14 to 18 pounds (6.35 to 8.1kg). It is important to note that the weight of a healthy Wire Fox Terrier depends on how large the Wire Fox Terrier is – taller Wire Fox Terrier should weigh more.

Breed Characteristics

The following section will give you a simplistic overview of the characteristics of a Fox Terrier. Our rating system is from 1 to 10 – with 1 being the lowest score and 10 being the highest.

- **Adaptability:** 6/10
- **Friendliness:** 8/10

- ➢ **Health:** 6/10
- ➢ **Ease of Grooming:** 3/10
- ➢ **Amount of Shedding:** 1/10
- ➢ **Trainability:** 6/10
- ➢ **Intelligence:** 8/10
- ➢ **Exercise Needed:** 8/10
- ➢ **Playfulness:** 8/10
- ➢ **Family Friendliness:** 10/10

The French Bulldog (commonly nicknamed *Frenchie*) is a small breed of short haired companion dog. The breed is a cross between the English Bulldog and French Terriers (and other breeds that hunt rats) and came into existence in the early 1800s. The French Bulldog ranked as the 9th most popular breed in the USA and the 4th most popular breed in the United Kingdom in 2014! The French Bulldog comes in a wide variety of coat colorations including: fawn, cream, black, brindle, white and even blue (a light steely gray color). The French Bulldog should appear small, muscular, heavy boned, active, compactly built and have a smooth coat. They should also have a large square shaped head with a broad, deep and well laid back muzzle. A French Bulldog should have a short nose with broad and well defined nostrils. The breed also has a deep, broad and square under-jaw. The combination of the short nose and large under-jaw makes the French Bulldog a breed that is prone to drooling!

Lifespan

As a breed, the French Bulldog will commonly live to be between 10 and 12 years old. However it is not uncommon for a Frenchie to live to be as old as 14 – providing they do not develop any serious health issues.

Size

Adult French Bulldogs should normally be around 11 to 12 inches (28 to 30cm) tall at the shoulder. An adult Frenchie will normally weigh between 16 and 28 pounds (7 to 13kg).

Frenchie Clubs

There are many French Bulldog clubs throughout the world. We recommended bringing your Frenchie to a gathering while it is a puppy to help socialize it with other dogs. French Bulldog clubs are also a great way to meet other owners and gain first hand grooming tips.

Personality

The French Bulldog is a smart, compassionate and affectionate breed that enjoys spending a lot of its time with people and other animals. The breed is very easy to train as long as training sessions are kept positive and full of praise, play and food based rewards.

Breed Characteristics

The following section will give you a simplistic overview of the characteristics of a French Bulldog. Our rating system is from 1 to 10 – with 1 being the lowest score and 10 being the highest.

- **Adaptability:** 6/10
- **Friendliness:** 8/10
- **Health:** 6/10
- **Ease of Grooming:** 10/10
- **Amount of Shedding:** 5/10
- **Trainability:** 6/10
- **Intelligence:** 6/10
- **Exercise Needed:** 8/10
- **Playfulness:** 10/10
- **Family Friendliness:** 10/10

Encyclopedia of Dog Breeds

THE GERMAN PINSCHER

The German Pinscher is a medium-sized breed of dog that is a member of the Pinscher typing. The breed is also commonly known as the 'Deutscher Pinscher' in reference to its country of origin, Germany. The German Pinscher is included in the origins for the Dobermann Pinscher, the Rottweiler, the Miniature Pinscher, the Affenpinscher and the Standard Schnauzer. The German Pinscher has been shown in dog book since the early 1880s, but drawings of the breed date back all the way to the early 1780s. However it is believed that the German Pinscher originated in the 15th century! The breed's ancestral history is believed to be connected to ratters, but was developed in Germany for the purposes of guardian and herding cattle. The German Pinscher also began to be used as a coach guardian due to their obedience, agility and strength. The breed has also always been used in homesteads for ratting purposes as they will instinctively hunt and kill small vermin – due to the German Pinscher's extremely high prey drive it is recommended to not leave it of a leash in an unfenced area. The breed is known to be an incredibly loving companion with an even temperament. Temperament is hereditary which means that when you are considering purchasing a German Pinscher it is important to physically meet and interact with the mother of the puppy to ensure that they is gentle and loving. The German Pinscher is a highly intelligent, friendly, confident and trainable breed. While a well-trained German Pinscher live happily with small animals and children it is still advisable to never leave your German Pinscher alone with either to minimize the chance of a potential accident. It is important to remember that the German Pinscher is a working dog and highly energetic, it is therefore likely to develop destructive behaviors if it is not exercised (both physically and mentally) due to an abundance of energy or general boredom. It is also important to note that as a whole, the German Pinscher, has a great dislike for water. They are known to take baths to appease their owners, but will generally shun water at all costs.

Lifespan

A German Pinscher will normally live to be between 12 and 14 years old. However it is not uncommon for a German Pinscher to live to be as old as 15, providing that it does not develop any serious health issues.

Height and Weight

A fully grown German Pinscher will normally stand between 17 to 20 inches (43 to 51cm) tall at the shoulder. A healthy adult German Pinscher will normally weigh between 25 to 45 pounds (11.25 to 20.5kg). It is important to note that the weight of a healthy German Pinscher depends on how large the German Pinscher is – taller German Pinscher should weigh more.

Breed Characteristics

The following section will give you a simplistic overview of the characteristics of a German Pinscher. Our rating system is from 1 to 10 – with 1 being the lowest score and 10 being the highest.

- ➢ **Adaptability:** 6/10
- ➢ **Friendliness:** 8/10
- ➢ **Health:** 6/10
- ➢ **Ease of Grooming:** 3/10
- ➢ **Amount of Shedding:** 1/10
- ➢ **Trainability:** 6/10
- ➢ **Intelligence:** 8/10
- ➢ **Exercise Needed:** 8/10
- ➢ **Playfulness:** 8/10
- ➢ **Family Friendliness:** 10/10

THE GERMAN SHEPHERD

The German Shepherd is a breed of medium to large-sized working dog that originates from Germany. The German spelling is *'Deutscher Schäferhund.'* The German Shepherd is a relatively new breed of dog that came into existence in 1899 and was put to work as a sheep herder. However due to their physical strength and intelligence they have become a popular choice for all lines of work: disability assistance, search and rescue, police, acting and military. It is also a popular household pet and is the second most popular breed of dog in the United States! German Shepherds come in two coat varieties: short-medium and long. The long haired variety is rarer due to the fact that the long-hair gene is recessive. Their coats are most commonly tan or red with black marking on their backs and face. However there are rarer color variations such as pure white, pure black and silver blue.

Lifespan

German Shepherds normally live for between 9 and 12 years. However it is not uncommon for a German Shepherd to live for as long as 13 years provided they do not develop any serious health issues.

Intelligence

German Shepherds have been breed specifically for their intelligence. They are consider to be the third most intelligent dog breed – behind the Border Collier and Poodle. A well trained German Shepherd will obey a command, without it needing to be repeated, about 95% of the time! Due to their intelligence, obedience and physical capabilities they have solidified themselves as police and military dogs.

Biting

German Shepherds are a potentially dangerous breed. Their bites have a force of over 1000 newtons which is almost three times as powerful as a human bite, which has a force of around 350 newtons. It is therefore imperative to train your German Shepherd to minimize the chance of it biting someone! It is considered best practice to enroll your German Shepherd in obedience school from puppyhood.

Size

Adult male German Shepherds stand at a height of between 24 and 26 inches (61 to 66cm). Females are slightly smaller and stand at a height of between 22 and 24 inches (55 to 61cm). The weight of both males and females so fall between the range of 75 to 95 pounds (34 to 43kg).

Breed Characteristics

The following section will give you a simplistic overview of the characteristics of a Labrador Retriever. Our rating system is from 1 to 10 – with 1 being the lowest score and 10 being the highest.

- **Adaptability:** 6/10
- **Friendliness:** 8/10
- **Health:** 8/10
- **Ease of Grooming:** 10/10
- **Amount of Shedding:** 10/10
- **Trainability:** 8/10
- **Intelligence:** 10/10
- **Exercise Needed:** 8/10
- **Playfulness:** 10/10
- **Family Friendliness:** 10/10

THE GERMAN SHORTHAIRED POINTER

The German Shorthaired Pointer is a medium to large sized breed of hunting dog that was developed during the 19th century in Germany. The breed is also commonly known as the 'Deutscher Kurzhaariger,' the 'Vorstehhund,' and the 'Kurzhaar.' The German Shorthaired Pointer is a descendant of the German Bird Dog and the Old Spanish Pointer. It is also believed that the breed has traces of hound and tracking dogs: such as the English Pointer and the Arkwright Pointer. The German Shorthaired Pointer was developed to be a versatile hunting breed and gun dog that is capable of hunting both on land and in the water. The breed has a streamlined build with powerful muscular legs that allow it to capable of running, swimming and changing direction rapidly. The German Shorthaired Pointer's powerful build also makes it capable of retrieving relatively heavy game. The German Shorthaired Pointer has a short, flat and dense undercoat which is protected by stiff guard hairs that make the breed's coat resistant to water, the cold and most other weathers. The breed's coat normally comes in the following colorations: dark brown, liver (colloquially called 'chocolate' or 'chestnut'), black, black roan, white, live roan, liver and white or black and white. The German Shorthaired Pointer normally has a solidly colored head and a speckled or 'ticked' body. It is also not uncommon for the German Shorthaired Pointer to have large patches of color known as 'saddles.' The temperament of dogs is normally affected by the following factors: individual personality, heredity, training and socialization. It is therefore important to make sure that you meet the puppy's mother before purchasing a German Shorthaired Pointer. It is also important to make sure to thoroughly socialize your German Shorthaired Pointer with strangers, children and other animals during its puppyhood. Generally speaking, the German Shorthaired Pointer is a highly intelligent, bold affectionate, enthusiastic and willing to please breed. The German Shorthaired Pointer loves interacting with humans and spending time with their family units. It is important to note that as a sporting breed, the German Shorthaired Pointer has a high amount of energy which needs to be expended. If the German Shorthaired Pointer has a buildup of energy it is likely to develop destructive behaviors due to boredom or hyperactivity.

Lifespan

A German Shorthaired Pointer will normally live to be between 12 and 14 years old. However it is not uncommon for a German Shorthaired Pointer to live to be as old as 15, providing that it does not develop any serious health issues.

Height and Weight

A fully grown German Shorthaired Pointer will normally stand between 21 to 25 inches (53.5 to 63.5cm) tall at the shoulder. A healthy adult German Shorthaired Pointer will normally weigh between 45 to 70 pounds (20.5 to 31.75kg). It is important to note that the weight of a healthy German Shorthaired Pointer depends on how large the German Shorthaired Pointer is – taller German Shorthaired Pointer should weigh more.

Breed Characteristics

The following section will give you a simplistic overview of the characteristics of a German Shorthaired Pointer. Our rating system is from 1 to 10 – with 1 being the lowest score and 10 being the highest.

- **Adaptability:** 5/10
- **Friendliness:** 8/10
- **Health:** 6/10
- **Ease of Grooming:** 10/10
- **Amount of Shedding:** 4/10
- **Trainability:** 10/10
- **Intelligence:** 10/10
- **Exercise Needed:** 10/10
- **Playfulness:** 10/10

➢ **Family Friendliness:** 10/10

THE GERMAN WIREHAIRED POINTER

The German Wirehaired Pointer is a breed of medium to large-sized dog that is a member of the griffon typing. As the name suggests the breed originates from Germany and was developed during the 19th century. The breed is also commonly known as the 'Deutsch Drahthaar,' and the 'Vorstehhund' in Germany. The breed was developed for the purposes of being a rugged and versatile hunting dog that was capable of working closely with either a single hunter or a small party of hunters. The German Wirehaired Pointer was developed to be able to traverse varied terrain (from the mountainous regions of the Alps, to the dense forests present with Germany, to open fields and farms surrounding small farms) on foot. The people who developed the breed wanted the German Wirehaired Pointer to have a coat that was both easy to maintain but would also be able to protect the dog from heavy cover and cold weather. The German Wirehaired Pointer therefore has a weather resistant, water-repellent wiry and dense undercoat. The German Wirehaired Pointer also have a straight, wiry, harsh and flat lying overcoat that is about two inches in length. The German Wirehaired Pointer was developed for the main purpose of point and location upland game, being fearless while hunting 'sharp' game (such as foxes), being able to retrieve water fowl and land birds and be a devoted and trainable companion. The temperament of dogs is normally affected by the following factors: individual personality, heredity, training and socialization. It is therefore important to make sure that you meet the puppy's mother before purchasing a German Wirehaired Pointer. It is also important to make sure to thoroughly socialize your German Wirehaired Pointer with strangers, children and other animals during its puppyhood. Generally speaking, the German Wirehaired Pointer thrives on human companionship and is very affectionate, loyal and playful. It is important to note that as a working breed, the German Wirehaired Pointer has a high amount of energy which needs to be expended. If the German Wirehaired Pointer has a buildup of energy it is likely to develop destructive behaviors due to boredom or hyperactivity.

Lifespan

A German Wirehaired Pointer will normally live to be between 12 and 13 years old. However it is not uncommon for a German Wirehaired Pointer to live to be as old as 14, providing that it does not develop any serious health issues.

Height and Weight

A fully grown German Wirehaired Pointer will normally stand between 22 to 26 inches (56 to 66cm) tall at the shoulder. A healthy adult German Wirehaired Pointer will normally weigh between 60 to 70 pounds (27 to 31.75kg). It is important to note that the weight of a healthy German Wirehaired Pointer depends on how large the German Wirehaired Pointer is – taller German Wirehaired Pointer should weigh more.

Breed Characteristics

The following section will give you a simplistic overview of the characteristics of a German Wirehaired Pointer. Our rating system is from 1 to 10 – with 1 being the lowest score and 10 being the highest.

- **Adaptability:** 6/10
- **Friendliness:** 7/10
- **Health:** 8/10
- **Ease of Grooming:** 8/10
- **Amount of Shedding:** 4/10
- **Trainability:** 8/10
- **Intelligence:** 10/10
- **Exercise Needed:** 10/10
- **Playfulness:** 10/10
- **Family Friendliness:** 10/10

THE GIANT SCHNAUZER

The Giant Schnauzer is a working breed of dog that originates from Germany and was developed during the 17th century. The breed is also commonly known as the 'Munich Schnauzer,' the 'Munchener' and the 'Russian Bear Schnauzer.' The breed has a large and varied ancestral history with the most notable breeds being: the Great Dane, the Bouvier des Flandres and the German Pinscher. The first Giant Schnauzer emerged from the German state of Bavaria and was originally considered to be a rough-coated variant of the German Pinscher breed. The breed's hair is believed to have been developed to help the Giant Schnauzer withstand the extreme coldness of the German winter and also to minimize damage from vermin bites. The breed was originally bred and developed to be a multipurpose farm dog and was mainly tasked with guardian property and driving animals to market. By the turn of the 20th century the Giant Schnauzer was a common choice for guarding and watching over factories, breweries, stockyards and butcheries throughout the state of Bavaria. The breed was widely unknown outside Bavaria, until it was used as a military dog during the course of the first and second World Wars. In modern times the Giant Schnauzer is mainly used as a police dog and as a general household companion. The breed makes an excellent police dog and household pet due to the fact that the Giant Schnauzer breed is known to be incredibly loyal, obedient and suspicious of strangers. The temperament of dogs is normally affected by the following factors: individual personality, heredity, training and socialization. It is therefore important to make sure that you meet the puppy's mother before purchasing a Giant Schnauzer. It is also important to make sure to thoroughly socialize your Giant Schnauzer with strangers, children and other animals during its puppyhood. It is important to note that as a working breed, the Giant Schnauzer has a high amount of energy which needs to be expended. If the Giant Schnauzer has a buildup of energy it is likely to develop destructive behaviors due to boredom or hyperactivity. The Giant Schnauzer's coat comes in two color variants: black and a pattern known as pepper and salt. The Giant Schnauzer is a breed of dog that has a double coat. The Giant Schnauzer's outer coat is short, wiry, dense and hard with hairs that stand up from the skin while its undercoat is generally very soft.

Lifespan

A Giant Schnauzer will normally live to be between 10 and 12 years old. However it is not uncommon for a Giant Schnauzer to live to be as old as 13, providing that it does not develop any serious health issues.

Height and Weight

A fully grown Giant Schnauzer will normally stand between 23 to 27 inches (58.5 to 68.5cm) tall at the shoulder. A healthy adult Giant Schnauzer will normally weigh between 55 to 80 pounds (25 to 36.25kg). It is important to note that the weight of a healthy Giant Schnauzer depends on how large the Giant Schnauzer is – taller Giant Schnauzer should weigh more.

Breed Characteristics

The following section will give you a simplistic overview of the characteristics of a Giant Schnauzer. Our rating system is from 1 to 10 – with 1 being the lowest score and 10 being the highest.

- **Adaptability:** 5/10
- **Friendliness:** 6/10
- **Health:** 8/10
- **Ease of Grooming:** 5/10
- **Amount of Shedding:** 8/10
- **Trainability:** 8/10
- **Intelligence:** 8/10
- **Exercise Needed:** 8/10
- **Playfulness:** 10/10
- **Family Friendliness:** 10/10

THE GLEN OF IMAAL TERRIER

The Glen of Imaal Terrier is a breed of dog that is a member of the terrier typing. The breed is also commonly known as the 'Irish Glen of Imaal Terrier' or the 'Wicklow Terrier' in reference to the breed originating from the Glen of Imaal in the County of Wicklow, Ireland. The breed was officially recognized by the Irish Kennel Club in 1934 but was only recently recognized by the American Kennel Club in 2004. The breed is belived to have been developed during the reign of Elizabeth I. Elizabeth I hired French and Hessian mercenaries to quell a rebellion in Ireland which lead to many of the mercenaries settling in the Wicklow area after the conflict. The mercenaries brought with them their low bodied hounds, which they bred with the local Irish terrier stock which eventually lead to the Glen of Imaal Terrier breed. Like many other terriers, the Glen of Imaal Terrier was originally used to hunt and kill vermin such as rats, mice, foxes, badges and otters. However the breed quickly started to be used as a general purpose farm dog due to its high levels of trainability and intelligence. In modern times the Glen of Imaal Terrier is mainly found as a household companion dog due to its affectionate and loving nature. The Glen of Imaal Terrier has a unique double coat that is wiry on the topside and much softer on the underside. The temperament of dogs is normally affected by the following factors: individual personality, heredity, training and socialization. It is therefore important to make sure that you meet the puppy's mother before purchasing a Glen of Imaal Terrier. It is also important to make sure to thoroughly socialize your Glen of Imaal Terrier with strangers, children and other animals during its puppyhood. Generally speaking, the Glen of Imaal Terrier tends to be much more easy going that most other breeds within the terrier typing. The Glen of Imaal Terrier is known to be undemanding, energetic and even-tempered which makes it a perfect household pet. It is important to note that as a working breed, the Glen of Imaal Terrier has a high amount of energy which needs to be expended. If the Glen of Imaal Terrier has a buildup of energy it is likely to develop destructive behaviors due to boredom or hyperactivity.

Lifespan

A Glen of Imaal Terrier will normally live to be between 12 and 14 years old. However it is not uncommon for a Glen of Imaal Terrier to live to be as old as 15, providing that it does not develop any serious health issues.

Height and Weight

A fully grown Glen of Imaal Terrier will normally stand between 12 to 14 inches (30.5 to 35.5cm) tall at the shoulder. A healthy adult Glen of Imaal Terrier will normally weigh between 25 to 35 pounds (11.5 to 16kg). It is important to note that the weight of a healthy Glen of Imaal Terrier depends on how large the Glen of Imaal Terrier is – taller Glen of Imaal Terrier should weigh more.

Breed Characteristics

The following section will give you a simplistic overview of the characteristics of a Glen of Imaal Terrier. Our rating system is from 1 to 10 – with 1 being the lowest score and 10 being the highest.

- **Adaptability:** 6/10
- **Friendliness:** 8/10
- **Health:** 10/10
- **Ease of Grooming:** 10/10
- **Amount of Shedding:** 1/10
- **Trainability:** 8/10
- **Intelligence:** 8/10
- **Exercise Needed:** 8/10
- **Playfulness:** 8/10
- **Family Friendliness:** 10/10

THE GOLDADOR

The Goldador is a relatively new breed of dog that has been developed within the last two decades. The Goldador is a mix of both the Labrador Retriever and the Golden Retriever. The aim of the breed's development was to create a sensitive, tolerant, intelligent and highly trainable working dog – the efforts proved to be highly successful! The Goldador is now considered one of the top choices for organizations that train guide and assistance dogs. Despite the Goldador's popularity as an assistance dog, the Goldador is not a popular household pet breed. As of January 2017, there are no breed clubs or breeding standards for the Goldador. The Goldador is a highly alert breed which also means that it makes an excellent watchdog, but the Goldador is also a highly inquisitive and friendly breed which means that it is not a very effective guard dog. The temperament of dogs is normally affected by the following factors: individual personality, heredity, training and socialization. It is therefore important to make sure that you meet the puppy's mother before purchasing a Goldador. It is also important to make sure to thoroughly socialize your Goldador with strangers, children and other animals during its puppyhood. Generally speaking, the Goldador has a desire to please its owner which makes it an incredibly easy breed to train. Despite its unpopularity as a household pet, the Goldador is known to get along well within a household enviroment due to the fact that it gets along well with strangers, children and other animals (providing that it has been socialized properly during its puppyhood). The Goldador has a double coat in a similar fashion to a Labrador Retriever. The breed's top coat is short, thick and straight while its undercoat is soft and dense. Generally the Goldador's coat will range from yellow to gold in coloration. However due to the lack of a breeding standard, the Goldador is also known to occasionally have a reddish brown coat. It is important to note that as a cross between two working breeds, the Goldador has a high amount of energy which needs to be expended. If the Goldador has a buildup of energy it is likely to develop destructive behaviors due to boredom or hyperactivity.

Lifespan

A Goldador will normally live to be between 10 and 13 years old. However it is not uncommon for a Goldador to live to be as old as 15, providing that it does not develop any serious health issues.

Height and Weight

A fully grown Goldador will normally stand between 22 to 24 inches (? to ?cm) tall at the shoulder.

A healthy adult Goldador will normally weigh between 60 to 80 pounds (? to ?kg). It is important to note that the weight of a healthy Goldador depends on how large the Goldador is – taller Goldador should weigh more.

Breed Characteristics

The following section will give you a simplistic overview of the characteristics of a Goldador. Our rating system is from 1 to 10 – with 1 being the lowest score and 10 being the highest.

- **Adaptability:** 8/10
- **Friendliness:** 10/10
- **Health:** 8/10
- **Ease of Grooming:** 9/10
- **Amount of Shedding:** 5/10
- **Trainability:** 7/10
- **Intelligence:** 10/10
- **Exercise Needed:** 10/10
- **Playfulness:** 10/10
- **Family Friendliness:** 10/10

THE GOLDEN RETRIEVER

The Golden Retriever is one of the most popular breeds of dog in the United States of America and United Kingdom. The Golden Retriever is a large breed of dog. It was bred for the purpose of being a gun dog that would be able to retriever shot waterfowl, ducks and upland game during hunting and shooting parties. The breed has been called 'retriever' due to the fact that they are capable of retrieving the prey without damaging it. They have a dense inner coat that allows them to stay warm in the outdoors and an outer coat that repels water. The Golden Retriever is a long-haired breed and shed copiously if not groomed on a regular basis. They are a highly intelligent breed and are often trained to be disability dogs (caring for the deaf and blind), search and rescue dogs, detection dogs and as previously mentioned hunting dogs. There are three types of Golden Retriever: The American type, the British type and the Canadian type.

The American Type

The American type of Golden Retriever is less muscular than the other two types. Males stand at a height of between 23 and 24 inches (58 and 61cm). Females are smaller and stand at a height of 21.5 to 22.5

inches (55 to 57cm). The American type has a darker golden colored coat and its legs will converge to the center of the dog's body as it runs. The eyes of the American type are slightly slanted and triangular.

The British Type

The British type of Golden Retriever is prevalent through the United Kingdom and Europe. The British type has a broader skull and a more muscular forequarters than the other types. The British type will nearly always have a light golden coat, however cream colorings are also common (red and mahogany colorations are not accepted by the UK's competitive standard). The British type has notably rounder eyes than its American counterpart. Males stand at a height of 22 to 24 inches (56 to 61cm) and females stand at a height of 20 to 22 inches (51 to 56cm).

The Canadian Type

The Canadian Golden Retriever has a thinner and darker coat that the other two types. It also stands at a taller height. Males stand at a height of between 24 and 25 inches (61 to 63.5cm). Females are slightly smaller and stand at a height of 21.5 to 22.5 inches (55 to 57).

Lifespan

Despite their physical differences, all three types have a similar life expectancy. A Golden Retriever will live for between 10 and 12 years on average. However it is not uncommon for them to live to be as old as 14 if they do not suffer from any serious health issues.

Breed Characteristics

The following section will give you a simplistic overview of the characteristics of a Labrador Retriever. Our rating system is from 1 to 10 – with 1 being the lowest score and 10 being the highest.

- **Adaptability:** 6/10
- **Friendliness:** 10/10
- **Health:** 9/10
- **Ease of Grooming:** 8/10
- **Amount of Shedding:** 10/10
- **Trainability:** 9/10
- **Intelligence:** 10/10
- **Exercise Needed:** 8/10
- **Playfulness:** 10/10
- **Family Friendliness:** 10/10

THE GOLDENDOODLE

The Goldendoodle is a cross-breed of dog that was obtained by breeding a Poodle with a Golden Retriever. The Goldendoodle began being developed during the 1990s in both North America and Australia. The breed was originally being developed to attempt to create a hypoallergenic guide dog suitable for visually impaired people who have an allergy to dog hair. The Goldendoodle has three main coat types: the straight coat, the wavy coat and the curly coat. The straight coat lies flat the Goldendoodle's body and resembles the coat of a Golden Retriever. The wavy coat is the most common coat type is a mixture of the Poodle's curly coat and the Golden Retriever's straight coat. The curly coat resembles the coat found on a standard Poodle. The Goldendoodle's coat can come in a plethora of colorations but will most commonly be: white, cream, gold, red, brown apricot or black. The Goldendoodle has mainly been used as a guide dogs, therapy dogs, search and rescue dogs and diabetic dogs as they have inherited the Golden Retriever's ease of training and the Poodle's relatively high level of intelligence. The temperament of dogs is normally affected by the following factors: individual personality, heredity, training and socialization. It is therefore important to make sure that you meet the puppy's mother before purchasing a Goldendoodle. It is also important to make sure to thoroughly socialize your Goldendoodle with strangers, children and other animals during its puppyhood. Generally speaking, the Goldendoodle is a highly loyal, affectionate and even tempered breed which has allowed the Goldendoodle to become an increasingly popular choice for a household pet. It is important to note that as a cross between two working breeds, the Goldendoodle has a high amount of energy which needs to be expended. If the Goldendoodle has a buildup of energy it is likely to develop destructive behaviors due to boredom or hyperactivity.

Lifespan

A Goldendoodle will normally live to be between 10 and 13 years old. However it is not uncommon for a Goldendoodle to live to be as old as 15, providing that it does not develop any serious health issues.

Height and Weight

A fully grown Goldendoodle will normally stand between 20 to 24 inches (50.8 to 61cm) tall at the shoulder. A healthy adult Goldendoodle will normally weigh between 50 to 90 pounds (22.5 to 40.8kg). It is important to note that the weight of a healthy Goldendoodle depends on how large the Goldendoodle is – taller Goldendoodle should weigh more.

Breed Characteristics

The following section will give you a simplistic overview of the characteristics of a Goldendoodle. Our rating system is from 1 to 10 – with 1 being the lowest score and 10 being the highest.

- **Adaptability:** 6/10
- **Friendliness:** 10/10
- **Health:** 6/10
- **Ease of Grooming:** 8/10
- **Amount of Shedding:** 4/10
- **Trainability:** 7/10
- **Intelligence:** 10/10
- **Exercise Needed:** 8/10
- **Playfulness:** 10/10
- **Family Friendliness:** 10/10

THE GORDON SETTER

The Gordon Setter is a large breed of dog that is a member of the setter family. The setter family is classified as either being made up of sporting dogs or gun dogs depending the preference of the national kennel club or council. It is believed that the Gordon Setter, and all setters, descends from the old Land Spaniel and that they came into existence during the late 1800s. The Gordon Setter was originally developed in Scotland for the purposes of hunting game birds. However the Gordon Setter was quickly imported into all sections of the United Kingdom, where the Gordon Setter was mainly used to hunt partridge, grouse, pheasant and woodcock. Due to the Gordon Setter's incredible hunting ability, it has been used to hunt 'sitting' birds all over the world – birds that 'sit' are defined as birds that will attempt to conceal themselves on land to avoid danger rather than taking flight. The modern Gordon Setter has a predominantly black coat with light tan markings on its chest, legs and muzzle. The breed is also commonly known as 'Black and Tans' due to its coat coloration. The Gordon Setter is also the largest breed within the setter family. The temperament of dogs is normally affected by the following factors: individual personality, heredity, training and socialization. It is therefore important to make sure that you meet the puppy's mother before purchasing a Gordon Setter. It is also important to make sure to thoroughly socialize your Gordon Setter with strangers, children and other animals during its puppyhood. Generally speaking, the Gordon Setter is an alert, confident, fearless, affectionate, intelligent and loyal breed. The breed thrives in a loving household environment as they love attention. Both puppy and adult Gordon Setters have the tendency to be boisterous and jumpy while playing, which means that the breed may not be suitable for household with very young children. It is important to note that as a working breed, the Gordon Setter has a high amount of energy which needs to be expended. If the Gordon Setter has a buildup of energy it is likely to develop destructive behaviors due to boredom or hyperactivity. The Gordon Setter was bred to run and it is therefore recommended to allow your Gordon Setter to run and exercise for between 60 and 90 minutes a day.

Lifespan

A Gordon Setter will normally live to be between 10 and 12 years old. However it is not uncommon for a Gordon Setter to live to be as old as 13, providing that it does not develop any serious health issues.

Height and Weight

A fully grown Gordon Setter will normally stand between 23 to 27 inches (58.5 to 68.5cm) tall at the shoulder. A healthy adult Gordon Setter will normally weigh between 45 to 80 pounds (20.5 to 36.25kg). It is important to note that the weight of a healthy Gordon Setter depends on how large the Gordon Setter is – taller Gordon Setter should weigh more.

Breed Characteristics

The following section will give you a simplistic overview of the characteristics of a Gordon Setter. Our rating system is from 1 to 10 – with 1 being the lowest score and 10 being the highest.

- **Adaptability:** 6/10
- **Friendliness:** 7/10
- **Health:** 8/10
- **Ease of Grooming:** 4/10
- **Amount of Shedding:** 10/10
- **Trainability:** 8/10
- **Intelligence:** 10/10
- **Exercise Needed:** 9/10
- **Playfulness:** 10/10
- **Family Friendliness:** 10/10

THE GREAT DANE

The modern Great Dane is a breed of large dog that originates from Germany. In the late 1600s the Great Dane was kept by German nobility and were used to hunt boars, bears and deer. Due to their gigantic size the Great Dane was used as a 'catch dog,' and would hold the prey in place until the hunter was able to kill it. It was also common for the nobility to employ the breed as guard dogs and would normally keep a few in their bed chambers. However, likenesses of the breed have been found on ancient Egyptian and Tibetan artifacts dating back to 3000 B.C! The breed is one of the largest domesticated dog breeds in the world. A Great Dane, named Zeus, is the current world record holder for the world's tallest dog – he measured gigantic 44 inches (112cm) from paw to shoulder! Overall the Great Dane is intelligent, playful, loving, eager to please and easy to house train.

Lifespan

Like many other large dog breeds, the Great Dane has a relatively short life. A Great Dane will normally live to be around 7 to 9 years old. However it is not uncommon for a Great Dane to live to be as old as 10, or even 11, years old providing that they do not develop any serious health issues.

Height and Weight

A fully grown Great Dane will normally be between 28 and 34 inches (71 to 86cm) tall at the shoulder. However as previously mentioned the world record holding Great Dane was over 40 inches (101.5cm) tall at the shoulder. Due to the discrepancy in their potential sizes, the potential healthy weight for a Great Dane has a large variable. It is common for a fully grown Great Dane to weigh between 100 and 200 pounds (45 to 90kg).

Space

Due to their gigantic size, the breed requires a lot of space. Even though they make good housedogs, they need a lot of room to just move around and navigate through an area. It is important to remember that a Great Dane can reach up on top of a kitchen table or counter. They have long tails that can easily sweep the contents off of a table.

Coat Colorations

The Great Dane will normally have a smooth, short-haired coat in one of the following six colorations:

- Fawn (a golden color with a black mask)
- Brindle (a mixture of fawn and black covering the entire of the dog's body in a pattern similar to tiger-stripes)
- Blue (blue-grey color)
- Black
- Mantle (a mixture of black and white with a solid black blanket over the body)
- Harlequin (white with irregular black patches over the dog's body)

Breed Characteristics

The following section will give you a simplistic overview of the characteristics of a Great Dane. Our rating system is from 1 to 10 – with 1 being the lowest score and 10 being the highest.

- **Adaptability:** 4/10
- **Friendliness:** 10/10
- **Health:** 8/10
- **Ease of Grooming:** 10/10
- **Amount of Shedding:** 10/10
- **Trainability:** 6/10
- **Intelligence:** 7/10
- **Exercise Needed:** 10/10
- **Playfulness:** 10/10
- **Family Friendliness:** 10/10

THE GREAT PYRENEES

The Pyrenean Mountain Dog, also more commonly known as the Great Pyrenees (especially in North America), is a large breed of dog that is mainly used as a livestock guardian. The Great Pyrenees is an incredibly old breed that has been used for hundreds of years for the purposes of protecting shepherd's livestock from predators. The earliest description of the breed dates back to as early as 1407 but was recorded for the first time by Fray Miguel Agustin, who was the 'prior' of the temple in Catalan, in his book which was published on the 1617. Agustin also states that the Great Pyrenees has a white coat to allow it be clearly visible during both night and day, which allows the shepherd to clearly see when the flock is in danger. The Great Pyrenees has a weather resistant double coat which consists of long, thick and coarse overcoat that lies flat the Great Pyrenees's body. The overcoat also covers the breed's wooly, fine and densely packed undercoat. The Great Pyrenees coat is much more profuse around its neck and shoulders which create the appearance of a mane. The Great Pyrenees also has a great deal of feathering along the back of its legs and thighs. The hair on the dog's face and ears is much shorter and finer than the hairs on the rest of its body. The temperament of dogs is normally affected by the following factors: individual personality, heredity, training and socialization. It is therefore important to make sure that you meet the puppy's mother before purchasing a Great Pyrenees. It is also important to make sure to thoroughly socialize your Great Pyrenees with strangers, children and other animals during its puppyhood. Generally speaking, the Great Pyrenees is a confident, gentle and affection breed. They are known to be incredibly territorial and protective due to their history as a flock guardian. The Great Pyrenees is also known to be a nocturnal breed, again, due to its history as a flock guardian. The breed's nocturnal nature is important to consider when choosing to own a Great Pyrenees. While the Great Pyrenees is known to be aggressive towards animals it deems to be a threat, the breed is typically very calm, docile and gentle around harmless animals and small children due to its natural guardian instinct. It is important to note that as a working breed, the Great Pyrenees has a high amount of energy which needs to be expended. If the Great Pyrenees has a buildup of energy it is likely to develop destructive behaviors due to boredom or hyperactivity.

Lifespan

A Great Pyrenees will normally live to be between

10 and 12 years old. However it is not uncommon for a Great Pyrenees to live to be as old as 13, providing that it does not develop any serious health issues.

Height and Weight

A fully grown Great Pyrenees will normally stand between 25 to 32 inches (63.5 to 81.25cm) tall at the shoulder. A healthy adult Great Pyrenees will normally weigh between 85 to 160 pounds (38.5 to 72.5kg). It is important to note that the weight of a healthy Great Pyrenees depends on how large the Great Pyrenees is – taller Great Pyrenees should weigh more.

Breed Characteristics

The following section will give you a simplistic overview of the characteristics of a Great Pyrenees. Our rating system is from 1 to 10 – with 1 being the lowest score and 10 being the highest.

- **Adaptability:** 6/10
- **Friendliness:** 8/10
- **Health:** 8/10
- **Ease of Grooming:** 8/10
- **Amount of Shedding:** 10/10
- **Trainability:** 8/10
- **Intelligence:** 8/10

- **Exercise Needed:** 10/10
- **Playfulness:** 8/10
- **Family Friendliness:** 10/10

THE GREATER SWISS MOUNTAIN DOG

The Greater Swiss Mountain Dog is a large breed of dog that was developed in the Swiss Alps. The Greater Swiss Mountain Dog is believed to be a product of mating the indigenous dog breeds found in the Swiss Alps with large mastiff types who were brought to Switzerland by foreign settlers. The breed is a member of the Sennenhund typing and is considered to be the largest and most ancient of the four breeds. The Greater Swiss Mountain Dog was originally used as an all-purpose farm dog. The Greater Swiss Mountain Dog was considered to be one of the most popular breeds within Switzerland but almost died out during the late 19th century due to the fact that all of the breed's duties were being performed by other breeds of dog or machines. The Greater Swiss Mountain Dog has a large heavy-boned physique with immense physical strength but is relatively agile which allowed it to easily complete any farm worked that it was tasked with. The temperament of dogs is normally affected by the following factors: individual personality, heredity, training and socialization. It is therefore important to make sure that you meet the puppy's mother before purchasing a Greater Swiss Mountain Dog. It is also important to make sure to thoroughly socialize your Greater Swiss Mountain Dog with strangers, children and other animals during its puppyhood. Generally speaking, the Greater Swiss Mountain Dog is sociable, affectionate, clam and dignified. The breed is also relatively healthy and tends to suffer dramatically less ailments that tend to hinder other large breeds of dog. It is important to note that as a working breed, the Greater Swiss Mountain Dog has a high amount of energy which needs to be expended. If the Greater Swiss Mountain Dog has a buildup of energy it is likely to develop destructive behaviors due to boredom or hyperactivity. The breed has a tricolored (black, white and tan) double coat. The breed's coat can range in length and texture from short, fine and straight to wavy, long and coarse.

The Other Breeds of Sennenhund

The Greater Swiss Mountain Dog is one of the four breeds within the Sennenhund-type of dog. The other three breeds within this typing are:

- Bernese Mountain Dog
- Appenzeller
- Entlebucher Mountain Dog

Lifespan

A Greater Swiss Mountain Dog will normally live to

be between 7 and 8 years old. However it is not uncommon for a Greater Swiss Mountain Dog to live to be as old as 9, providing that it does not develop any serious health issues.

Height and Weight

A fully grown Greater Swiss Mountain Dog will normally stand between 23 to 28 inches (58.5 to 71cm) tall at the shoulder. A healthy adult Greater Swiss Mountain Dog will normally weigh between 85 to 140 pounds (38.5 to 63.5kg). It is important to note that the weight of a healthy Greater Swiss Mountain Dog depends on how large the Greater Swiss Mountain Dog is – taller Greater Swiss Mountain Dog should weigh more.

Breed Characteristics

The following section will give you a simplistic overview of the characteristics of a Greater Swiss Mountain Dog. Our rating system is from 1 to 10 – with 1 being the lowest score and 10 being the highest.

- **Adaptability:** 6/10
- **Friendliness:** 10/10
- **Health:** 6/10
- **Ease of Grooming:** 10/10

- **Amount of Shedding:** 5/10
- **Trainability:** 6/10
- **Intelligence:** 6/10
- **Exercise Needed:** 8/10
- **Playfulness:** 10/10
- **Family Friendliness:** 10/10

THE GREYHOUND

The Greyhound is a breed of dog that is a member of the sighthound typing which has been bred for racing purposes. Historically, the Greyhound was used primarily for hunting purposes. They were employed in the open as it allowed them to most efficiently use their keen sense of sight. The Greyhound was originally tasked with hunting and coursing deer and hare. However in the 1920s the breed was introduced to the United Kingdom, Ireland and Australia where there was a significant racing culture. Greyhound racing has been a popular past time for many people over the years but in 2016 it was announced that most countries would stop racing Greyhound due to the fact that it is considered animal cruelty. All modern pure-bred Greyhounds are derived from the Greyhound stock recorded and registered in the 18th century. The temperament of dogs is normally affected by the following factors: individual personality, heredity, training and socialization. It is therefore important to make sure that you meet the puppy's mother before purchasing a Greyhound. It is also important to make sure to thoroughly socialize your Greyhound with strangers, children and other animals during its puppyhood. Generally speaking, Greyhounds tend to be gentle, loyal, loving and quiet pets. They have a tendency to be aloof with strangers but revel in the company other their owners and other dogs. It is important to note that Greyhounds are hunting dogs developed in recent years to chase small animals – which can lead to them not coexisting peacefully with other household pets (such as cats). However some Greyhound seem to have a dramatically lower 'prey drive' than others, so whether or not a Greyhound can live with small animals seems to be dependent completely on the induvial nature and training of the Greyhound. It is important to note that as a hunting and racing breed, the Greyhound has a high amount of energy which needs to be expended. If the Greyhound has a buildup of energy it is likely to develop destructive behaviors due to boredom or hyperactivity. However, retired racing Greyhound tend to have a calm and lazy temperament and spend most of their time sleeping. Retired Greyhounds tend to never be hyperactive and make much better 'apartment dogs' than many smaller breeds.

Lifespan

A Greyhound will normally live to be between 12 and 14 years old. However it is not uncommon for a Greyhound to live to be as old as 15, providing that it does not develop any serious health issues.

Height and Weight

A fully grown Greyhound will normally stand between 25 to 30 inches (63.5 to 76cm) tall at the shoulder. A healthy adult Greyhound will normally weigh between 50 to 85 pounds (22.5 to 38.5kg). It is important to note that the weight of a healthy Greyhound depends on how large the Greyhound is – taller Greyhound should weigh more.

Breed Characteristics

The following section will give you a simplistic overview of the characteristics of a Greyhound. Our rating system is from 1 to 10 – with 1 being the lowest score and 10 being the highest.

- **Adaptability:** 6/10
- **Friendliness:** 10/10
- **Health:** 8/10
- **Ease of Grooming:** 10/10
- **Amount of Shedding:** 8/10
- **Trainability:** 8/10
- **Intelligence:** 10/10
- **Exercise Needed:** 8/10
- **Playfulness:** 8/10
- **Family Friendliness:** 10/10

Encyclopedia of Dog Breeds

THE HARRIER

The Harrier is a medium-sized breed of dog that is classified as a hound. The breed greatly resembles the English Foxhound but is much smaller in size. The origin of the breed is widely disputed. Some theories suggest that the Harrier was created by cross-breeding the English Foxhound, the Greyhound and the Fox Terrier. While other theories suggest that the Harrier descends from a mixture of the Talbot Hound, the Bloodhound and the Basset Hound. The first Harrier pack was established in England during the mid-1200s and the breed quickly spread throughout England and Whales. Despite England being the point of origin for the first Harrier pack, England does not actually recognize the Harrier as a breed but the American Kennel Club first registered a Harrier in 1885. The modern Harrier is between the English Foxhound and the Beagle in size and was developed primarily for the purpose of hunting hares, although it has also been commonly used to hunt foxes. The Harrier has a muscular body with a hard and short coat. The breed is large boned to allow it to have both stamina and strength during a hunt. The temperament of dogs is normally affected by the following factors: individual personality, heredity, training and socialization. It is therefore important to make sure that you meet the puppy's mother before purchasing a Harrier. It is also important to make sure to thoroughly socialize your Harrier with strangers, children and other animals during its puppyhood. Generally speaking, the Harrier is an affectionate, loyal and cheerful breed. They are highly tolerant dogs and will become friendly with strangers very quickly. It is important to note that the Harrier is a hound dog, which means that it enjoys exploring, sniffing and trailing – so it is important to make sure that you keep your Harrier on a leash or in a safely fenced enclosed area. It is also important to note that as a working breed, the Harrier has a high amount of energy which needs to be expended. If the Harrier has a buildup of energy it is likely to develop destructive behaviors due to boredom or hyperactivity.

Lifespan

A Harrier will normally live to be between 9 and 11 years old. However it is not uncommon for a Harrier to live to be as old as 12, providing that it does not develop any serious health issues.

Height and Weight

A fully grown Harrier will normally stand between 19 to 21 inches (48.25 to 30.5cm) tall at the shoulder. A healthy adult Harrier will normally weigh between 45 to

60 pounds (20.5 to 27.25kg). It is important to note that the weight of a healthy Harrier depends on how large the Harrier is – taller Harrier should weigh more.

Breed Characteristics

The following section will give you a simplistic overview of the characteristics of a Harrier. Our rating system is from 1 to 10 – with 1 being the lowest score and 10 being the highest.

- **Adaptability:** 6/10
- **Friendliness:** 10/10
- **Health:** 10/10
- **Ease of Grooming:** 10/10
- **Amount of Shedding:** 6/10
- **Trainability:** 8/10
- **Intelligence:** 8/10
- **Exercise Needed:** 10/10
- **Playfulness:** 10/10
- **Family Friendliness:** 10/10

THE HAVANESE

The Havanese is a breed of dog that is a member of the Bichon typing. The breed is also commonly known as the 'Havanese Cuban Bichon' and the 'Youcef Sorry.' The Havanese originates from Cuba and is actually Cuba's national dog. Like many other breeds within the Bichon typing, the Havanese's progenitors are believed to have come from Tenerife. However there is a theory that the Havanese descends from breeds of dog from Malta, as there are ancient texts written by Aristotle that allude to a breed similar to the Havanese. During the Cuban Revolution, upper-class and middle-class Cubans fled to the United States, but few were able to bring their dogs with them. American breeders became extremely interested in the rarity of the Havanese as there were only 11 Havanese in America by the 1970s. Despite the interest in the breed, the American Kennel Club officially recognized the Havanese breed in 1996. In modern times the Havanese is employed mainly as a therapy dog, a tracking dog and an assistance dog (such as signaling for the hearing impaired) but the Havanese is mainly found as a household companion. The Havanese has a long, soft, lightweight, profuse and silky coat. The breed's coat is slightly wavy. The Havanese has a double coat but is unique in the fact that its outer coat is neither coarse or overly dense. The temperament of dogs is normally affected by the following factors: individual personality, heredity, training and socialization. It is therefore important to make sure that you meet the puppy's mother before purchasing a Havanese. It is also important to make sure to thoroughly socialize your Havanese with strangers, children and other animals during its puppyhood. Generally speaking, the Havanese is easy to train, intelligent, loyal, empathetic and affectionate. The breed tends to take emotional ques from their owner: the Havanese is happy and satisfied when their owner is happy and satisfied. The Havanese has a love for performing as they highly desire attention. The Havanese is happy to play outside and inside, but generally prefers being inside with their owners and should never be left outside overnight. As a whole the Havanese can happily and easily fit into any size household.

Lifespan

A Havanese will normally live to be between 12 and 13 years old. However it is not uncommon for a Havanese to live to be as old as 15, providing that it does not develop any serious health issues.

Height and Weight

A fully grown Havanese will normally stand between 8 to 11 inches (20.3 to 28cm) tall at the shoulder. A healthy adult Havanese will normally weigh between 7 to 13 pounds (3 to 6kg). It is important to note that the weight of a healthy Havanese depends on how large the Havanese is – taller Havanese should weigh more.

Breed Characteristics

The following section will give you a simplistic overview of the characteristics of a Havanese. Our rating system is from 1 to 10 – with 1 being the lowest score and 10 being the highest.

- **Adaptability:** 8/10
- **Friendliness:** 10/10
- **Health:** 6/10
- **Ease of Grooming:** 2/10
- **Amount of Shedding:** 3/10
- **Trainability:** 6/10
- **Intelligence:** 8/10
- **Exercise Needed:** 5/10
- **Playfulness:** 10/10
- **Family Friendliness:** 10/10

THE IBIZAN HOUND

The Ibizan Hound, like the name suggests, is a breed of dog that is a member of the hound family. The Ibizan Hound originated on the island of Elvissa and has been traditionally put to use in the Catalan-speaking areas of Spain and France. The Ibizan Hound is a lean and agile breed that is capable of hunting on all types of terrain and was mainly employed to hunt rabbits and other small game. The breed has an incredibly good sense of sight and smell which allows it to easy track small game. Hunters traditionally use packs of Ibizan Hound females as the female Ibizan Hound is considered to be a much better hunter. The Ibizan Hound will normally be completely silent during a hunt as it also uses its sense of hearing to locate prey, however once the prey is located and trapped the Ibizan Hound will normally bark as a signal to the hunter. While the need for hunting rabbits has died down, the Ibizan Hound is still a popular breed within Spain and France. The Ibizan Hound is now mainly used in dog shows, especially for agility trials, as it has a great degree of discipline, a high level of obedience, great agility and has a very powerful vertical jump. The Ibizan Hound has an elegant and agile frame but also has good bone girth which makes it a hardy and all around rugged breed. The breed's distinguishing feature is its large upright ears. The Ibizan

Hound's coat can come in two varieties: wiry and smooth. Smooth coats tend to be very short while wiry coats (which are dramatically more rare) can range in length from 1 to 3 inches. The temperament of dogs is normally affected by the following factors: individual personality, heredity, training and socialization. It is therefore important to make sure that you meet the puppy's mother before purchasing a Ibizan Hound. It is also important to make sure to thoroughly socialize your Ibizan Hound with strangers, children and other animals during its puppyhood. Generally speaking, the Ibizan Hound is a very affectionate, intelligent and loyal companion that can fit in easily to any household environment. It is important to note that they breed has a relatively high prey drive and should therefore not be left alone with other small household pets to avoid any potential accidents. It is important to note that as a working breed, the Ibizan Hound has a high amount of energy which needs to be expended. If the Ibizan Hound has a buildup of energy it is likely to develop destructive behaviors due to boredom or hyperactivity.

Lifespan

A Ibizan Hound will normally live to be between 10 and 12 years old. However it is not uncommon for a Ibizan Hound to live to be as old as 14, providing that it does not develop any serious health issues.

Height and Weight

A fully grown Ibizan Hound will normally stand between 21 to 27 inches (53.5 to 68.5cm) tall at the shoulder. A healthy adult Ibizan Hound will normally weigh between 45 to 50 pounds (20.5 to 22.75kg). It is important to note that the weight of a healthy Ibizan Hound depends on how large the Ibizan Hound is – taller Ibizan Hound should weigh more.

Breed Characteristics

The following section will give you a simplistic overview of the characteristics of a Ibizan Hound. Our rating system is from 1 to 10 – with 1 being the lowest score and 10 being the highest.

- **Adaptability:** 6/10
- **Friendliness:** 10/10
- **Health:** 8/10
- **Ease of Grooming:** 10/10
- **Amount of Shedding:** 5/10
- **Trainability:** 8/10
- **Intelligence:** 8/10
- **Exercise Needed:** 10/10
- **Playfulness:** 10/10
- **Family Friendliness:** 10/10

THE ICELANDIC SHEEPDOG

The Icelandic Sheepdog is a breed of dog that is a member of the Spitz typing. The breed is also commonly known as the 'Icelandic Spitz' and the 'Friaar Dog.' The Icelandic Sheepdog very much resembles the bodies of dogs found in graves in Denmark and Sweden dating back to about 8000 B.C. It is therefore believed that the Icelandic Sheepdog is a descendant from Viking dog breeds. The Icelandic Sheepdog is commonly used to herd sheep and other cattle in the Icelandic countryside. When herding, the Icelandic Sheepdog was mainly used to prevent the cattle from straying away from the pack rather than driving the cattle. The Icelandic Sheepdog would tend to bark at animals that began to stray, this barking habit is still present within the Icelandic Sheepdog nature as they tend to bark when they want something. The Icelandic Sheepdog was also used to find and retrieve cattle that got lost in the countryside, which means that the breed is used to working alone and without the presence of humans. The breed was very popular up until the the 19th century where the plague and canine distemper destroyed over 75% of the breed! The breeds number continued to dwindle to the point where the Icelandic Dog Breeder Association (HRFI) was established to preserve the breed. The temperament of dogs is normally affected by the following factors:

individual personality, heredity, training and socialization. It is therefore important to make sure that you meet the puppy's mother before purchasing a Icelandic Sheepdog. It is also important to make sure to thoroughly socialize your Icelandic Sheepdog with strangers, children and other animals during its puppyhood. Generally speaking, the Icelandic Sheepdog is an incredibly loyal, friendly and enthusiastic breed. They are also known to be incredibly inquisitive, trainable and intelligent due to their working history. It is important to note that as a working breed, the Icelandic Sheepdog has a high amount of energy which needs to be expended. If the Icelandic Sheepdog has a buildup of energy it is likely to develop destructive behaviors due to boredom or hyperactivity.

Lifespan

A Icelandic Sheepdog will normally live to be between 12 and 14 years old. However it is not uncommon for a Icelandic Sheepdog to live to be as old as 15, providing that it does not develop any serious health issues.

Height and Weight

A fully grown Icelandic Sheepdog will normally stand between 16 to 18 inches (40.5 to 45.75cm) tall at the shoulder. A healthy adult Icelandic Sheepdog will normally weigh between 20 to 30 pounds (9 to 13.5kg). It is important to note that the weight of a healthy Icelandic Sheepdog depends on how large the Icelandic Sheepdog is – taller Icelandic Sheepdog should weigh more.

Breed Characteristics

The following section will give you a simplistic overview of the characteristics of a Icelandic Sheepdog. Our rating system is from 1 to 10 – with 1 being the lowest score and 10 being the highest.

- **Adaptability:** 6/10
- **Friendliness:** 7/10
- **Health:** 6/10
- **Ease of Grooming:** 3/10
- **Amount of Shedding:** 10/10
- **Trainability:** 7/10
- **Intelligence:** 8/10
- **Exercise Needed:** 8/10
- **Playfulness:** 8/10
- **Family Friendliness:** 10/10

THE IRISH RED AND WHITE SETTER

The Irish Red and White Setter is a breed of dog that is a member of the Setter typing. As with all Setters, the Irish Red and White Setter is classified as a gundog and is included in the sporting group in Canada and America. The breed is virtually identical in temperament and use to its related breeds: the Irish Setter, the English Setter and the Gordon Setter. The Irish Red and White Setter was developed to be able to locate the whereabouts of game birds and then indicate where the birds are to the hunters. The Irish Red and White Setter mainly uses its incredible sense of smell to track game birds throughout varied terrain. Within the United Kingdom, the Irish Red and White Setter is mainly used to hunt grouse, partridge, pheasant and woodcock. The breed was incredibly popular but has become virtually extinct in recent years. There are multiple dedicated organizations that are working to maintain the Irish Red and White Setter breed and it has now been recognized by all major kennel clubs. The Irish Red and White Setter is less athletically built than most other setters: it has a heavy body and a broad head. However despite this, the Irish Red and White Setter is still a relatively athletic breed and has high levels of endurance. As the name suggests: the Irish Red and White Setter must have a red and white coat – it is actually a white dog with red patches! The temperament of dogs is normally affected by the following factors: individual personality, heredity, training and socialization. It is therefore important to make sure that you meet the puppy's mother before purchasing a Irish Red and White Setter. It is also important to make sure to thoroughly socialize your Irish Red and White Setter with strangers, children and other animals during its puppyhood. Generally speaking, the Irish Red and White Setter is a devoted, affectionate and loyal breed which makes them a perfect household pet. It is important to note that as a working breed, the Irish Red and White Setter has a high amount of energy which needs to be expended. If the Irish Red and White Setter has a buildup of energy it is likely to develop destructive behaviors due to boredom or hyperactivity.

Lifespan

A Irish Red and White Setter will normally live to be between 10 and 12 years old. However it is not uncommon for a Irish Red and White Setter to live to be as old as 14, providing that it does not develop any serious health issues.

Height and Weight

A fully grown Irish Red and White Setter will normally stand between 22 to 26 inches (56 to 66cm) tall at the shoulder. A healthy adult Irish Red and White Setter will normally weigh between 50 to 70 pounds (22.5 to 31.75kg). It is important to note that the weight of a healthy Irish Red and White Setter depends on how large the Irish Red and White Setter is – taller Irish Red and White Setter should weigh more.

Breed Characteristics

The following section will give you a simplistic overview of the characteristics of a Irish Red and White Setter. Our rating system is from 1 to 10 – with 1 being the lowest score and 10 being the highest.

- **Adaptability:** 6/10
- **Friendliness:** 8/10
- **Health:** 4/10
- **Ease of Grooming:** 6/10
- **Amount of Shedding:** 6/10
- **Trainability:** 8/10
- **Intelligence:** 8/10
- **Exercise Needed:** 10/10
- **Playfulness:** 10/10
- **Family Friendliness:** 10/10

THE IRISH SETTER

The Irish Setter is a breed of dog that is a member of the setter typing. The term 'Irish Setter' is commonly used to describe both the field-bred Red Setter recognized in the 'Field Dog Study Book,' and the show-bred dog recognized by the American Kennel Club. The Irish Setter was bred for hunting purposes; specifically for the purposes of locating and pointing out upland gamebirds. The breed uses its incredible sense of smell to locate their prey. They are a wide-ranging hunter who is more than capable of hunting in both fields and wet or dry moorland terrain. The Irish Setter has a moderately long, silky double coat that is normally either of a red or chestnut coloration. The breed's undercoat is abundant in winter weather, while the top coat is fine all year around. The Irish Setter's coat feathers around their tail, chest, ears, legs and body. The temperament of dogs is normally affected by the following factors: individual personality, heredity, training and socialization. It is therefore important to make sure that you meet the puppy's mother before purchasing a Irish Setter. It is also important to make sure to thoroughly socialize your Irish Setter with strangers, children and other animals during its puppyhood. Generally speaking, the Irish Setter is an incredibly friendly, intelligent, enthusiastic and loyal household pet. They get along well with strangers and small children. However it is important to note that the Irish Setter has a high prey drive, due to their hunting history. It is therefore not recommend to keep an Irish Setter in the same household as a smaller pet (such as a cat) – although it is possible to socialize your Irish Setter with small animals during its puppyhood which could lead to the Irish Setter living peacefully with smaller household pets. The Irish Setter responds well to human interaction and companionship. The breed is therefore relatively easy to train with positive reinforcement. It is important to note that as a working breed, the Irish Setter has a high amount of energy which needs to be expended. If the Irish Setter has a buildup of energy it is likely to develop destructive behaviors due to boredom or hyperactivity.

Lifespan

A Irish Setter will normally live to be between 10 and 13 years old. However it is not uncommon for a Irish Setter to live to be as old as 15, providing that it does not develop any serious health issues.

Height and Weight

A fully grown Irish Setter will normally stand between 25 to 27 inches (63.5 to 68.5cm) tall at the shoulder. A healthy adult Irish Setter will normally weigh between 60 to 70 pounds (27.25 to 31.75kg). It is important to note that the weight of a healthy Irish Setter depends on how large the Irish Setter is – taller Irish Setter should weigh more.

Breed Characteristics

The following section will give you a simplistic overview of the characteristics of a Irish Setter. Our rating system is from 1 to 10 – with 1 being the lowest score and 10 being the highest.

- **Adaptability:** 6/10
- **Friendliness:** 10/10
- **Health:** 5/10
- **Ease of Grooming:** 6/10
- **Amount of Shedding:** 8/10
- **Trainability:** 10/10
- **Intelligence:** 10/10
- **Exercise Needed:** 10/10
- **Playfulness:** 10/10
- **Family Friendliness:** 10/10

The Irish Terrier

The Irish Terrier is a breed of dog that is a member of the Terrier typing. The breed originates from Ireland and is considered to be one of the oldest breeds of terrier. The Irish Terrier was originally developed for its gameness, as it has a great innate instinct to hunt and kill vermin. The Irish Terrier was famously described as 'the poor man's sentinel, the farmer's friend, and the gentleman's favorite,' by F. M. Jowett in their work 'The Irish Terrier.' Breed standards describe the Irish Terrier as racy, rectangular shaped and of a red coloration. The breed is powerful without being overly heavy. The breed's double coat comes in a variety of red colorations and its one of its most unique features. The outer coat is wiry in texture and should never been silky, woolly or wavy. The inner part of the breed's coat, called the 'underwood,' should be densely packed and also of a red coloration. The temperament of dogs is normally affected by the following factors: individual personality, heredity, training and socialization. It is therefore important to make sure that you meet the puppy's mother before purchasing a Irish Terrier. It is also important to make sure to thoroughly socialize your Irish Terrier with strangers, children and other animals during its puppyhood. Generally speaking, the Irish Terrier is very good with people and has a high sense of loyalty towards their family unit. The Irish Terrier is a great choice for families with young children, as the Irish Terrier is an extremely tolerant breed and can handle a fair deal of 'rough housing.' However it is important to note that the Irish Terrier has a high prey drive, due to their hunting history. It is therefore not recommend to keep an Irish Terrier in the same household as a smaller pet (such as a cat) – although it is possible to socialize your Irish Terrier with small animals during its puppyhood which could lead to the Irish Terrier living peacefully with smaller household pets. It is important to note that as a working breed, the Irish Terrier has a high amount of energy which needs to be expended. If the Irish Terrier has a buildup of energy it is likely to develop destructive behaviors due to boredom or hyperactivity.

Lifespan

A Irish Terrier will normally live to be between 12 and 14 years old. However it is not uncommon for a Irish Terrier to live to be as old as 16, providing that it does not develop any serious health issues.

Height and Weight

A fully grown Irish Terrier will normally stand

between 18 to 20 inches (45.75 to 50.8cm) tall at the shoulder. A healthy adult Irish Terrier will normally weigh between 25 to 27 pounds (11.3 to 12.25kg). It is important to note that the weight of a healthy Irish Terrier depends on how large the Irish Terrier is – taller Irish Terrier should weigh more.

Breed Characteristics

The following section will give you a simplistic overview of the characteristics of a Irish Terrier. Our rating system is from 1 to 10 – with 1 being the lowest score and 10 being the highest.

- **Adaptability:** 6/10
- **Friendliness:** 8/10
- **Health:** 10/10
- **Ease of Grooming:** 5/10
- **Amount of Shedding:** 8/10
- **Trainability:** 6/10
- **Intelligence:** 8/10
- **Exercise Needed:** 10/10
- **Playfulness:** 10/10
- **Family Friendliness:** 10/10

THE IRISH WATER SPANIEL

The Irish Water Spaniel is a breed of dog that is a member of the Spaniel typing – the Irish Water Spaniel is actually the largest Spaniel! As the breed's name suggests, the Irish Water Spaniel is native to Ireland and is believed to have originated around 1000 years ago. Irish folklore suggests that the Irish Water Spaniel is a descendant of Dobhar-chu. Dobar-chu is believed to be a water dwelling creature that is half dog and half fish. The Dobhar-chu is also believed to have fur that has incredible protective qualities. However it is much more likely that the Irish Water Spaniel is a mixture of the Poodle, the English Water Spaniel, the Barbet and the Portuguese Water Dog. The breed's coat consists of very densely packed curly hair which sheds very little. Due to the fact that the breed's coat hardly ever sheds – the Irish Water Spaniel is considered to be a hypoallergenic breed. The Irish Water Spaniel's dense coat allows it to stay warm in cold waters. The breed is muscular and sturdily built. Interestingly, the Irish Water Spaniel has webbed feet which aid in its ability to swim. The Irish Water Spaniel was originally employed as a water fowling dog and was set to work on marshes, bogs, estuaries and rivers. The temperament of dogs is normally affected by the following factors: individual personality, heredity, training and socialization. It is therefore important to make sure that you meet the puppy's mother before purchasing a Irish Water Spaniel. It is also important to make sure to thoroughly socialize your Irish Water Spaniel with strangers, children and other animals during its puppyhood. Generally speaking, the Irish Water Spaniel is an active, loving, protective and respectful breed. The Irish Water Spaniel make a perfect household pet for families with children, and other small animals, as it is highly respectful of them. It has to be noted that the Irish Water Spaniel is sometimes considered to be aggressive due to its fierce-sounding bark – however the breed is not known to be aggressive in any way! It is important to note that as a working breed, the Irish Water Spaniel has a high amount of energy which needs to be expended. If the Irish Water Spaniel has a buildup of energy it is likely to develop destructive behaviors due to boredom or hyperactivity.

Lifespan

A Irish Water Spaniel will normally live to be between 10 and 11 years old. However it is not uncommon for a Irish Water Spaniel to live to be as old as 12, providing that it does not develop any serious health issues.

Height and Weight

A fully grown Irish Water Spaniel will normally stand between 21 to 24 inches (53.3 to 61cm) tall at the shoulder. A healthy adult Irish Water Spaniel will normally weigh between 45 to 65 pounds (20.5 to 29.5kg). It is important to note that the weight of a healthy Irish Water Spaniel depends on how large the Irish Water Spaniel is – taller Irish Water Spaniel should weigh more.

Breed Characteristics

The following section will give you a simplistic overview of the characteristics of a Irish Water Spaniel. Our rating system is from 1 to 10 – with 1 being the lowest score and 10 being the highest.

- **Adaptability:** 6/10
- **Friendliness:** 10/10
- **Health:** 5/10
- **Ease of Grooming:** 6/10
- **Amount of Shedding:** 1/10
- **Trainability:** 8/10
- **Intelligence:** 8/10
- **Exercise Needed:** 8/10
- **Playfulness:** 8/10
- **Family Friendliness:** 10/10

THE IRISH WOLFHOUND

The Irish Wolfhound is a large breed of domestic sighthound that originates from Ireland. The breed's name originates from its purpose – wolf hunting with dogs – rather than from the breed's wolf-like appearance. The Irish Wolfhound is a very old breed and it is believed that the breed's ancestors were brought to Ireland as early as 7000 B.C. The breed's ancestors were originally bred to be war hounds and hunting dogs. The Irish continued this tradition, but also began to breed the Irish Wolfhound for the purposes of guarding their homes and protecting their livestock. During the British conquest of Ireland, it became law that only nobility could own a Irish Wolfhound which made the breed an unpopular national symbol due to its connection to the British invasion. However in modern years, the Irish Wolfhound has had an increase in popularity and has actually been used as the symbol for both rugby codes. The American Kennel Club states that the Irish Wolfhound is the tallest of all dog breeds. The breed has a muscular build similar to that of a Greyhound. The breed is also known to be incredibly athletic, active and agile. The breed's coat comes in the following colorations: red, brindle, grey, black, fawn, white and wheaten. Due to the breed's hunting history, the Irish Wolfhound is both fast enough to catch a wolf, and muscular enough to kill it. The temperament of dogs is normally affected by the following factors: individual personality, heredity, training and socialization. It is therefore important to make sure that you meet the puppy's mother before purchasing a Irish Wolfhound. It is also important to make sure to thoroughly socialize your Irish Wolfhound with strangers, children and other animals during its puppyhood. Generally speaking, the Irish Wolfhound is known to be an intelligent, introverted, quiet and reserved breed. They are an easygoing animal that can easily create a strong loving bond with their family unit. It is important to note that as a working breed, the Irish Wolfhound has a high amount of energy which needs to be expended. If the Irish Wolfhound has a buildup of energy it is likely to develop destructive behaviors due to boredom or hyperactivity.

Lifespan

A Irish Wolfhound will normally live to be between 6 and 8 years old. However it is not uncommon for a Irish Wolfhound to live to be as old as 9, providing that it does not develop any serious health issues.

Height and Weight

A fully grown Irish Wolfhound will normally stand

between 32 to 35 inches (81.25 to 89cm) tall at the shoulder. A healthy adult Irish Wolfhound will normally weigh between 115 to 180 pounds (52 to 81.5kg). It is important to note that the weight of a healthy Irish Wolfhound depends on how large the Irish Wolfhound is – taller Irish Wolfhound should weigh more.

Breed Characteristics

The following section will give you a simplistic overview of the characteristics of a Irish Wolfhound. Our rating system is from 1 to 10 – with 1 being the lowest score and 10 being the highest.

- **Adaptability:** 3/10
- **Friendliness:** 10/10
- **Health:** 2/10
- **Ease of Grooming:** 6/10
- **Amount of Shedding:** 6/10
- **Trainability:** 6/10
- **Intelligence:** 8/10
- **Exercise Needed:** 7/10
- **Playfulness:** 8/10
- **Family Friendliness:** 10/10

THE ITALIAN GREYHOUND

The Italian Greyhound is a small breed of dog that is a member of the sighthound typing. The breed is commonly referred to as 'Iggy' or simply as the 'I.G.' The breed's name, the Italian Greyhound, is a reference to the breed's popularity in Renaissance Italy. Mummified dogs, very similar to the Italian Greyhound, have been found in Egypt and clay pictorials of small Greyhound like dogs have been found in Pompeii – which means that the Italian Greyhound is most likely not a native Italian breed. The Italian Greyhound is believed to have originated over 2000 years ago. The Italian Greyhound is the smallest member of the sighthound typing and are considered to be a 'toy' breed. The Italian Greyhound has a deep chest, long slender legs and a long neck that tapers down to its small head. The breed's face is pointed in a similar fashion to a full sized Greyhound - the breed is actually aesthetically a miniature version of the Greyhound. While many Italian owners dispute the term 'Miniature Greyhound,' the American Kennel Club states that the Italian Greyhound have the same genetic bloodline as the Greyhound. The temperament of dogs is normally affected by the following factors: individual personality, heredity, training and socialization. It is therefore important to make sure that you meet the puppy's mother before purchasing a Italian Greyhound.

It is also important to make sure to thoroughly socialize your Italian Greyhound with strangers, children and other animals during its puppyhood. Generally speaking, the Italian Greyhound makes a great companion dog as it enjoys the company of people. However the Italian Greyhound has an extremely fragile build which makes it not a decent choice for families with small children – as rough play is likely to harm an Italian Greyhound. The Italian Greyhound is also known to be incredibly loving, affectionate and loyal to its family unit. It is important to note that as a sporting breed, the Italian Greyhound has a high amount of energy which needs to be expended. If the Italian Greyhound has a buildup of energy it is likely to develop destructive behaviors due to boredom or hyperactivity.

Lifespan

A Italian Greyhound will normally live to be between 12 and 13 years old. However it is not uncommon for a Italian Greyhound to live to be as old as 15, providing that it does not develop any serious health issues.

Height and Weight

A fully grown Italian Greyhound will normally stand between 13 to 15 inches (33 to 38cm) tall at the shoulder. A healthy adult Italian Greyhound will normally weigh between 6 to 15 pounds (2.75 to 6.8kg). It is important to note that the weight of a healthy Italian Greyhound depends on how large the Italian Greyhound is – taller Italian Greyhound should weigh more.

Breed Characteristics

The following section will give you a simplistic overview of the characteristics of a Italian Greyhound. Our rating system is from 1 to 10 – with 1 being the lowest score and 10 being the highest.

- **Adaptability:** 6/10
- **Friendliness:** 10/10
- **Health:** 6/10
- **Ease of Grooming:** 10/10
- **Amount of Shedding:** 4/10
- **Trainability:** 8/10
- **Intelligence:** 6/10
- **Exercise Needed:** 8/10
- **Playfulness:** 8/10
- **Family Friendliness:** 10/10

Encyclopedia of Dog Breeds

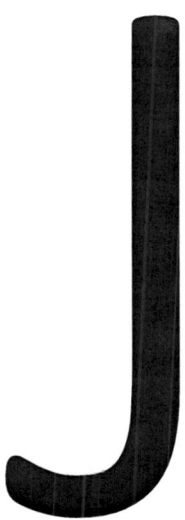

THE JACK RUSSELL

The Jack Russell is a small breed of dog that is a member of the Terrier typing. The Jack Russell is also commonly known by its initials, 'JRT,' or simply as a 'Jack.' The Jack Russell was originally developed for the purpose of hunting foxes. The breed was designed to be athletic enough to be able to chase and intimidate their quarry while also having an even unaggressive temperament, which keeps it from attacking the fox and effectively ending the hunt. Both the Jack Russell and the Fox Terrier descend from the same group of dogs owned by Reverend Jack Russell in 1795. Originally Jack Russell's with white coat colorations were favored due to the fact that there was a need to be able to distinguish between the dog and their prey. Due to the fact that the Jack Russell has a working background, the breed has hardly changed over the last 200 years. The breed still has a predominately white coat with black, brown or tan markings. The Jack Russell has three potential coat types: rough, smooth and broken (which is a combination of the rough and smooth coats). In modern times the breed is still commonly used for working purposes – however it is more commonly used for vermin control purposes rather than sporting/hunting purposes. The Jack Russell is commonly used to trap vermin, such as foxes and groundhogs, in their dens while their owners dig to the vermin. The temperament of dogs is normally affected by the following factors: individual personality, heredity, training and socialization. It is therefore important to make sure that you meet the puppy's mother before purchasing a Jack Russell. It is also important to make sure to thoroughly socialize your Jack Russell with strangers, children and other animals during its puppyhood. Generally speaking, the Jack Russell is a highly intelligent, friendly and energetic breed. They make a good pet for households with an active lifestyle. It is important to note that the Jack Russell was developed for hunting purposes and therefore has a high prey drive. The Jack Russell will commonly pursue smaller animals, such as squirrels or cats, which can make it an unsuitable pet for household with multiple animals. It is also important to note that as a working breed, the Jack Russell has a high amount of energy which needs to be expended. If the Jack Russell has a buildup of energy it is likely to develop destructive behaviors due to boredom or hyperactivity.

Lifespan

A Jack Russell will normally live to be between 10 and 13 years old. However it is not uncommon for a Jack Russell to live to be as old as 15, providing that it does not develop any serious health issues.

Height and Weight

A fully grown Jack Russell will normally stand between 10 to 15 inches (2.5.5 to 38cm) tall at the shoulder. A healthy adult Jack Russell will normally weigh between 13 to 17 pounds (6 to 7.75kg). It is important to note that the weight of a healthy Jack Russell depends on how large the Jack Russell is – taller Jack Russell should weigh more.

Breed Characteristics

The following section will give you a simplistic overview of the characteristics of a Jack Russell. Our rating system is from 1 to 10 – with 1 being the lowest score and 10 being the highest.

- **Adaptability:** 6/10
- **Friendliness:** 10/10
- **Health:** 7/10
- **Ease of Grooming:** 6/10
- **Amount of Shedding:** 5/10
- **Trainability:** 8/10
- **Intelligence:** 10/10
- **Exercise Needed:** 10/10
- **Playfulness:** 10/10
- **Family Friendliness:** 10/10

THE JAPANESE CHIN

The Japanese Chin is a breed of toy dog that originates from China. The breed is commonly known as the 'Japanese Spaniel,' and was highly popular with Japanese nobility – hence why the breed's name alludes to the 'Japanese.' It is believed that the Japanese Chin breed could have originated in around 732 AD! However, other records indicate that the Japanese Chin probably would have come into existence during the mid-6th century as this is when the breed was gifted to a Japanese Empress. Within Japanese culture dogs are mainly viewed as working or helper animals. This makes the Japanese Chin unique as the breed was developed for the purpose of companionship. Traditionally the ownership of a Japanese Chin was restricted to only Japanese nobility and royalty. Each group of nobles or royals bred the Japanese Chin to their own standard which has resulted in the Japanese Chin breed being high varied: differences in size, body type, eye set and coat density are common. Generally speaking, the Japanese Chin has a single overcoat that grows to a medium-long length. The breed's coat is commonly colored black and white, or red and white. The Japanese Chin is known for its unique state of permanent Strabismus of the eyes (cross eye). The temperament of dogs is normally affected by the following factors:

individual personality, heredity, training and socialization. It is therefore important to make sure that you meet the puppy's mother before purchasing a Japanese Chin. It is also important to make sure to thoroughly socialize your Japanese Chin with strangers, children and other animals during its puppyhood. Generally speaking, the Japanese Chin is an alert, independent and intelligent breed. The Japanese Chin's temperament has been related to that of a cat, as it uses its paws to clean its face, enjoys resting on high surfaces, have a good sense of stability and is highly independent. The breed also is known to be incredibly loyal and affectionate towards its owners and family unit.

Lifespan

A Japanese Chin will normally live to be between 10 and 12 years old. However it is not uncommon for a Japanese Chin to live to be as old as 14, providing that it does not develop any serious health issues.

Height and Weight

A fully grown Japanese Chin will normally stand between 8 to 11 inches (20.3 to 28cm) tall at the shoulder. A healthy adult Japanese Chin will normally weigh between 4 to 9 pounds (1.8 to 4kg). It is important to note that the weight of a healthy Japanese

Chin depends on how large the Japanese Chin is – taller Japanese Chin should weigh more.

Breed Characteristics

The following section will give you a simplistic overview of the characteristics of a Japanese Chin. Our rating system is from 1 to 10 – with 1 being the lowest score and 10 being the highest.

- **Adaptability:** 6/10
- **Friendliness:** 7/10
- **Health:** 6/10
- **Ease of Grooming:** 6/10
- **Amount of Shedding:** 6/10
- **Trainability:** 6/10
- **Intelligence:** 6/10
- **Exercise Needed:** 3/10
- **Playfulness:** 8/10
- **Family Friendliness:** 8/10

K

THE KEESHOND

The Keeshond is a medium sized breed of dog that originates from Germany. The breed is commonly also known as the 'Dutch Barge Dog' and the 'Smiling Dutchman.' The breed is known for its unique plush two-layered coat, curled tail and its silver and black fur with a ruff around its neck. The breed is closely related to other breeds within the Spitz typing such as the Mittelsplitz, Kleinspitz and Pomeranian. The breed was originally called the 'German Spitz,' but the breed's name was changed in 1926 to the Keeshond. The first breed standard for the Keeshond was posted at a dog show in Berlin in 1880. The breed is sturdily built with a wedge-shaped head, a medium-sized muzzle, a tightly curled tail and a pair of small pointed ears. The Keeshond's ruff is a good way to guess the dog's gender: males tend to have a much thicker and more pronounced ruff than females. The temperament of dogs is normally affected by the following factors: individual personality, heredity, training and socialization. It is therefore important to make sure that you meet the puppy's mother before purchasing a Keeshond. It is also important to make sure to thoroughly socialize your Keeshond with strangers, children and other animals during its puppyhood. Generally speaking, the Keeshond is known to be an extremely playful breed with a love of physical exercise and athletics. The breed as a whole seems very eager to please humans, which actually leads to the Keeshond being a highly trainable breed. Their intelligence and trainability has led to the Keeshond being used as a guide dog. The Keeshond makes an excellent family dog as they love human contact and get along very well with children and other household pets. The breed is also known to be incredibly empathetic as was actually the first choice for 'comfort dogs' to help the rescue works after the tragedy of 9/11. It is important to note that as a working and sporting breed, the Keeshond has a high amount of energy which needs to be expended. If the Keeshond has a buildup of energy it is likely to develop destructive behaviors due to boredom or hyperactivity.

Lifespan

A Keeshond will normally live to be between 12 and 14 years old. However it is not uncommon for a Keeshond to live to be as old as 15, providing that it does not develop any serious health issues.

Height and Weight

A fully grown Keeshond will normally stand between 16 to 19 inches (40.5 to 48.25cm) tall at the shoulder. A healthy adult Keeshond will normally weigh between 35 to 45 pounds (16 to 20.5kg). It is important to note that the weight of a healthy Keeshond depends on how large the Keeshond is – taller Keeshond should weigh more.

Breed Characteristics

The following section will give you a simplistic overview of the characteristics of a Keeshond. Our rating system is from 1 to 10 – with 1 being the lowest score and 10 being the highest.

- **Adaptability:** 8/10
- **Friendliness:** 10/10
- **Health:** 6/10
- **Ease of Grooming:** 6/10
- **Amount of Shedding:** 10/10
- **Trainability:** 7/10
- **Intelligence:** 8/10
- **Exercise Needed:** 8/10
- **Playfulness:** 10/10
- **Family Friendliness:** 10/10

THE KERRY BLUE TERRIER

The Kerry Blue Terrier is a breed of dog that is a member of the Terrier typing. The breed is also commonly known as the 'Irish Blue Terrier.' The Kerry Blue Terrier was originally developed for the purpose of controlling 'vermin,' which includes rats, badgers, foxes, hares, rabbits and otters. Due to the fact that the Kerry Blue Terrier is capable of hunting 'vermin' both on land and in water, the breed quickly became popular as a general purpose working dog due its high levels of adaptability. The breed has been known to be a guard dog, a companion dog and a cattle herder. The breed was first used in the mountains of Kerry, in Ireland, hence the breed's name - the Kerry Blue Terrier is actually the national dog of Ireland. The Kerry Blue Terrier is known to have a long head with a flat skull, a deep chest, and a soft wavy-to-curly coat. The Kerry Blue Terrier's most unique feature is its coat. The breed has no undercoat and its coat has a texture similar to human hair or fine wool. Interestingly, the Kerry Blue Terrier does not tend to shed but will continuously grow its coat throughout the year which makes the Kerry Blue Terrier a hypoallergenic breed. The breed's coat comes in various shades of 'blue,' however all Kerry Blue Terrier puppies are born with black coats that slowly shift to a blue coloration. The temperament of dogs is normally affected by the following factors: individual personality, heredity, training and socialization. It is therefore important to make sure that you meet the puppy's mother before purchasing a Kerry Blue Terrier. It is also important to make sure to thoroughly socialize your Kerry Blue Terrier with strangers, children and other animals during its puppyhood. Generally speaking, the Kerry Blue Terrier is known to be an incredibly affectionate, loyal and gentle breed. The Kerry Blue Terrier makes a perfect household pet for families with small children as the breed is incredibly hardy and gentle. However it is important to note that the Kerry Blue Terrier has a high prey instinct and does not live happily with other small animals. It is important to note that as a working breed, the Kerry Blue Terrier has a high amount of energy which needs to be expended. If the Kerry Blue Terrier has a buildup of energy it is likely to develop destructive behaviors due to boredom or hyperactivity.

Lifespan

A Kerry Blue Terrier will normally live to be between 12 and 13 years old. However it is not uncommon for a Kerry Blue Terrier to live to be as old as 15, providing that it does not develop any serious health issues.

Height and Weight

A fully grown Kerry Blue Terrier will normally stand between 17 to 19 inches (43 to 48cm) tall at the shoulder. A healthy adult Kerry Blue Terrier will normally weigh between 33 to 40 pounds (15 to 18kg). It is important to note that the weight of a healthy Kerry Blue Terrier depends on how large the Kerry Blue Terrier is – taller Kerry Blue Terrier should weigh more.

Breed Characteristics

The following section will give you a simplistic overview of the characteristics of a Kerry Blue Terrier. Our rating system is from 1 to 10 – with 1 being the lowest score and 10 being the highest.

- **Adaptability:** 6/10
- **Friendliness:** 8/10
- **Health:** 6/10
- **Ease of Grooming:** 5/10
- **Amount of Shedding:** 1/10
- **Trainability:** 8/10
- **Intelligence:** 8/10
- **Exercise Needed:** 8/10
- **Playfulness:** 8/10
- **Family Friendliness:** 10/10

THE KOMONDOR

The Komondor is a large breed of molossers dog that originates from Hungary. The breed is commonly known as the 'Mop Dog,' the 'Hungarian Sheepdog,' and as the 'Hungarian Komondor.' In Hungarian the plural for the breed's name is the Komondorok. The Komondor was originally brought into Hungary by the Cuman, the Turkic speaking nomadic people, during the 12th century. The breed's name references this as 'Korman' translates to 'Cuman' and 'Dor' translates to 'Dog'. Despite the breed being relatively popular in modern times, the Komondor went nearly extinct during World War II due to the fact that invading German troops has to kill the Komondor before they were able to capture the house or farm that the dog guarded. The Komondor has an innate guardian instinct and has therefore traditionally been used to guard livestock. The Komondor is an athletic breed that is powerful enough to chase of any predators that may threaten the livestock it guard. The Komondor has been commonly used to guard sheep from wolves and bears! The Komondor has a long cord-like white coat which provides it with protection against vegetation, predators and the weather. The breed's unique coat also gives it a sheep-like appearance which allows the Komondor to easily camouflage itself amongst the sheep it guards. The breed's ability to camouflage itself allows it to easily surprise potential predators. In modern times the Komondor is an extremely popular choice for a flock guardian in the United States of America, as it easily can protect sheep from coyotes, bears and cougars. The temperament of dogs is normally affected by the following factors: individual personality, heredity, training and socialization. It is therefore important to make sure that you meet the puppy's mother before purchasing a Komondor. It is also important to make sure to thoroughly socialize your Komondor with strangers, children and other animals during its puppyhood. Generally speaking, the Komondor is known to be a calm, steady and protective breed. It is also known to be loyal to its owner but also independent enough to make its own decisions while guarding a flock. The Komondor is also known to be an incredibly fearless breed and will often put itself in danger to defend its flock. It is important to note that as a working breed, the Komondor has a high amount of energy which needs to be expended. If the Komondor has a buildup of energy it is likely to develop destructive behaviors due to boredom or hyperactivity.

Lifespan

A Komondor will normally live to be between ? and ? years old. However it is not uncommon for a

Komondor to live to be as old as ?, providing that it does not develop any serious health issues.

Height and Weight

A fully grown Komoncor will normally stand between ? to ? inches (? to ?cm) tall at the shoulder. A healthy adult Komondor will normally weigh between ? to ? pounds (? to ?kg). It is important to note that the weight of a healthy Komordor depends on how large the Komondor is – taller Komondor should weigh more.

Breed Characteristics

The following section will give you a simplistic overview of the characteristics of a Komondor. Our rating system is from 1 to 10 – with 1 being the lowest score and 10 being the highest.

- ➢ **Adaptability:** 6/10
- ➢ **Friendliness:** 6/10
- ➢ **Health:** 6/10
- ➢ **Ease of Grooming:** 5/10
- ➢ **Amount of Shedding:** 6/10
- ➢ **Trainability:** 8/10
- ➢ **Intelligence:** 8/10
- ➢ **Exercise Needed:** 6/10
- ➢ **Playfulness:** 8/10

➤ **Family Friendliness:** 10/10

THE KOOIKERHONDJE

The Kooikerhondje is a small bred of Spaniel-type dog that originates from the Netherlands. The breed is also commonly known as the 'Kooiker,' and by its literal English translation, the 'Little Cager Hound.' The breed was developed during the 16th century in its country of origin to be a tolling breed. The Kooikerhondje was primarily used to lure and drive ducks into 'koolen' (cage which are in the form of canals with traps at the end), so their owner, or the hunter, could easy catch them. The hunters who employed this duck hunting technique were known as the 'Kooikers,' hence the breed being known as the 'Kooikerhondje' as 'hondje' means dog. The Kooikerhondje was also used on farmers to catch and exterminate vermin. The breed nearly went extinct during World War II as there was little need for the Kooikerhondje and breeding therefore stopped. The breed was officially recognized by the Dutch Kennel Club in 1971, and has since been imported to many other countries including Canada and the United States of America. The Kooikerhondje has a bright orange and white coat with a heavily plumed white tail, which the breed wags to entice ducks to follow it into the caged canals. The temperament of dogs is normally affected by the following factors: individual personality, heredity, training and socialization. It is therefore important to make sure that you meet the puppy's mother before purchasing a Kooikerhondje. It is also important to make sure to thoroughly socialize your Kooikerhondje with strangers, children and other animals during its puppyhood. Generally speaking, the Kooikerhondje is known to be a good natured, quiet and well behaved breed of dog. The breed is also known to be intelligent, trainable and highly willing to please its owner. It is important to note that as a working breed, the Kooikerhondje has a high amount of energy which needs to be expended. If the Kooikerhondje has a buildup of energy it is likely to develop destructive behaviors due to boredom or hyperactivity. However the Kooikerhondje is known to be quiet and relaxed indoors if it has been properly exercised.

Lifespan

A Kooikerhondje will normally live to be between 11 and 13 years old. However it is not uncommon for a Kooikerhondje to live to be as old as 14, providing that it does not develop any serious health issues.

Height and Weight

A fully grown Kooikerhondje will normally stand between 14 to 16 inches (35.5 to 40.5cm) tall at the shoulder. A healthy adult Kooikerhondje will normally weigh between 20 to 25 pounds (9 to 11.3kg). It is important to note that the weight of a healthy Kooikerhondje depends on how large the Kooikerhondje is – taller Kooikerhondje should weigh more.

Breed Characteristics

The following section will give you a simplistic overview of the characteristics of a Kooikerhondje. Our rating system is from 1 to 10 – with 1 being the lowest score and 10 being the highest.

- **Adaptability:** 6/10
- **Friendliness:** 5/10
- **Health:** 6/10
- **Ease of Grooming:** 5/10
- **Amount of Shedding:** 6/10
- **Trainability:** 7/10
- **Intelligence:** 8/10
- **Exercise Needed:** 10/10
- **Playfulness:** 8/10
- **Family Friendliness:** 8/10

THE KOREAN JINDO

The Korean Jindo is a breed of hunting dog that originates from the Jindo Island, which is located in South Korea. The breed is celebrated throughout South Korea for having an extremely brave and loyal nature. The Korean Jindo was traditionally used for hunting purposes due to its courage, intelligence and pack sensibility. The breed was normally used to hunt medium to large sized game, such as deer and boar, but there is actually a South Korean legend that tells of how three Korean Jindos killed a Siberian Tiger during a hunt! Despite this legend seeming unrealistic, there are multiple reports of Korean Jindo killing deer or coyotes without the knowledge or direction of their owners. During a hunt, a pack of Korean Jindo will use their combined strength to take down the prey and then will send a single Jindo back to the hunter to lead him to the prey. The Korean Jindo is a breed of double coated spitz-type dog. The breed is split into two typing: Tonggot (which have a more muscular body) and Hudu (which have more slender and agile bodies). The breed's coat normally comes in white, fawn, grey, black and brindle. The temperament of dogs is normally affected by the following factors: individual personality, heredity, training and socialization. It is therefore important to make sure that you meet the puppy's mother before purchasing a Korean Jindo. It is also important to make sure to thoroughly socialize your Korean Jindo with strangers, children and other animals during its puppyhood. Generally speaking, the Korean Jindo is an incredibly energetic, affectionate and loyal breed of dog. It is important to note that when keeping a Korean Jindo it is important to have a fenced garden (a fence of at least 6ft is recommended), as the Korean Jindo is likely to explore its surroundings due to its innate hunting instinct. It is important to note that as a working breed, the Korean Jindo has a high amount of energy which needs to be expended. If the Korean Jindo has a buildup of energy it is likely to develop destructive behaviors due to boredom or hyperactivity.

Lifespan

A Korean Jindo will normally live to be between 12 and 14 years old. However it is not uncommon for a Korean Jindo to live to be as old as 15, providing that it does not develop any serious health issues.

Height and Weight

A fully grown Korean Jindo will normally stand between 18 to 21 inches (45.75 to 53.3cm) tall at the shoulder. A healthy adult Korean Jindo will normally weigh between 35 to 60 pounds (15.85 to 27.2kg). It is important to note that the weight of a healthy Korean Jindo depends on how large the Korean Jindo is – taller Korean Jindo should weigh more.

Breed Characteristics

The following section will give you a simplistic overview of the characteristics of a Korean Jindo. Our rating system is from 1 to 10 – with 1 being the lowest score and 10 being the highest.

- **Adaptability:** 6/10
- **Friendliness:** 8/10
- **Health:** 8/10
- **Ease of Grooming:** 2/10
- **Amount of Shedding:** 10/10
- **Trainability:** 6/10
- **Intelligence:** 10/10
- **Exercise Needed:** 8/10
- **Playfulness:** 8/10
- **Family Friendliness:** 10/10

THE KUVASZ

The Kuvasz is an ancient breed of dog that originates from Hungary. The Kuvasz predeceasing breed is believed to date back to 200 B.C. as they are known to have been used by the Magyar tribe. The Magyar tribe conquered Hungary in 896 A.D. and with their conquering force came the Kuvasz-type dogs. The Kuvasz has traditionally been used as a livestock guardian and to also guard royal palaces. In 1978, a fossilized skeleton of a 9th Century Kuvasz-type dog was discover near Keszthely. The morphology of the fossilized dog's skeleton is almost identical to that of the modern Kuvasz, which makes the Kuvasz one of the oldest identifiable dog breeds as few breeds date back as far as the 9th Century! The Kuvasz breed became almost extinct during World War II. The Kuvasz breed was known to fiercely defend their families and were therefore often exterminated by the invading German and Soviet armies. After the war fewer than thirty Kuvasz remained in Hungary. Since the breed's near extermination, dedicated breeds have actively worked to revitalize the Kuvasz breed. Fortunately, the Kuvasz has seen an increase in popularity due to the successful work of the dedicated breeders! The Kuvasz is a large breed of dog that has an extremely dense white double coat that is known to be odorless. Despite the breed's coat being white, the Kuvasz's skin is actually of a blackish pigment and they have a large round black nose. The breed's coat and skin coloration are signifiers of the breed's history in livestock guarding, as they look very similar to sheep and could therefore camouflage themselves amongst them. The temperament of dogs is normally affected by the following factors: individual personality, heredity, training and socialization. It is therefore important to make sure that you meet the puppy's mother before purchasing a Kuvasz. It is also important to make sure to thoroughly socialize your Kuvasz with strangers, children and other animals during its puppyhood. Generally speaking, the Kuvasz is known to be an intelligent, loyal, patient and humorous breed. Due to their history in livestock guarding, the Kuvasz is also known to be a highly intelligent, independent and trainable breed that is more than capable of looking after itself. While the Kuvasz is highly affectionate towards its family and people it known, the breed is very wary of strangers and unknown dogs. It is important to closely monitor your Kuvasz whenever it meets someone new or when it is off its leash. It is important to note that as a working breed, the Kuvasz has a high amount of energy which needs to be expended. If the Kuvasz has a buildup of energy it is likely to develop destructive behaviors due to boredom or hyperactivity.

Lifespan

A Kuvasz will normally live to be between 10 and 11 years old. However it is not uncommon for a Kuvasz to live to be as old as 12, providing that it does not develop any serious health issues.

Height and Weight

A fully grown Kuvasz will normally stand between 26 to 30 inches (66 to 76.2cm) tall at the shoulder. A healthy adult Kuvasz will normally weigh between 70 to 115 pounds (31.75 to 51.2kg). It is important to note that the weight of a healthy Kuvasz depends on how large the Kuvasz is – taller Kuvasz should weigh more.

Breed Characteristics

The following section will give you a simplistic overview of the characteristics of a Kuvasz. Our rating system is from 1 to 10 – with 1 being the lowest score and 10 being the highest.

- **Adaptability:** 6/10
- **Friendliness:** 4/10
- **Health:** 8/10
- **Ease of Grooming:** 8/10
- **Amount of Shedding:** 8/10
- **Trainability:** 6/10

- **Intelligence:** 8/10
- **Exercise Needed:** 8/10
- **Playfulness:** 8/10
- **Family Friendliness:** 10/10

Encyclopedia of Dog Breeds

THE LABRADOODLE

The Labradoodle is a designer breed of dog that was created by cross breeding the Labrador Retriever and the Standard, Miniature or Toy Poodle. The breed was first developed in 1955, but did not gain popularity until 1988, when the Labradoodle started to be used as a hypoallergenic guide dog. The breed was developed by an Australian breeder named Wally Conron. Conron's aim was to combined the low shedding coat and intelligence of the Poodle with the gentleness and trainability of the Labrador. Despite the breed's popularity, the Labradoodle is not recognized as a breed by any of the world's major Kennel Clubs. Due to the fact that there is no standardization in the Labradoodle breed, puppies do not have predictable characteristics. While most Labradoodle puppies share common traits, their behavioral and physical characteristics remain somewhat unpredictable. Due to the lack of a breed standard, the Labradoodle's coat can be short, long, wiry, curly, smooth or rough. The Labradoodle's with straight coats are known as 'hair' Labradoodles. The Labradoodle's with wiry coats are known as 'fleece' Labradoodles. The temperament of dogs is normally affected by the following factors: individual personality, heredity, training and socialization. It is therefore important to make sure that you meet the puppy's mother before purchasing a Labradoodle. It is also important to make sure to thoroughly socialize your Labradoodle with strangers, children and other animals during its puppyhood. Generally speaking, the Labradoodle has the temperament qualities of a Poodle mixed with a Labrador Retriever and is therefore playful, friendly, energetic and good with strangers, children and other animals. The Labradoodle is also considered to be highly intelligent due to the fact that both of its parent breeds are likewise highly intelligent – the Poodle is often considered the most intelligent dog breed. It is important to note that as a crossbreed of two working dog breeds, the Labradoodle has a high amount of energy which needs to be expended. If the Labradoodle has a buildup of energy it is likely to develop destructive behaviors due to boredom or hyperactivity.

Lifespan

A Labradoodle will normally live to be between 12 and 13 years old. However it is not uncommon for a Labradoodle to live to be as old as 14, providing that it does not develop any serious health issues.

Height and Weight

A fully grown Labradoodle will normally stand between 21 to 24 inches (53.3 to 61cm) tall at the shoulder. A healthy adult Labradoodle will normally weigh between 50 to 65 pounds (22.7 to 29.5kg). It is important to note that the weight of a healthy Labradoodle depends on how large the Labradoodle is – taller Labradoodle should weigh more.

Breed Characteristics

The following section will give you a simplistic overview of the characteristics of a Labradoodle. Our rating system is from 1 to 10 – with 1 being the lowest score and 10 being the highest.

- **Adaptability:** 8/10
- **Friendliness:** 10/10
- **Health:** 8/10
- **Ease of Grooming:** 8/10
- **Amount of Shedding:** 1/10
- **Trainability:** 7/10
- **Intelligence:** 8/10
- **Exercise Needed:** 10/10
- **Playfulness:** 10/10
- **Family Friendliness:** 10/10

THE LABRADOR RETRIEVER

The Labrador Retriever is among one of the most popular breeds of dog worldwide. The Labrador Retriever originates from the island of Newfoundland, off the northeastern Atlantic coast of Canada, and have been used as work dogs since the early 1700s. The Labrador Retriever was quickly recognized for its intelligence, good disposition and loyalty. English Sportsmen imported many Labrador Retrievers to service the purpose of retrieving prey during gun hunts. Labrador Retrievers come in a large variety of colors such as black, chocolate, white, a foxlike red and their iconic yellow. They are one of the most intelligent and empathetic breeds and are often used in therapy and aiding the disabled. Due to their intelligence, ease of training and good nature they have become the most popular family dog breed in the United States of America.

Lifespan

Labrador Retrievers normally live for between 10 and 12 years. However it is not uncommon for them to live for as long as 14 years if they do not develop any major health issues.

Adult Size

Labrador Retrievers are a medium-large breed. Males stand at a height of between 22.5 and 24.5 inches (57 to 62.5cm) and weigh between 65 and 80 pounds (30 to 36kg). Females are generally smaller than males. They normally stand at a height of between 21.5 and 23.5 (54.5 to 60cm) and weight between 55 and 70 pounds (25 to 32kg).

Official Breed Standards

As the above averages suggest, there is a great deal of variation within the Labrador Retriever breed. The following characteristics are based upon the standards created by the American Kennel Club.

- **Size:** A Labrador Retriever should be as long from the withers to the base of the tail as they are form the floor to the withers. The weight and size standards are the same as from the previous section.
- **Body:** The body of a Labrador Retriever should be muscular and powerful.
- **Head:** A Labrador Retrievers head should be bread with slightly pronounced eyebrows. The eyes should appear bright, intelligent, healthy and expressive. The eyes should be

circled in black and be colored either brown or hazel. The ears should hang close to the head and be set slightly above the eyes.
- ➤ **Jaw:** The jaws should be strong and powerful. A Labrador Retriever's muzzle should not be overly tapered and of a medium length. There should be a slight curve to the jaw as it goes back.
- ➤ **Coat:** A Labrador Retriever's coat should be made up of short and dense hair. The coat should also be water-resistant which leads to the coat being slightly oil when dry.

Breed Characteristics

The following section will give you a simplistic overview of the characteristics of a Labrador Retriever. Our rating system is from 1 to 10 – with 1 being the lowest score and 10 being the highest.

- ➤ **Adaptability:** 6/10
- ➤ **Friendliness:** 10/10
- ➤ **Health:** 8/10
- ➤ **Ease of Grooming:** 8/10
- ➤ **Amount of Shedding:** 10/10
- ➤ **Trainability:** 8/10
- ➤ **Intelligence:** 10/10
- ➤ **Exercise Needed:** 10/10

- **Playfulness:** 10/10
- **Family Friendliness:** 10/10

THE LAKELAND TERRIER

The Lakeland Terrier is a breed of dog that originates from the Lake District in England, hence the breed's name. The Lakeland Terrier is a small-to-medium sized breed and is a member of the Terrier family. The Lakeland Terrier is considered to be the most hypoallergenic breed of Terrier. The Lakeland Terrier was first registered in the United Kingdom in 1921. The breed was developed to be able to hunt foxes while traversing the mountainous and rocky terrain of the Lake District. Due to the terrain being unsuitable for horseback hunting, the Lakeland Terrier would work closely with hunters and is therefore a highly trainable breed. The Lakeland Terrier is incredibly energetic and has a great amount of stamina. It is believed that the breed's athleticism is due to the fact that the Lakeland Terrier would have to run all day during hunts, whereas its close cousin, the Fox Terrier, would normally have been carried in a saddle bag until it was needed. The Lakeland Terrier was also used throughout the United Kingdom to exterminate 'vermin' on farmland. The temperament of dogs is normally affected by the following factors: individual personality, heredity, training and socialization. It is therefore important to make sure that you meet the puppy's mother before purchasing a Lakeland Terrier. It is also important to make sure to thoroughly socialize your Lakeland Terrier with strangers, children and other animals during its puppyhood. Generally speaking, the Lakeland Terrier is a highly energetic, confident and friendly breed. It is highly atypical for a Lakeland Terrier to show signs of shyness or aggression, which makes it a very popular household companion breed. The breed is also known to be highly intelligent and independently minded. It is not uncommon for a Lakeland Terrier to exhibit 'selective deafness' if they are particularly interested in something. It is important to note that as a working breed, the Lakeland Terrier has a high amount of energy which needs to be expended. If the Lakeland Terrier has a buildup of energy it is likely to develop destructive behaviors due to boredom or hyperactivity.

Lifespan

A Lakeland Terrier will normally live to be between 12 and 13 years old. However it is not uncommon for a Lakeland Terrier to live to be as old as 15, providing that it does not develop any serious health issues.

Height and Weight

A fully grown Lakeland Terrier will normally stand between 12 to 14 inches (30.5 to 35.5cm) tall at the shoulder. A healthy adult Lakeland Terrier will normally weigh between 15 to 17 pounds (6.8 to 7.7kg). It is important to note that the weight of a healthy Lakeland Terrier depends on how large the Lakeland Terrier is – taller Lakeland Terrier should weigh more.

Breed Characteristics

The following section will give you a simplistic overview of the characteristics of a Lakeland Terrier. Our rating system is from 1 to 10 – with 1 being the lowest score and 10 being the highest.

- **Adaptability:** 6/10
- **Friendliness:** 8/10
- **Health:** 10/10
- **Ease of Grooming:** 5/10
- **Amount of Shedding:** 4/10
- **Trainability:** 7/10
- **Intelligence:** 8/10
- **Exercise Needed:** 8/10
- **Playfulness:** 8/10
- **Family Friendliness:** 10/10

THE LANCASHIRE HEELER

The Lancashire Heeler is a small breed of dog that originated in Lancashire, in England. The breed is believed to be a descendant of the Welsh Corgi, due to the fact that the Welsh Corgi was used to drive livestock from Whales to the north western regions of England. In the Ormskirk area, a type of black and tan terrier, known as the 'Manchester Terrier,' was introduced. It is believed that the Lancashire Heeler breed was created by mixing the Welsh Corgi and the Manchester Terrier. The Lancashire Heeler breed is known to be at least 150 years old. The Lancashire Heeler has traditionally been used as a general purpose farm dog and is capable of both exterminating small vermin, such as rats, and herding cattle. The Lancashire Heeler breed was recognized as being a vulnerable native breed by the English Kennel Club in 2006, which means that there are under 300 registrations of Lancashire Heelers on a yearly basis. The Lancashire Heeler has been known to compete in dog agility trials, obedience trials, showmanship competitions, flyball and herding events. The breed has a short and harsh top coat and a short and smooth undercoat that keeps it warm and dry in any weather. The temperament of dogs is normally affected by the following factors: individual personality, heredity, training and socialization. It is therefore important to make sure that you meet the puppy's mother before purchasing a Lancashire Heeler. It is also important to make sure to thoroughly socialize your Lancashire Heeler with strangers, children and other animals during its puppyhood. Generally speaking, the Lancashire Heeler is known to be an alert, friendly, energetic and intelligent breed. The Lancashire Heeler is also known to be incredibly affectionate and playful when it is around its direct family unit. Despite its small size, the Lancashire Heeler is a relatively strong breed that enjoys physical exertion. It is important to note that as a working breed, the Lancashire Heeler has a high amount of energy which needs to be expended. If the Lancashire Heeler has a buildup of energy it is likely to develop destructive behaviors due to boredom or hyperactivity.

Lifespan

A Lancashire Heeler will normally live to be between 9 and 11 years old. However it is not uncommon for a Lancashire Heeler to live to be as old as 14, providing that it does not develop any serious health issues.

Height and Weight

A fully grown Lancashire Heeler will normally stand between 10 to 12 inches (25.5 to 30.5cm) tall at the shoulder. A healthy adult Lancashire Heeler will normally weigh between 13 to 15 pounds (5.9 to 6.8kg). It is important to note that the weight of a healthy Lancashire Heeler depends on how large the Lancashire Heeler is – taller Lancashire Heeler should weigh more.

Breed Characteristics

The following section will give you a simplistic overview of the characteristics of a Lancashire Heeler. Our rating system is from 1 to 10 – with 1 being the lowest score and 10 being the highest.

- **Adaptability:** 6/10
- **Friendliness:** 7/10
- **Health:** 8/10
- **Ease of Grooming:** 8/10
- **Amount of Shedding:** 6/10
- **Trainability:** 7/10
- **Intelligence:** 8/10
- **Exercise Needed:** 8/10
- **Playfulness:** 8/10
- **Family Friendliness:** 10/10

THE LEONBERGER

The Leonberger is a giant breed of dog that originates from Germany. The breed is also commonly known as the 'Gentle Giant,' the 'Gentle Lion,' and as simply the 'Leo.' The Leonberger's name is derived from the city of Leonberg which is in the Baden-Wurttemberg region of Germany. The Leonberger is believed to have come into existence in the mid-1850s when a Landseer Newfoundland was mixed with a Saint Bernard, and later a Pyrenean Mountain Dog. Traditionally the Leonberger has a long white coat, which was considered very fashionable at the time. The modern Leonberger has a much darker coat and will usually have a black mask covering most of its face and muzzle. The breed's numbers suffered dramatically during World War I and World War II as most of the Leonberger breeders were killed, fled Germany or enrolled in the military. During the World Wars, the Leonberger was mainly used to pull carts full of ammunition to and from the front line. Traditionally the Leonberger breed was employed as a general purpose farm dog or a guard dog. The Leonberger has a very unique water-resistant double coat on its body and very short fine hairs on its muzzle and limbs. The breed's durable outer coat is relatively straight and lies flat to the dog's body. Interestingly the Leonberger is a dimorphic breed as it possesses either a strongly masculine or elegantly feminine form, which allows the breed's gender to be immediately discernible. The temperament of dogs is normally affected by the following factors: individual personality, heredity, training and socialization. It is therefore important to make sure that you meet the puppy's mother before purchasing a Leonberger. It is also important to make sure to thoroughly socialize your Leonberger with strangers, children and other animals during its puppyhood. Generally speaking, the Leonberger is known to be a friendly, submissive, obedient and hardworking breed. They are also known to be incredibly playful under the right circumstances. The breed is also known to be intelligent, loyal and robust and is capable of performing a wide variety of work related tasks. It is important to note that as a working breed, the Leonberger has a high amount of energy which needs to be expended. If the Leonberger has a buildup of energy it is likely to develop destructive behaviors due to boredom or hyperactivity.

Lifespan

A Leonberger will normally live to be between 10 and 11 years old. However it is not uncommon for a Leonberger to live to be as old as 12, providing that it does not develop any serious health issues.

Height and Weight

A fully grown Leonberger will normally stand between 25 to 31 inches (? to ?cm) tall at the shoulder. A healthy adult Leonberger will normally weigh between 120 to 170 pounds (? to ?kg). It is important to note that the weight of a healthy Leonberger depends on how large the Leonberger is – taller Leonberger should weigh more.

Breed Characteristics

The following section will give you a simplistic overview of the characteristics of a Leonberger. Our rating system is from 1 to 10 – with 1 being the lowest score and 10 being the highest.

- **Adaptability:** 3/10
- **Friendliness:** 8/10
- **Health:** 2/10
- **Ease of Grooming:** 8/10
- **Amount of Shedding:** 10/10
- **Trainability:** 6/10
- **Intelligence:** 8/10
- **Exercise Needed:** 8/10
- **Playfulness:** 8/10
- **Family Friendliness:** 10/10

THE LHASA APSO

The Lhasa Apso is a companion breed of dog that originates from Tibet and is believed to be over 4000 years old. In Tibet, the Lhasa Apso is known as the 'Apso Seng Kyl,' which translates to the 'Bearded Lion Dog.' The breed was developed for the purposes of being a household, or a monetary, sentinel that was tasked with letting people know if any intruders enter the property. The Lhasa Apso has an incredible sense of hearing and a loud sharp bark, which makes it a perfect burglar alarm. Traditionally in Tibet, the Lhasa Apso was never sold and the only way to obtain one was for it to be received as a gift. The Lhasa Apso breed was introduced to the United States of America in 1933, when Thubten Gyatso, 13th Dalai Lama gifted a pair of Lhasa Apso to C. Suydam Cutting. Due to the fact that the Lhasa Apso was developed in incredibly harsh conditions found within the Himalaya region, the breed is surprisingly hardy and long living. The Lhasa Apso is known for its unique looking coat. The breed's coat has a heavy and hard texture and the hairs lie straight. It is considered a fault if a Lhasa Apso coat is wooly or silky to the touch. The breed's coat comes in a wide variety of colorations that includes black, white, red and various shades of gold. Despite the breed having a dense long haired coat it is actually considered to be a hypo-allergenic breed. This is due to the fact that the Lhasa Apso's coat hair is relatively heavy which decreases the chance of airborne hairs, dander and allergens. The Lhasa Apso's coat shed continuously in a similar fashion to human hair. The temperament of dogs is normally affected by the following factors: individual personality, heredity, training and socialization. It is therefore important to make sure that you meet the puppy's mother before purchasing a Lhasa Apso. It is also important to make sure to thoroughly socialize your Lhasa Apso with strangers, children and other animals during its puppyhood. Generally speaking, the Lhasa Apso is affectionate, intelligent, independent and assertive. The breed is incredibly loyal towards its family unit but is highly suspicious of strangers, due to their history as a sentinel dog.

Lifespan

A Lhasa Apso will normally live to be between 12 and 14 years old. However it is not uncommon for a Lhasa Apso to live to be as old as 15, providing that it does not develop any serious health issues.

Height and Weight

A fully grown Lhasa Apso will normally stand between 9 to 11 inches (23to 28cm) tall at the shoulder.

A healthy adult Lhasa Apso will normally weigh between 12 to 15 pounds (5.5 to 6.8kg). It is important to note that the weight of a healthy Lhasa Apso depends on how large the Lhasa Apso is – taller Lhasa Apso should weigh more.

Breed Characteristics

The following section will give you a simplistic overview of the characteristics of a Lhasa Apso. Our rating system is from 1 to 10 – with 1 being the lowest score and 10 being the highest.

- **Adaptability:** 8/10
- **Friendliness:** 6/10
- **Health:** 6/10
- **Ease of Grooming:** 2/10
- **Amount of Shedding:** 6/10
- **Trainability:** 6/10
- **Intelligence:** 8/10
- **Exercise Needed:** 8/10
- **Playfulness:** 10/10
- **Family Friendliness:** 9/10

THE LOWCHEN

The Lowchen is a small breed of dog that originates from Germany. The breed is also commonly known as the 'Petit Chien Lion' and the 'Little Lion Dog.' The Lowchen is considered by most registries as a toy dog breed, but in America the Lowchen is registered as a non-sporting dog. The Lowchen can be traced back as far as the early 1440s! It is known that the Lowchen is related to the Bichon Frise, but the breed's history remains obscure. The breed traditionally was kept as a companion dog by the wealthy, elite and aristocrats of Germany. Despite being a relatively old breed, the Lowchen did not enter England until 1968 and the United States of America until 1971! The temperament of dogs is normally affected by the following factors: individual personality, heredity, training and socialization. It is therefore important to make sure that you meet the puppy's mother before purchasing a Lowchen. It is also important to make sure to thoroughly socialize your Lowchen with strangers, children and other animals during its puppyhood. Generally speaking, the Lowchen is a friendly, healthy and affectionate breed of dog. The Lowchen is known to be highly intelligent and playful. The breed makes a perfect house pet as it is known to get along well with other animals, strangers and small children. Due to the breed's history as a companion dog, the Lowchen craves human companionship and attention. The Lowchen should therefore not be left alone for extended periods of time. The Lowchen is suitable to keep in an apartment due to its small size and quiet nature.

Lion Cut

The Lowchen has a long and wavy coat that is traditionally groomed, and presented, in a lion cut. This means that the dog's haunches, back legs, front legs, and 1/3-1/2 of the dog's tail closet to the body are shaved while the rest of the dog's coat is left natural. This creates a mane around the dog's head and gives the Lowchen a unique lion-like appearance.

Lifespan

A Lowchen will normally live to be between 12 and 13 years old. However it is not uncommon for a Lowchen to live to be as old as 15, providing that it does not develop any serious health issues.

Height and Weight

A fully grown Lowchen will normally stand between 12 to 14 inches (30.5 to 35.5cm) tall at the shoulder. A healthy adult Lowchen will normally weigh between 9 to 18 pounds (23 to 46kg). It is important to note that the weight of a healthy Lowchen depends on how large the Lowchen is – taller Lowchen should weigh more.

Breed Characteristics

The following section will give you a simplistic overview of the characteristics of a Lowchen. Our rating system is from 1 to 10 – with 1 being the lowest score and 10 being the highest.

- **Adaptability:** 6/10
- **Friendliness:** 10/10
- **Health:** 10/10
- **Ease of Grooming:** 7/10
- **Amount of Shedding:** 6/10
- **Trainability:** 8/10
- **Intelligence:** 8/10
- **Exercise Needed:** 8/10
- **Playfulness:** 10/10
- **Family Friendliness:** 10/10

THE MALTESE

The Maltese is a small breed of 'Toy Dog.' The breed is a descends from dogs that originally came from the Central Mediterranean Area. The name 'Maltese' reflects the breeds ancestral history as it is derived from the Mediterranean island nation of Malta. The Maltese has been recognized by the WCO (World Canine Organization) as being under the patronage of Italy since 1954. The Maltese has a slightly rounded skull, with a finger-wide dome, a black button nose and brown eyes. If a Maltese is not exposed to sunlight on a regular basis it is possible for their nose to become a pale pink or light brown color. This nose coloration is normally referred to as 'winter nose' as it normally develops during the darker and colder months of the year. They have a compact body with relatively long drop ears. The Maltese also has a slight discoloration of fur around its eyes which give the breed its signature expressive look.

Lifespan

A Maltese will normally live to be between 10 and 13 years old. However it is not uncommon for a Maltese to live to be as old as 15, providing that they do not develop any serious health issues.

Height and Weight

A fully grown Maltese will normally be between 8 to 10 inches tall at the shoulder (). An adult Maltese will normally weigh up to 7 pounds ().

Coat

The coat of the Maltese is long and silky. They do not have an undercoat which is somewhat uncommon for a long haired breed. Some Maltese have curly hair, which is most commonly found behind the dog's ears. Curly hair is considered a 'fault' in terms of Dog Show breed standards. A Maltese will normally have a white coat but it is not uncommon for their coats to be tinted slightly with a tan coloration. The Maltese does not shed which makes it a perfect choice for anyone who has allergies. The most common cut for a Maltese is called 'the puppy cut,' which involves trimming the dog's entire body to a single short length. There will be a more detailed section on grooming in a later section of this book.

Breed Characteristics

The following section will give you a simplistic overview of the characteristics of a Maltese. Our rating system is from 1 to 10 – with 1 being the lowest score

and 10 being the highest.

- ➤ **Adaptability:** 6/10
- ➤ **Friendliness:** 8/10
- ➤ **Health:** 6/10
- ➤ **Ease of Grooming:** 4/10
- ➤ **Amount of Shedding:** 4/10
- ➤ **Trainability:** 6/10
- ➤ **Intelligence:** 8/10
- ➤ **Exercise Needed:** 6/10
- ➤ **Playfulness:** 8/10
- ➤ **Family Friendliness:** 10/10

THE MALTESE SHIH TZU

The Maltese Shih Tzu is a 'designer' breed of dog that is a cross between a Maltese and a Shih Tzu. When purchasing a designer breed it is important to note that you are not purchasing a 'true,' or 'pure,' breed and there are no breeding standards for the Maltese Shih Tzu. Maltese Shih Tzu puppies come in a wide variety of sizes, looks and temperaments. However, a Maltese Shih Tzu puppy will generally not have the Shih Tzu's short nose and bulging eyes while also being less prone to the tear staining found in pure bred Maltese. The Maltese Shih Tzu was originally developed in 1990 with the purpose of creating a nonshedding breed – which is physically impossible. The Maltese Shih Tzu is one of the most popular crossbreeds within Australia and North America. The temperament of dogs is normally affected by the following factors: individual personality, heredity, training and socialization. It is therefore important to make sure that you meet the puppy's mother before purchasing a Maltese Shih Tzu. It is also important to make sure to thoroughly socialize your Maltese Shih Tzu with strangers, children and other animals during its puppyhood. Generally speaking, the Maltese Shih Tzu is known to be an adaptable, intelligent and outgoing breed. Despite their small size, the Maltese Shih Tzu like to exercise on a regular basis and will fit into an active family lifestyle.

Lifespan

A Maltese Shih Tzu will normally live to be between 11 and 13 years old. However it is not uncommon for a Maltese Shih Tzu to live to be as old as 14, providing that it does not develop any serious health issues.

Height and Weight

A fully grown Maltese Shih Tzu will normally stand between 6 to 10 inches (15.25 to 25.5cm) tall at the shoulder. A healthy adult Maltese Shih Tzu will normally weigh between 6 to 12 pounds (2.75 to 5.5kg). It is important to note that the weight of a healthy Maltese Shih Tzu depends on how large the Maltese Shih Tzu is – taller Maltese Shih Tzu should weigh more.

Breed Characteristics

The following section will give you a simplistic overview of the characteristics of a Maltese Shih Tzu. Our rating system is from 1 to 10 – with 1 being the lowest score and 10 being the highest.

- **Adaptability:** 6/10
- **Friendliness:** 7/10
- **Health:** 5/10

- **Ease of Grooming:** 5/10
- **Amount of Shedding:** 1/10
- **Trainability:** 8/10
- **Intelligence:** 7/10
- **Exercise Needed:** 7/10
- **Playfulness:** 6/10
- **Family Friendliness:** 8/10

THE MALTIPOO

The Maltipoo is a 'designer' breed of dog that is a cross between a Maltese and a Poodle. The breed is also commonly known as the 'Moodle' or the 'Maltapoo.' When purchasing a designer breed it is important to note that you are not purchasing a 'true,' or 'pure,' breed and there are no breeding standards for the Maltipoo. Maltipoo puppies come in a wide variety of sizes, looks and temperaments. The Maltipoo is considered to be a hypoallergenic breed due to the fact that its coat is a mix between the low shedding Maltese and the hypoallergenic Poodle. The Maltipoo is known to bark frequently, which has therefore lead to it being commonly used as a watchdog. The temperament of dogs is normally affected by the following factors: individual personality, heredity, training and socialization. It is therefore important to make sure that you meet the puppy's mother before purchasing a Maltipoo. It is also important to make sure to thoroughly socialize your Maltipoo with strangers, children and other animals during its puppyhood. Generally speaking, the Maltipoo is known to be an intelligent, affectionate and calm natured breed. The Maltipoo is also known to be a gentle breed and is therefore a perfect pet for any family with small children or other small animals.

Lifespan

A Maltipoo will normally live to be between 10 and 12 years old. However it is not uncommon for a Maltipoo to live to be as old as 13, providing that it does not develop any serious health issues.

Height and Weight

A fully grown Maltipoo will normally stand between 8 to 14 inches (20.3 to 35.5cm) tall at the shoulder. A healthy adult Maltipoo will normally weigh between 5 to 20 pounds (2.25 to 9kg). It is important to note that the weight of a healthy Maltipoo depends on how large the Maltipoo is – taller Maltipoo should weigh more.

Breed Characteristics

The following section will give you a simplistic overview of the characteristics of a Maltipoo. Our rating system is from 1 to 10 – with 1 being the lowest score and 10 being the highest.

- **Adaptability:** 8/10
- **Friendliness:** 8/10
- **Health:** 5/10
- **Ease of Grooming:** 7/10

- **Amount of Shedding:** 1/10
- **Trainability:** 8/10
- **Intelligence:** 8/10
- **Exercise Needed:** 6/10
- **Playfulness:** 8/10
- **Family Friendliness:** 10/10

THE MANCHESTER TERRIER

The Manchester Terrier is a breed of short-haired dog that is a member of the Terrier typing. The Manchester Terrier is considered by many people to be the oldest recognizable Terrier breed. The Manchester Terrier is very similar in appearance to the Doberman and German Pinschers – however the Manchester Terrier is more similar in size to Miniatures. During the early 19th century, England went through a period of extremely poor sanitation which lead to an increase in the rat population which lead to widespread diseases. The increase in the rat population lead to rat hunting becoming a very popular sport. John Hulme, an enthusiastic member of the sport of rat-baiting and rabbit coursing, crossed a whippet and a terrier with the purpose of developing a more streamlined dog breed that was better suited to rat hunting. Hulme's cross proved to be highly successful and was continued until the Manchester Terrier was developed. The Manchester Terrier was initially used in rat pits until they were made illegal which lead to the breed being commonly used in inns and pubs to deal with their rat infestations. The first Manchester Terrier was registered by the English Kennel Club in 1860 and by the American Kennel Club in 1887. The temperament of dogs is normally affected by the following factors: individual personality, heredity, training and socialization. It is therefore important to make sure that you meet the puppy's mother before purchasing a Manchester Terrier. It is also important to make sure to thoroughly socialize your Manchester Terrier with strangers, children and other animals during its puppyhood. Generally speaking, the Manchester Terrier is known to be very social creature that is incredibly affectionate towards people. Thought the Manchester Terrier is not an aggressive breed it is not a suitable breed to be kept in a household with other small animals, due to its history and development revolving around the extermination of small 'vermin.' To eliminate any chance that your Manchester Terrier may attack, or harass, other small animals it is highly advisable to bring it to obedience training classes during its early puppyhood. The obedience classes will teach your Manchester Terrier to obey your commands as well as allowing it to socialize with other dog breeds of various sizes. It is important to note that as a working breed, the Manchester Terrier has a high amount of energy which needs to be expended. If the Manchester Terrier has a buildup of energy it is likely to develop destructive behaviors due to boredom or hyperactivity.

Lifespan

A Manchester Terrier will normally live to be between 12 and 14 years old. However it is not uncommon for a Manchester Terrier to live to be as old as 16, providing that it does not develop any serious health issues.

Height and Weight

A fully grown Manchester Terrier will normally stand between 15 to 17 inches (38 to 43cm) tall at the shoulder. A healthy adult Manchester Terrier will normally weigh between 12 to 22 pounds (5.5 to 10kg). It is important to note that the weight of a healthy Manchester Terrier depends on how large the Manchester Terrier is – taller Manchester Terrier should weigh more.

Breed Characteristics

The following section will give you a simplistic overview of the characteristics of a Manchester Terrier. Our rating system is from 1 to 10 – with 1 being the lowest score and 10 being the highest.

- **Adaptability:** 6/10
- **Friendliness:** 7/10
- **Health:** 5/10

- ➢ **Ease of Grooming:** 10/10
- ➢ **Amount of Shedding:** 6/10
- ➢ **Trainability:** 6/10
- ➢ **Intelligence:** 8/10
- ➢ **Exercise Needed:** 8/10
- ➢ **Playfulness:** 8/10
- ➢ **Family Friendliness:** 10/10

THE MASTIFF

The term 'Mastiff' refers to a large breed of dog that is a member of the Molossers typing. The term 'Mastiff' has been used throughout history synonymously with the term 'Molossers.' For example, the Bulldog breeds, the Great Dane, the Boston Terrier and the Pit Bull may be considered 'Mastiff' types. It is believed that all Mastiff types share a single common ancestor which is thought to be an ancient, and extinct, breed known as the 'Molossus' which originated from Ancient Greece. The temperament of dogs is normally affected by the following factors: individual personality, heredity, training and socialization. It is therefore important to make sure that you meet the puppy's mother before purchasing a Mastiff. It is also important to make sure to thoroughly socialize your Mastiff with strangers, children and other animals during its puppyhood. Generally speaking, breeds within the Mastiff typing are known to be intelligent, affectionate and hard working. It is important to note that as a working breed, the Mastiff has a high amount of energy which needs to be expended. If the Mastiff has a buildup of energy it is likely to develop destructive behaviors due to boredom or hyperactivity.

Lifespan

Generally speaking, most Mastiff breeds will normally live to be between 6 and 10 years old. However it is not uncommon for a Mastiff to live to be as old as 14, providing that it does not develop any serious health issues and dependent on the breed of Mastiff.

Height and Weight

There are multiple different types of Mastiff and it is therefore impossible to give specific standardized heights and weights. However, generally a fully grown Mastiff will normally stand between 20 to 32 inches (50.8 to 81.25cm) tall at the shoulder. A healthy adult Mastiff will normally weigh between 100 to 220 pounds (45.35 to 100kg). It is important to note that the weight of a healthy Mastiff depends on how large the Mastiff is – taller Mastiff should weigh more.

List of Mastiff Breeds

- Abruzzese Mastiff – originating from the Italian region of the Abruzzi.
- Alpine Mastiff – an extinct breed that originated from Sweden.
- American Mastiff – originating from the

United States of America.
- Bordeaux Mastiff – originating from France and also commonly known as the 'French Mastiff.'
- Brazilian Mastiff – originating from Brazil.
- Bullmastiff – a cross between a Bulldog and a Mastiff
- Cuban Mastiff – originating from Cuba
- Dogo Argentino – originating from Argentina and also commonly known as the 'Argentinian Mastiff.'
- Dutch Mastiff – also commonly known as the 'Pug.'
- English Mastiff – originating from England.
- German Mastiff – originating from Germany.
- Italian Mastiff – originating from Italy and also commonly known as the 'Cane Corso.'
- Japanese Mastiff – originating from Japan and also commonly known as the 'Tosa Inu.'
- Korean Mastiff – originating from Korea and also commonly known as the 'Dosa Gae.'
- Kumaon Mastiff – a very rare breed originating from India.
- Neapolitan Mastiff – originating from the Naples region of Italy.
- Pakistani Mastiff – originating from the Punjab region of Pakistan and also commonly

known as the 'Bully Kutta.'
- Persian Mastiff – originating from north Iran and also commonly known as the 'Iranian Mastiff.'
- Portuguese Mastiff – originating from the Alentejo region of Portugal.
- Perro de Presa Canario – originating from the Canary Islands and also commonly known as the 'Canary Mastiff.'
- Puerto Rican Mastiff – originating from Puerto Rico.
- Pyrenean Mastiff – originating from Spain.
- South African Mastiff – originating from South Africa and also commonly known as the 'Boerboel.'
- Spanish Mastiff – originating from Spain.
- Tibetan Mastiff – originating from Tibet.

Breed Characteristics

The following section will give you a simplistic overview of the characteristics generally found within the Mastiff typing. Our rating system is from 1 to 10 – with 1 being the lowest score and 10 being the highest.

- **Adaptability:** 4/10
- **Friendliness:** 8/10
- **Health:** 6/10

- ➢ **Ease of Grooming:** 6/10
- ➢ **Amount of Shedding:** 6/10
- ➢ **Trainability:** 5/10
- ➢ **Intelligence:** 6/10
- ➢ **Exercise Needed:** 8/10
- ➢ **Playfulness:** 8/10
- ➢ **Family Friendliness:** 10/10

THE MINIATURE PINSCHER

The Miniature Pinscher is a small toy breed of dog that originates from Germany. The Miniature Pinscher is also commonly known as the 'Zwergpinscher,' the 'Min Pin' and as the 'King of the Toys.' It is believed that the Miniature Pinscher was developed through the process of cross breeding the German Pinscher, the Italian Greyhound and the Dachshund. The Miniature Pinscher was first registered as a unique breed about 200 years ago, however there is a plethora of historical evidence that suggests that the Miniature Pinscher is actually a very old breed. The Miniature Pinscher is often believed to be a miniature version of the Doberman Pinscher, but this is actually incorrect. This common misconception is due to the fact that the two breeds look very similar and the fact that the Doberman Pinscher was introduced to the United States of America and England about 50 years before the Miniature Pinscher. The Miniature Pinscher has a sturdily built, compact and athletic body that is covered in a smooth coat. The Miniature Pinscher's coat comes in a wide variety of colorations that includes: solid red, stag red, chocolate stag red, black, blue and fawn. Traditionally the show standard for the Miniature Pinscher stated that the breed needed its tail docked and ears cropped – however due to the cruelty involved in the cropping and docking process this is no longer a breed standard and has fallen out of fashion. The temperament of dogs is normally affected by the following factors: individual personality, heredity, training and socialization. It is therefore important to make sure that you meet the puppy's mother before purchasing a Miniature Pinscher. It is also important to make sure to thoroughly socialize your Miniature Pinscher with strangers, children and other animals during its puppyhood. Generally speaking, the Miniature Pinscher is known to be assertive, outgoing, independent and energetic. It is considered best practice for the Miniature Pinscher to not be owned by anyone except experienced dog owners due to their assertive nature. The breed makes an excellent watchdog due to their innate suspicion of strangers. It is important to note that the Miniature Pinscher has a high amount of energy which needs to be expended. If the Miniature Pinscher has a buildup of energy it is likely to develop destructive behaviors due to boredom or hyperactivity. It is advised to have a medium-to-large sized garden with a secure fence to allow your Miniature Pinscher to have access to vigorous exercise whenever it chooses.

Lifespan

A Miniature Pinscher will normally live to be between 10 and 12 years old. However it is not uncommon for a Miniature Pinscher to live to be as old as 14, providing that it does not develop any serious health issues.

Height and Weight

A fully grown Miniature Pinscher will normally stand between 10 to 12 inches (25.4 to 30.5cm) tall at the shoulder. A healthy adult Miniature Pinscher will normally weigh between 8 to 12 pounds (3.6 to 5.5kg). It is important to note that the weight of a healthy Miniature Pinscher depends on how large the Miniature Pinscher is – taller Miniature Pinscher should weigh more.

Breed Characteristics

The following section will give you a simplistic overview of the characteristics of a Miniature Pinscher. Our rating system is from 1 to 10 – with 1 being the lowest score and 10 being the highest.

- **Adaptability:** 6/10
- **Friendliness:** 6/10
- **Health:** 6/10
- **Ease of Grooming:** 10/10
- **Amount of Shedding:** 3/10
- **Trainability:** 6/10
- **Intelligence:** 6/10

- ➢ **Exercise Needed:** 8/10
- ➢ **Playfulness:** 10/10
- ➢ **Family Friendliness:** 10/10

THE MINIATURE SCHNAUZER

The Miniature Schnauzer is a small breed of Schnauzer that originates from Germany. It is believed that the Miniature breed was developed in the mid-to-late 19th century by crossing the Standard Schnauzer and a smaller breed, like the Poodle or Affenpinscher. The breed is described as family orientated, aloof and friendly. It is also known for having good guarding tendencies without a predisposition to bite. The breed is recognized as having three different coat colorations: solid black, black and silver and a coloration known as 'salt and pepper.' The breed is extremely popular worldwide due to its temperament and relatively small size. The Miniature Schnauzer is ranked within the top 20 most popular breeds in the United Sates of American since 2013.

Lifespan

A Miniature Schnauzer will common live to be between 11 and 13 years old. However it is not uncommon for a Miniature Schnauzer to live to be as old as 14 or 15, providing that they do not develop any serious health issues.

Height and Weight

An adult Miniature Schnauzer will normally be between 12 and 15 inches (30 to 38cm) tall at the shoulder. This is dramatically smaller than the Standard Schnauzer that normally stands between 17 and 20 inches (43 to 51cm) tall at the shoulder. The Miniature's relatively small size aids in its popularity. A healthy Miniature Schnauzer will normally weigh between 11 and 20 pounds (5 to 13.5kg).

Temperament

The Miniature Schnauzer is known to be people-oriented and good with small children and other animals of a similar size. The breed is also known to be highly affectionate, intelligent and stubborn. They are also known to be highly protective of their homes and family units – a Miniature Schnauzer will often bark at any unfamiliar sound.

Breed Characteristics

The following section will give you a simplistic overview of the characteristics of a Miniature Schnauzer. Our rating system is from 1 to 10 – with 1 being the lowest score and 10 being the highest.

➢ **Adaptability:** 8/10

- ➢ **Friendliness:** 8/10
- ➢ **Health:** 6/10
- ➢ **Ease of Grooming:** 4/10
- ➢ **Amount of Shedding:** 4/10
- ➢ **Trainability:** 8/10
- ➢ **Intelligence:** 9/10
- ➢ **Exercise Needed:** 8/10
- ➢ **Playfulness:** 8/10
- ➢ **Family Friendliness:** 10/10

Encyclopedia of Dog Breeds

THE NEAPOLITAN MASTIFF

The Neapolitan Mastiff is a large, ancient breed of dog that originates from Italy. The Neapolitan Mastiff is also commonly known as the 'Mastino,' the 'Mastino Neapolitan,' the 'Italian Molosso' and the 'Can'e Presa.' The breed has been popular across Europe for hundreds of years and has traditionally been used to guard and defend both people and property due to the Neapolitan Mastiff's innate protective instinct and intimidating appearance and gigantic size. In ancient times the Neapolitan Mastiff has also been used to bait bulls, bears and jaguars. Despite the breed's popularity, the Neapolitan Mastiff nearly went extinct during World War II. Soon after the war, an Italian painter, Piero Scanziani, established a breeding kennel with the specific purpose of turning the Mastiff-type dogs of Italy into a standardized breed which lead to the creation of the Neapolitan Mastiff's breeding standard. The Neapolitan Mastiff is a large, well-muscled and powerful breed of dog. The breed's body is covered in loose skin that is covered in a smooth short coat. The Neapolitan Mastiff's coat comes in the following colorations: blue, black, tawny and mahogany. The temperament of dogs is normally affected by the following factors: individual personality, heredity, training and socialization. It is therefore important to make sure that you meet the puppy's mother before purchasing a Neapolitan Mastiff. It is also important to make sure to thoroughly socialize your Neapolitan Mastiff with strangers, children and other animals during its puppyhood. Generally speaking, is a protective, fearless and family orientated breed. The Neapolitan Mastiff enjoys nothing more than spending time with its family unit. The Neapolitan Mastiff is known to be an incredibly intelligent breed with the tendency to be independent thinkers. The Neapolitan Mastiff is a fast learning breed - which is both a positive and a negative thing. It is important to not allow your Neapolitan Mastiff to develop bad habits as it take a lot more time to 'unlearn' bad behaviors than initially to learn them. It is important to make sure that you properly socialize your Neapolitan Mastiff from early puppyhood as the Neapolitan Mastiff is known to be highly suspicious, and in some cases even aggressive, towards strangers and unknown dogs. Despite its large size, the Neapolitan Mastiff is relatively adaptable to apartment living due to the fact that it rarely ever barks. However if you do choose to keep your Neapolitan Mastiff in an apartment it is important to make sure that you provide your Neapolitan Mastiff with adequate exercise on a regular basis as if the Neapolitan Mastiff has a buildup of energy it is likely to develop destructive behaviors due to boredom or hyperactivity.

Lifespan

A Neapolitan Mastiff will normally live to be between 7 and 8 years old. However it is not uncommon for a Neapolitan Mastiff to live to be as old as 10, providing that it does not develop any serious health issues.

Height and Weight

A fully grown Neapolitan Mastiff will normally stand between 24 to 31 inches (61 to 78.75cm) tall at the shoulder. A healthy adult Neapolitan Mastiff will normally weigh between 120 to 200 pounds (54.5 to 90.7kg). It is important to note that the weight of a healthy Neapolitan Mastiff depends on how large the Neapolitan Mastiff is – taller Neapolitan Mastiff should weigh more.

Breed Characteristics

The following section will give you a simplistic overview of the characteristics of a Neapolitan Mastiff. Our rating system is from 1 to 10 – with 1 being the lowest score and 10 being the highest.

- **Adaptability:** 5/10
- **Friendliness:** 5/10
- **Health:** 5/10

- **Ease of Grooming:** 6/10
- **Amount of Shedding:** 6/10
- **Trainability:** 5/10
- **Intelligence:** 7/10
- **Exercise Needed:** 6/10
- **Playfulness:** 8/10
- **Family Friendliness:** 10/10

THE NEWFOUNDLAND

The Newfoundland is a large breed of working dog that originates from Newfoundland, Canada. The breed's coat comes in three main colorations: black, brown, or white-and-black (which is known as a 'Landseer'). The Newfoundland is a breed of Mastiff and shares many similar traits to other Mastiffs, such as the St. Bernard, the Great Pyrenees and the English Mastiff, including stout legs, a broad snout, a relatively large head, a thick neck and a sturdy, musical body structure. The Newfoundland has a water-resistant coat and webbed feet which makes the breed extremely adept at swimming. The breed's heavy bone structure, muscular form and webbed feet allow the Newfoundland to easy combat rough ocean waves and powerful tides which has lead the Newfoundland to be a common choice for sea related rescues. The Newfoundland is so adept at sea based rescues that it can still be found on boats in St. John's. The Newfoundland has a profuse, waterproof, longhaired and double coat which means that it sheds regularly and is somewhat hard to groom. The Newfoundland's ancestry is believed to be a mixture of the Portuguese Mastiffs and a wild breed of dog found in Newfoundland. Some breed enthusiast believe that the Newfoundland descends from a breed of large and black coated bear dog that was introduced into Canada around 1000 A.D – however it is widely accepted that this is probably nothing more than a romantic fantasy. The breed has been relatively popular, especially in the United States of America and Canada, but went almost extinct during the Second World War due to wartime breeding restrictions. The temperament of dogs is normally affected by the following factors: individual personality, heredity, training and socialization. It is therefore important to make sure that you meet the puppy's mother before purchasing a Newfoundland. It is also important to make sure to thoroughly socialize your Newfoundland with strangers, children and other animals during its puppyhood. Generally speaking, the Newfoundland breed is known to be clam, docile, highly loyal and sweet tempered. The breed is so gentle that it has commonly been nicknamed the 'Gentle Giant.' The Newfoundland makes a perfect addition to any family with small children as they are too sturdy to be hurt during play and are also very gentle and respectful of children's wellbeing. The Newfoundland is also a highly empathetic breed and is seeing increasing use as a therapy dog. Its use in therapy and childminding has lead the breed to be anecdotally known as the 'Nanny Dog.' Despite the fact that the Newfoundland is a generally very good around strangers and unknown dogs, it is still important to make sure that your properly socialize your Newfoundland during its puppyhood as its large and power form could be potentially hazardous if it is unsocalized and untrained! It is important to note that as a working breed, the Newfoundland has a high amount of energy which needs to be expended. If the Newfoundland has a buildup of energy it is likely to develop destructive behaviors due to boredom or hyperactivity.

Lifespan

A Newfoundland will normally live to be between 7 and 8 years old. However it is not uncommon for a Newfoundland to live to be as old as 10, providing that it does not develop any serious health issues.

Height and Weight

A fully grown Newfoundland will normally stand between 24 to 29 inches (? to ?cm) tall at the shoulder. A healthy adult Newfoundland will normally weigh between 100 to 160 pounds (? to ?kg). It is important to note that the weight of a healthy Newfoundland depends on how large the Newfoundland is – taller Newfoundland should weigh more.

Breed Characteristics

The following section will give you a simplistic overview of the characteristics of a Newfoundland. Our

rating system is from 1 to 10 – with 1 being the lowest score and 10 being the highest.

- **Adaptability:** 6/10
- **Friendliness:** 10/10
- **Health:** 3/10
- **Ease of Grooming:** 5/10
- **Amount of Shedding:** 10/10
- **Trainability:** 9/10
- **Intelligence:** 8/10
- **Exercise Needed:** 7/10
- **Playfulness:** 8/10
- **Family Friendliness:** 10/10

THE NORFOLK TERRIER

The Norfolk Terrier is a breed of dog that is a member of the Terrier typing. The breed originates from Norfolk, England. The Norfolk Terrier is closely related to the Norwich Terrier and was actually considered to be a variant of the Norwich Terrier until 1964 when it became a breed in its own right. The main distinguishing difference between the Norfolk Terrier and the Norwich Terrier is the elevation of their ears: the Norfolk Terrier has 'drop ears' (or folded ears) while the Norwich Terrier has 'pricked ears' (ears that sit upright). Both the Norfolk Terrier and the Norfolk Terrier are the smallest of the working terrier breeds. The Norfolk Terrier has a wire-haired coat which, according to multiple breeding standards from all over the world, can come in a variety of colorations including all shades of red, black, black and tan or grizzle. The Norfolk Terrier has a very small compact body with good substance and bone. 'Good substance' means that the Norfolk Terrier has a good amount of spring in their ribs, hips and bones which allows the Norfolk Terrier to be an incredibly agile ratter. The Norfolk Terrier has traditionally been used as a ratter and as an all-purpose earth-dog. The breed also became a very popular choice of pet for people who live in apartments or small homes. The temperament of dogs is normally affected by the following factors:

individual personality, heredity, training and socialization. It is therefore important to make sure that you meet the puppy's mother before purchasing a Norfolk Terrier. It is also important to make sure to thoroughly socialize your Norfolk Terrier with strangers, children and other animals during its puppyhood. Generally speaking, the Norfolk Terrier is known to be a fearless breed with an independent streak. The Norfolk Terrier is also considered to have the most affectionate and gentle temperament out of all the terrier breeds (except for maybe the Border Terrier). The Norfolk Terrier makes a perfect household pet due to the fact that they are very friendly towards children, strangers and unknown dogs. The Norfolk Terrier makes a perfect addition to any household with other dog breeds due to the fact that the Norfolk Terrier was traditionally put to work in packs, which makes the breed very easy to socialize. It is important to note that as a working breed, the Norfolk Terrier has a high amount of energy which needs to be expended. If the Norfolk Terrier has a buildup of energy it is likely to develop destructive behaviors due to boredom or hyperactivity.

Lifespan

A Norfolk Terrier will normally live to be between 10 and 12 years old. However it is not uncommon for a Norfolk Terrier to live to be as old as 15, providing that it does not develop any serious health issues.

Height and Weight

A fully grown Norfolk Terrier will normally stand between 9 to 10 inches (22.86 to 25.5cm) tall at the shoulder. A healthy adult Norfolk Terrier will normally weigh between 10 to 12 pounds (4.5 to 5.5kg). It is important to note that the weight of a healthy Norfolk Terrier depends on how large the Norfolk Terrier is – taller Norfolk Terrier should weigh more.

Breed Characteristics

The following section will give you a simplistic overview of the characteristics of a Norfolk Terrier. Our rating system is from 1 to 10 – with 1 being the lowest score and 10 being the highest.

- **Adaptability:** 8/10
- **Friendliness:** 10/10
- **Health:** 10/10
- **Ease of Grooming:** 8/10
- **Amount of Shedding:** 1/10
- **Trainability:** 6/10
- **Intelligence:** 8/10
- **Exercise Needed:** 8/10
- **Playfulness:** 10/10

➢ **Family Friendliness:** 10/10

THE NORWEGIAN BUHUND

The Norwegian Buhund is a breed of dog that is a member of the Spitz typing. The Norwegian Buhund is also commonly known as the 'Norsk Buhund' and the 'Norwegian Sheepdog.' The breed is closely related to the Icelandic Sheepdog. In the excavation of the ancient Gokstad, a Viking grave from about the year 900 A.D, in Norway multiple skeletons of dogs that closely resemble the Norwegian Buhund were discovered which suggests that the Norwegian Buhund is an ancient breed of dog. The Norwegian Buhund has traditionally been used for the purpose of herding sheep and other cattle. However it has also been commonly used as a watch dog, a nanny dog and as a companion dog. The breed is medium-sized and has a square profile that has a high set tail that curls over the center of its back. The Norwegian Buhund's coat comes in either a black or wheaten coloration: which is any shade from pale cream to a bright orange. The temperament of dogs is normally affected by the following factors: individual personality, heredity, training and socialization. It is therefore important to make sure that you meet the puppy's mother before purchasing a Norwegian Buhund. It is also important to make sure to thoroughly socialize your Norwegian Buhund with strangers, children and other animals during its puppyhood. Generally speaking, the

Norwegian Buhund is known to be an active, cheerful and loyal breed. The Norwegian Buhund makes a great addition to any family home due to their affectionate nature and love of children. However it is important to always supervise a Norwegian Buhund while it is interacting with children due to the breed's high levels of energy and hyperactivity – while the Norwegian Buhund is not known to be an aggressive breed it is not uncommon for a Norwegian Buhund to become overly excited and knock small children over in playful excitement. The Norwegian Buhund forms extremely close bonds with its family unit and may be aloof with strangers. The Norwegian Buhund is also an incredibly head strong and intelligent breed that desires to learn new things on a regular basis. It is important to note that as a working breed, the Norwegian Buhund has a high amount of energy which needs to be expended. If the Norwegian Buhund has a buildup of energy it is likely to develop destructive behaviors due to boredom or hyperactivity. It is also important to note that the Norwegian Buhund does not tire easily and it is therefore a full time pursuit to keep your Norwegian Buhund well exercised.

Lifespan

A Norwegian Buhund will normally live to be between 12 and 13 years old. However it is not uncommon for a Norwegian Buhund to live to be as old as 15, providing that it does not develop any serious health issues.

Height and Weight

A fully grown Norwegian Buhund will normally stand between 16 to 18 inches (40.6 to 45.7cm) tall at the shoulder. A healthy adult Norwegian Buhund will normally weigh between 25 to 40 pounds (11.3 to 18.1kg). It is important to note that the weight of a healthy Norwegian Buhund depends on how large the Norwegian Buhund is – taller Norwegian Buhund should weigh more.

Breed Characteristics

The following section will give you a simplistic overview of the characteristics of a Norwegian Buhund. Our rating system is from 1 to 10 – with 1 being the lowest score and 10 being the highest.

- **Adaptability:** 6/10
- **Friendliness:** 8/10
- **Health:** 8/10
- **Ease of Grooming:** 5/10
- **Amount of Shedding:** 6/10
- **Trainability:** 6/10

- ➢ **Intelligence:** 7/10
- ➢ **Exercise Needed:** 10/10
- ➢ **Playfulness:** 10/10
- ➢ **Family Friendliness:** 10/10

THE NORWEGIAN ELKHOUND

The Norwegian Elkhound is an ancient breed of Spitz type dog that originates from Norway. The Norwegian Elkhound is actually the National Dog of Norway. The breed is also commonly known as the 'Norsk Elkhound,' the 'Norwegian Moose Dog' and the 'Small Grey Elk Dog.' The Norwegian Elkhound has traditionally served as a hunter, herder, flock guardian and as a defender of both people and property. The breed was developed for the specific purpose of hunting large game and is known to hunt elk, bears and wolves fearlessly. The Norwegian Elkhound is an incredibly independent and intelligent breed that was tasked with hunting large game completely by themselves. When the Norwegian Elkhound had tracked the game it would then begin to bay to alert the hunter to the location of the game. The Norwegian Elkhound has an incredible ability to both keep large game stationary and to herd large game towards the hunter. In the excavation of the ancient Gokstad, a Viking grave from about the year 900 A.D, in Norway multiple skeletons of dogs that closely resemble the Norwegian Elkhound were discovered which suggests that the Norwegian Elkhound is an ancient breed of dog. The Norwegian Elkhound has a double coat which is made up of an underlying smooth and dense coat and an overlying coat made up of protective and coarse guard hairs. The breed's coat comes in the following colorations: grey, black, white and tan. The Norwegian Elkhound is known for its characteristically curled tail that curls onto its back. The temperament of dogs is normally affected by the following factors: individual personality, heredity, training and socialization. It is therefore important to make sure that you meet the puppy's mother before purchasing a Norwegian Elkhound. It is also important to make sure to thoroughly socialize your Norwegian Elkhound with strangers, children and other animals during its puppyhood. Generally speaking, the Norwegian Elkhound breed is known to be incredibly loyal, hardy and strong headed. Traditionally the Norwegian Elkhound would live in a pack, which makes it an excellent family dog as it enjoys nothing more than spending time with its family unit. The Norwegian Elkhound makes a terrible pet for anyone who lives in an apartment due to the breeds high levels of energy and loud bark – which is likely to lead to a noise complaint. It is important to note that as a working breed, the Norwegian Elkhound has a high amount of energy which needs to be expended. If the Norwegian Elkhound has a buildup of energy it is likely to develop destructive behaviors due to boredom or hyperactivity.

Lifespan

A Norwegian Elkhound will normally live to be between 12 and 13 years old. However it is not uncommon for a Norwegian Elkhound to live to be as old as 15, providing that it does not develop any serious health issues.

Height and Weight

A fully grown Norwegian Elkhound will normally stand between 19.5 to 20.5 inches (50 to 52cm) tall at the shoulder. A healthy adult Norwegian Elkhound will normally weigh between 44 to 51 pounds (20 to 23kg). It is important to note that the weight of a healthy Norwegian Elkhound depends on how large the Norwegian Elkhound is – taller Norwegian Elkhound should weigh more.

Breed Characteristics

The following section will give you a simplistic overview of the characteristics of a Norwegian Elkhound. Our rating system is from 1 to 10 – with 1 being the lowest score and 10 being the highest.

- **Adaptability:** 8/10
- **Friendliness:** 8/10
- **Health:** 8/10

- ➢ **Ease of Grooming:** 7/10
- ➢ **Amount of Shedding:** 10/10
- ➢ **Trainability:** 8/10
- ➢ **Intelligence:** 8/10
- ➢ **Exercise Needed:** 8/10
- ➢ **Playfulness:** 8/10
- ➢ **Family Friendliness:** 10/10

THE NORWEGIAN LUNDEHUND

The Norwegian Lundehund is a small breed of dog that is a member of the Spitz typing and originates from Norway. The Norwegian Lundehund is also commonly known as the 'Norsk Lundehund' and the 'Norwegian Puffin Dog.' The Norwegian Lundehund's name is a compound noun that is composes of the elements 'Lunde,' which means 'Puffin' and 'Hund,' which means dog. The breed has an incredibly long history and is believed to have been in existence since before the last Ice Age. The Norwegian Lundehund's wild ancestors survived through the harsh winters found in Norway by eating fish and sea birds. The Norwegian Lundehund has extra toes on its feet and an incredible agile body which allows it to easily hunt puffins, and other sea birds, on cliffs and in caves. The Norwegian Lundehund was mainly employed by the Vikings for the purpose of hunting sea birds for food and commerce. The Norwegian Lundehund breed almost went extinct during World War II due to canine distemper. However in the late 1960s an effort was made to revitalize the breed and dedicated breeding organization were created. Due to its hunting history, the Norwegian Lundehund has an incredibly agile body: the breed has a great range of motion in its joints and is actually capable of turning its head backwards along their own spine! The Norwegian

Lundehund has a soft undercoat and a overcoat made up of short, coarse and densely packed hairs. The temperament of dogs is normally affected by the following factors: individual personality, heredity, training and socialization. It is therefore important to make sure that you meet the puppy's mother before purchasing a Norwegian Lundehund. It is also important to make sure to thoroughly socialize your Norwegian Lundehund with strangers, children and other animals during its puppyhood. Generally speaking, the Norwegian Lundehund is known to be an incredibly friendly breed that happily gets along with strangers, unknown dogs and children. The Norwegian Lundehund is also known to be an incredibly playful breed. Due to their unique style of hunting, the Norwegian Lundehund is also a highly intelligent breed as it would normally have to independently problem solve while hunting puffin. It is important to note that as a working breed, the Norwegian Lundehund has a high amount of energy which needs to be expended. If the Norwegian Lundehund has a buildup of energy it is likely to develop destructive behaviors due to boredom or hyperactivity.

Lifespan

A Norwegian Lundehund will normally live to be between 10 and 12 years old. However it is not uncommon for a Norwegian Lundehund to live to be as old as 13, providing that it does not develop any serious health issues.

Height and Weight

A fully grown Norwegian Lundehund will normally stand between 12 to 15 inches (30.5 to 38.1cm) tall at the shoulder. A healthy adult Norwegian Lundehund will normally weigh between 13 to 16 pounds (5.9 to 7.25kg). It is important to note that the weight of a healthy Norwegian Lundehund depends on how large the Norwegian Lundehund is – taller Norwegian Lundehund should weigh more.

Breed Characteristics

The following section will give you a simplistic overview of the characteristics of a Norwegian Lundehund. Our rating system is from 1 to 10 – with 1 being the lowest score and 10 being the highest.

- **Adaptability:** 6/10
- **Friendliness:** 10/10
- **Health:** 6/10
- **Ease of Grooming:** 9/10
- **Amount of Shedding:** 10/10
- **Trainability:** 8/10
- **Intelligence:** 10/10

- **Exercise Needed:** 10/10
- **Playfulness:** 10/10
- **Family Friendliness:** 10/10

THE NORWICH TERRIER

The Norwich Terrier is a small breed of Terrier that originates from Norwich, United Kingdom. The Norwich Terrier breed has existed since at the least the 19th century and has traditionally been used throughout East Anglia, England, to hunt vermin. The Norwich Terrier has commonly been used in stable yards as a general purpose ratter, as a fox bolter during fox hunts and as general household companions. The Norwich Terrier is one of the smallest breeds within the Terrier typing and are relatively rare despite their popularity. The main reason that the Norwich Terrier is a rare breed is due to the fact that Norwich Terrier females have small litter sizes and there is often a need for them to have caesarian sections due to the breed's small body size. However, the Norwich Terrier is actually a relatively healthy and hardy breed. The Norwich Terrier can either have pricked or dropped ears – however for showing purposes pricked ears are highly favored. The breed has a thick double coat that comes in the following colorations: red, tan, black and tan, grizzle and wheaten. The temperament of dogs is normally affected by the following factors: individual personality, heredity, training and socialization. It is therefore important to make sure that you meet the puppy's mother before purchasing a Norwich Terrier. It is also important to make sure to thoroughly socialize your Norwich Terrier with strangers, children and other animals during its puppyhood. Generally speaking, the Norwich Terrier is known to be an incredibly intelligent, affectionate and courageous breed of dog. They can be highly assertive and it is incredibly uncommon to find an aggressive, shy or quarrelsome Norwich Terrier. The Norwich Terrier makes a perfect pet for anyone living in an apartment due to the fact that the breed rarely barks. It is important to watch your Norwich Terrier closely around other small household pets (such as kittens, rabbits and rodents) as the Norwich Terrier has a high prey drive and may mistake smaller pets as prey. It is important to note that as a working breed, the Norwich Terrier has a high amount of energy which needs to be expended. If the Norwich Terrier has a buildup of energy it is likely to develop destructive behaviors due to boredom or hyperactivity.

Lifespan

A Norwich Terrier will normally live to be between 10 and 12 years old. However it is not uncommon for a Norwich Terrier to live to be as old as 14, providing that it does not develop any serious health issues.

Height and Weight

A fully grown Norwich Terrier will normally stand between 8 to 10 inches (20.3 to 25.4cm) tall at the shoulder. A healthy adult Norwich Terrier will normally weigh between 8 to 12 pounds (3.6 to 5.4kg). It is important to note that the weight of a healthy Norwich Terrier depends on how large the Norwich Terrier is – taller Norwich Terrier should weigh more.

Breed Characteristics

The following section will give you a simplistic overview of the characteristics of a Norwich Terrier. Our rating system is from 1 to 10 – with 1 being the lowest score and 10 being the highest.

- **Adaptability:** 8/10
- **Friendliness:** 10/10
- **Health:** 8/10
- **Ease of Grooming:** 5/10
- **Amount of Shedding:** 3/10
- **Trainability:** 8/10
- **Intelligence:** 9/10
- **Exercise Needed:** 10/10
- **Playfulness:** 10/10
- **Family Friendliness:** 10/10

THE NOVA SCOTIA DUCK TOLLING RETRIEVER

The Nova Scotia Duck Tolling Retriever is a medium-sized breed of gun dog that was bred and developed primarily for the purpose of hunting. The breed is also commonly known as the 'Yarmoth Toller,' the 'Tolling Retriever,' the 'Little Red Duck Dog' and as simply the 'Toller.' The Nova Scotia Duck Tolling Retriever is the smallest member of the Retriever typing and is often mistaken for being a small bodied, or adolescent, Golden Retriever. The Nova Scotia Duck Tolling Retriever was developed during the 19th century in the community of Little River Harbour in Yarmouth County, Nova Scotia. The breed was developed for the purpose of hunting waterfowl and was extremely adept at luring water birds into the range of the hunter's guns. Once the water bird has been shot the Nova Scotia Duck Tolling Retriever was then tasked with retrieving the bird's body without damaging it. The Nova Scotia Duck Tolling Retriever is an incredibly active breed: both mentally and physically. The breed should have an athletic, well built, muscular and compact body that allows it to be both powerful and agile. The Nova Scotia Duck Tolling Retriever's coat normally comes in shades of red and gold, but may have lighter colors feathered throughout its coat. It is not uncommon for a Nova

Scotia Duck Tolling Retriever to have white patches on its tail and chest. The breed has a medium-to-long coat which is water-repellent which aids the Nova Scotia Duck Tolling Retriever in its water based work. The temperament of dogs is normally affected by the following factors: individual personality, heredity, training and socialization. It is therefore important to make sure that you meet the puppy's mother before purchasing a Nova Scotia Duck Tolling Retriever. It is also important to make sure to thoroughly socialize your Nova Scotia Duck Tolling Retriever with strangers, children and other animals during its puppyhood. Generally speaking, the Nova Scotia Duck Tolling Retriever breed is known to be incredibly intelligent, alert and active. The Nova Scotia Duck Tolling Retriever is also a very social and curious breed that is known to be very accepting of new people – shyness within an adult Nova Scotia Duck Tolling Retriever is actually considered a breeding fault! The Nova Scotia Duck Tolling Retriever makes a perfect household pet due to the fact that it is very loyal, trainable, affectionate, respectful and patient with children. It is important to note that as a working breed, the Nova Scotia Duck Tolling Retriever has a high amount of energy which needs to be expended. If the Nova Scotia Duck Tolling Retriever has a buildup of energy it is likely to develop destructive behaviors due to boredom or hyperactivity.

Lifespan

A Nova Scotia Duck Tolling Retriever will normally live to be between 10 and 12 years old. However it is not uncommon for a Nova Scotia Duck Tolling Retriever to live to be as old as 14, providing that it does not develop any serious health issues.

Height and Weight

A fully grown Nova Scotia Duck Tolling Retriever will normally stand between 17 to 21 inches (43 to 53.3cm) tall at the shoulder. A healthy adult Nova Scotia Duck Tolling Retriever will normally weigh between 35 to 50 pounds (15.87 to 22.68kg). It is important to note that the weight of a healthy Nova Scotia Duck Tolling Retriever depends on how large the Nova Scotia Duck Tolling Retriever is – taller Nova Scotia Duck Tolling Retriever should weigh more.

Breed Characteristics

The following section will give you a simplistic overview of the characteristics of a Nova Scotia Duck Tolling Retriever. Our rating system is from 1 to 10 – with 1 being the lowest score and 10 being the highest.

- **Adaptability:** 8/10
- **Friendliness:** 10/10
- **Health:** 8/10
- **Ease of Grooming:** 10/10
- **Amount of Shedding:** 6/10
- **Trainability:** 8/10
- **Intelligence:** 10/10
- **Exercise Needed:** 10/10
- **Playfulness:** 10/10
- **Family Friendliness:** 10/10

Encyclopædia of Dog Breeds

THE OLD ENGLISH SHEEPDOG

The Old English Sheepdog is a large breed of dog that was developed in England. The breed is also commonly known as the 'OES' and as simply the 'English Sheepdog.' The breed descends from an old line of pastoral type dogs, but there is no record of which breeds actually were used in the development of the Old English Sheepdog – however there is some speculation that the Russian Owtchar is within the breed's ancestral history. The Old English Sheepdog was first exhibited at a dog show in Birmingham, England, in 1873 and the breed quickly became a popular show breed. The Old English Sheepdog's general appearance has changed very little of the years, but in the dog show community elaborate grooming techniques have developed: including backcombing, powdering the Old English Sheepdog's fur and dreading the breed's hair. The Old English Sheepdog was exported to the United States of America in the 1880s, and by the turn of the 20th century 50% of the 10 wealthiest American families bred and showed the Old English Sheepdog. The Old English Sheepdog has an extremely long, shaggy and thick grey and white coat which makes it immediately recognizable and iconic. The breed has relatively large ears that lie flat against the side of its head. Traditionally the Old English Sheepdog's tail was docked (which resulted in the breed looking similar to a Panda), but it is now much more common to find a tailed Old English Sheepdog due to the fact that many countries have outlawed cosmetic tail docking due to the cruelty involved. The Old English Sheepdog has a profuse double coat that has a water resistant undercoat. It is important to note that the Old English Sheepdog's coat only sheds when it is being groomed. The temperament of dogs is normally affected by the following factors: individual personality, heredity, training and socialization. It is therefore important to make sure that you meet the puppy's mother before purchasing an Old English Sheepdog. It is also important to make sure to thoroughly socialize your Old English Sheepdog with strangers, children and other animals during its puppyhood. Generally speaking, the Old English Sheepdog is known to be an incredibly docile and calm breed that is never known to be aggressive, shy or nervous. The breed is also known to be intelligent and highly adaptable which makes it a popular choice as a show breed. It is important to note that the Old English Sheepdog was traditionally used as a work dog, and as a working breed, the Old English Sheepdog has a high amount of energy which needs to be expended. If the Old English Sheepdog has a buildup of energy it is likely to develop destructive behaviors due to boredom or hyperactivity.

Lifespan

A Old English Sheepdog will normally live to be between 10 and 11 years old. However it is not uncommon for an Old English Sheepdog to live to be as old as 12, providing that it does not develop any serious health issues.

Height and Weight

A fully grown Old English Sheepdog will normally stand between 24 to 28 inches (61 to 71cm) tall at the shoulder. A healthy adult Old English Sheepdog will normally weigh between 90 to 110 pounds (40.8 to 50kg). It is important to note that the weight of a healthy Old English Sheepdog depends on how large the Old English Sheepdog is – taller Old English Sheepdog should weigh more.

Breed Characteristics

The following section will give you a simplistic overview of the characteristics of a Old English Sheepdog. Our rating system is from 1 to 10 – with 1 being the lowest score and 10 being the highest.

- **Adaptability:** 8/10

- **Friendliness:** 8/10
- **Health:** 8/10
- **Ease of Grooming:** 3/10
- **Amount of Shedding:** 10/10
- **Trainability:** 6/10
- **Intelligence:** 8/10
- **Exercise Needed:** 8/10
- **Playfulness:** 8/10
- **Family Friendliness:** 10/10

THE OTTERHOUND

The Otterhound is an old breed of dog that originates from England. The breed's ancestral history is not known but it is believed that the breed dates back to as early as the medieval period. The Otterhound has traditionally been used as a scent hound and is currently recognized by the English Kennel Club as being a vulnerable native breed, which means that there are less than 600 Otterhounds worldwide! The Otterhound is a large, rough-coated breed with a relatively large head. The breed has an strong, sturdy body with large legs that allows it to move quickly and powerfully while hunting. Otterhound hunts its prey both on land and in water and it has a combination of characteristics that are unique to most hounds: it has an oily rough double coat which is water resistant and webbed feet that allow it to powerfully swim through the water. The Otterhound has an amazingly sensitive nose that allows it to track its prey through mud for up to 72 hours! The temperament of dogs is normally affected by the following factors: individual personality, heredity, training and socialization. It is therefore important to make sure that you meet the puppy's mother before purchasing a Otterhound. It is also important to make sure to thoroughly socialize your Otterhound with strangers, children and other animals during its puppyhood.

Generally speaking, the Otterhound is known to be an incredibly affectionate, docile and family orientated breed of dog. The Otterhound is known to enjoy the company of children and will become very excitable if it is allowed to play with them. An Otterhound should always be supervised while it is playing with children as its size can lead to unintentionally rough play – although its size also means that the Otterhound is highly unlikely to suffer an injury during any play. The Otterhound is known to enthusiastically greet its owners when they come home, but it is still a highly independent breed that is unlikely to form a 'clingy' attachment. It is important to note that as a working breed, the Otterhound has a high amount of energy which needs to be expended. If the Otterhound has a buildup of energy it is likely to develop destructive behaviors due to boredom or hyperactivity.

Lifespan

A Otterhound will normally live to be between 10 and 11 years old. However it is not uncommon for a Otterhound to live to be as old as 12, providing that it does not develop any serious health issues.

Height and Weight

A fully grown Otterhound will normally stand

between 24 to 27 inches (? to ?cm) tall at the shoulder. A healthy adult Otterhound will normally weigh between 80 to 115 pounds (36.25 to 52kg). It is important to note that the weight of a healthy Otterhound depends on how large the Otterhound is – taller Otterhound should weigh more.

Breed Characteristics

The following section will give you a simplistic overview of the characteristics of a Otterhound. Our rating system is from 1 to 10 – with 1 being the lowest score and 10 being the highest.

- **Adaptability:** 6/10
- **Friendliness:** 10/10
- **Health:** 8/10
- **Ease of Grooming:** 5/10
- **Amount of Shedding:** 8/10
- **Trainability:** 8/10
- **Intelligence:** 8/10
- **Exercise Needed:** 10/10
- **Playfulness:** 10/10
- **Family Friendliness:** 10/10

THE PAPILLON

The Papillon is a breed of dog that is a member of the Spaniel typing. The Papillon is also commonly known as the 'Continental Toy Spaniel,' the 'Butterfly Eared Dog' and as the 'Phalene' (which translates to 'Drop Ear Type'). The Papillon's history can be traced through art. The earliest paintings of dogs that resemble the Papillon were found in Italy and date back to the early 1500s. The Papillon has always been highly favored by nobility and the wealthy throughout history. The Papillon was first recognized by the American Kennel Club in 1935 and an organization called the 'Papillon Club of America' was founded. The Papillon is a popular choice for conformation, agility and obedience shows. The Papillon is a single coated breed and does therefore not withstand the cold very well. A Papillon's coat will normally be parti-colored or white with patches of virtually any other color. The temperament of dogs is normally affected by the following factors: individual personality, heredity, training and socialization. It is therefore important to make sure that you meet the puppy's mother before purchasing a Papillon. It is also important to make sure to thoroughly socialize your Papillon with strangers, children and other animals during its puppyhood. Generally speaking, the Papillon is known to be an adventurous, happy and friendly breed of dog. They are never known to be shy or aggressive. The Papillon breed is perfect for any family household due to their docile nature. However it is recommended to monitory any interactions between children and your Papillon to ensure that the children are not too rough.

Lifespan

A Papillon will normally live to be between 12 and 13 years old. However it is not uncommon for a Papillon to live to be as old as 16, providing that it does not develop any serious health issues.

Height and Weight

A fully grown Papillon will normally stand between 8 to 11 inches (3.6 to 5cm) tall at the shoulder. A healthy adult Papillon will normally weigh between 4 to 9 pounds (1.8 to 4kg). It is important to note that the weight of a healthy Papillon depends on how large the Papillon is – taller Papillon should weigh more.

Breed Characteristics

The following section will give you a simplistic overview of the characteristics of a Papillon. Our rating system is from 1 to 10 – with 1 being the lowest score and 10 being the highest.

- **Adaptability:** 6/10
- **Friendliness:** 8/10
- **Health:** 6/10
- **Ease of Grooming:** 6/10
- **Amount of Shedding:** 5/10
- **Trainability:** 6/10
- **Intelligence:** 8/10
- **Exercise Needed:** 8/10
- **Playfulness:** 10/10
- **Family Friendliness:** 10/10

THE PEEKAPOO

The Peekapoo is a cross breed of dog that is a mixture of a Pekingese and a Miniature Toy Poodle. The Peekapoo is considered to be one of the oldest breeds of designer, or hybrid, dog and was developed during the 1950s. The goal was to create a breed with a non-to low-shedding coat that would be suitable for people with dog hair allergies. The Peekapoo is a relatively popular breed within the United States of America, but there is actually no breed organization, standard or club. The Peekapoo's coat will generally have a very soft texture with a cotton-like feel. The breed only has a single coat or wavy hair that is of a medium-to-long length. As previously mentioned, the Peekapoo was produced with the intent of creating a low shedding breed but due to the unpredictable nature of genetics a Peekapoo's coat will normally be low to average shedding. The Peekapoo's coat can come in a wide variety of colors including: silver, white, gray, red, cream, chocolate and black. The temperament of dogs is normally affected by the following factors: individual personality, heredity, training and socialization. It is therefore important to make sure that you meet the puppy's mother before purchasing a Peekapoo. It is also important to make sure to thoroughly socialize your Peekapoo with strangers, children and other animals during its puppyhood. Generally speaking, the Peekapoo is a loving and loyal breed that is dedicated to their family unit. The Peekapoo is commonly kept as a lap dog and therefore thrives in close contact with its family members. The Peekapoo is a happy and confident breed that is not known to be shy or aggressive. A Peekapoo can make a loving companion for any child providing that it has been properly socialized during its puppyhood. The breed is known to be somewhat suspicious of new people and an older Peekapoo may have trouble dealing with a loud an unknown child. Despite getting along with children relatively easily, it is still not recommended to keep a Peekapoo in a household with very small children due to the fact that the children may unintentionally hurt the Peekapoo- a Peekapoo has a small and fragile build!

Lifespan

A Peekapoo will normally live to be between 10 and 12 years old. However it is not uncommon for a Peekapoo to live to be as old as 15, providing that it does not develop any serious health issues.

Height and Weight

A fully grown Peekapoo will normally stand between 5 to 11 inches (12.7 to 27.9cm) tall at the shoulder. A healthy adult Peekapoo will normally weigh between 4 to 20 pounds (1.8 to 9kg). It is important to note that the weight of a healthy Peekapoo depends on how large the Peekapoo is – taller Peekapoo should weigh more.

Breed Characteristics

The following section will give you a simplistic overview of the characteristics of a Peekapoo. Our rating system is from 1 to 10 – with 1 being the lowest score and 10 being the highest.

- **Adaptability:** 8/10
- **Friendliness:** 8/10
- **Health:** 6/10
- **Ease of Grooming:** 5/10
- **Amount of Shedding:** 3/10
- **Trainability:** 6/10
- **Intelligence:** 8/10
- **Exercise Needed:** 6/10
- **Playfulness:** 8/10
- **Family Friendliness:** 10/10

THE PEKINGESE

The Pekingese is an ancient breed of toy dog that originates from China. The Pekingese is also commonly known as the 'Lion Dog,' the 'Peking Lion Dog,' the 'Chinese Spaniel' and as simply the 'Peke.' The reason the breed is commonly known as the 'Lion Dog' is due to its resemblance to the Chinese guardian lions. Interestingly the Pekingese and the Shih Tzu are both referred to as the 'Lion Dog' in Chinese, despite the fact that the breeds are not related. Recent DNA analysis confirms that the Pekingese breed is one of the oldest breeds of dog and is actually one of the least genetically divergent breeds from the wolf – despite its small size. It is believed that the Pekingese is over 2000 years old! In their country of origin it was outlawed for anyone except members of the Chinese Imperial Palace to own a Pekingese. The Pekingese was introduced to England and America as either gifts, from Chinese Emperors or Empresses, or as rescued dogs during World War II. There is a smaller variant of the Pekingese, known as the 'Sleeve Pekingese.' The name 'Sleeve Pekingese' came from the fact that it was not uncommon for members of the Chinese Imperial Palace to conceal Pekingese in the capacious sleeves of their robes. The Pekingese has a flat face with large eyes. The breed also has a small, compact, durable and muscular body that sits low to the ground. The majority of Pekingese come in either a gold, red or sable coat coloration however it is not uncommon for their coats to be black, white and sable. The Pekingese can either come in a long variety or in a shorter, but relatively still long haired, Spaniel type coat. The temperament of dogs is normally affected by the following factors: individual personality, heredity, training and socialization. It is therefore important to make sure that you meet the puppy's mother before purchasing a Pekingese. It is also important to make sure to thoroughly socialize your Pekingese with strangers, children and other animals during its puppyhood. Generally speaking, the Pekingese is a self-important, confident, good natured and affectionate breed. They are known to be highly independent, stubborn and are likely to only show respect to people who respect them. The Pekingese is known to be an incredibly loyal and protective breed and will bark at unknown dogs and strangers.

Lifespan

A Pekingese will normally live to be between 10 and 12 years old. However it is not uncommon for a Pekingese to live to be as old as 15, providing that it does not develop any serious health issues.

Height and Weight

A fully grown Pekingese will normally stand between 6 to 9 inches (15.25 to 22.86cm) tall at the shoulder. A healthy adult Pekingese will normally weigh between 7 to 14 pounds (3.2 to 6.4kg). It is important to note that the weight of a healthy Pekingese depends on how large the Pekingese is – taller Pekingese should weigh more.

Breed Characteristics

The following section will give you a simplistic overview of the characteristics of a Pekingese. Our rating system is from 1 to 10 – with 1 being the lowest score and 10 being the highest.

- **Adaptability:** 6/10
- **Friendliness:** 6/10
- **Health:** 4/10
- **Ease of Grooming:** 2/10
- **Amount of Shedding:** 9/10
- **Trainability:** 8/10
- **Intelligence:** 8/10
- **Exercise Needed:** 3/10
- **Playfulness:** 5/10
- **Family Friendliness:** 10/10

THE PEMBROKE WELSH CORGI

The Pembroke Welsh Corgi is a breed of cattle herding dog that originates from the Pembrokeshire region of Wales. The breed is one of two breed known as 'Welsh Corgi.' The other breed is the Cardigan Welsh Corgi, and both breeds descend from northern Spitz-type dogs (such as the Siberian Husky). The Pembroke Welsh Corgi has been traced back as far as 1100 A.D! It is believed that Vikings and Flemish weavers brought the dogs with them as they traveled to reside in the Pembrokeshire region. The Pembroke Welsh Corgi is also one of the oldest herding breeds as it has been recorded that the Pembroke Welsh Corgi has been used to herd sheep, geese, ducks, horses and cattle as far back as the 10th century. Both the Pembroke Welsh Corgi and the Cardigan Welsh Corgi were officially recognized by the Kennel Club in 1928, but were grouped together as the 'Welsh Corgi. The two breeds were not recognized as separate and unique until 1934. The Pembroke Welsh Corgi ranks as the 20th most popular breed based upon registrations to the American Kennel Club. However in the United Kingdom, the Pembroke Welsh Corgi is actually considered to be a vulnerable breed and it is believed this is due to a lack of dedicated breeders in the United Kingdom. The Pembroke Welsh Corgi has erect ears, a triangular head and a relatively long and low slung body. Some Pembroke Welsh Corgi are born without a tail but it is important to ask that your Pembroke Welsh Corgi's lack of tail is a birth defect rather than due to docking, as the act of docking (removing a dogs tail) is illegal in most countries! The temperament of dogs is normally affected by the following factors: individual personality, heredity, training and socialization. It is therefore important to make sure that you meet the puppy's mother before purchasing a Pembroke Welsh Corgi. It is also important to make sure to thoroughly socialize your Pembroke Welsh Corgi with strangers, children and other animals during its puppyhood. Generally speaking, the Pembroke Welsh Corgi is known to be a highly affectionate breed that loves spending time with its family unit. They are actually known to follow their owners wherever they go. The breed seems to have an innate desire to please their owners and a relatively high level of intelligence, which makes the Pembroke Welsh Corgi a very easy dog to train. Most Pembroke Welsh Corgi will behave very well around small children, strangers and other animals however it is still highly important to properly socialize your Pembroke Welsh Corgi during its puppyhood to minimize the chance of any negative social behaviors. It is important to note that as a working breed, the Pembroke Welsh Corgi has a high amount of energy which needs to be expended. If the Pembroke Welsh Corgi has a buildup of energy it is likely to develop destructive behaviors due to boredom or hyperactivity.

Lifespan

A Pembroke Welsh Corgi will normally live to be between 12 and 13 years old. However it is not uncommon for a Pembroke Welsh Corgi to live to be as old as 14, providing that it does not develop any serious health issues.

Height and Weight

A fully grown Pembroke Welsh Corgi will normally stand between 10 to 12 inches (25.4 to 30.5cm) tall at the shoulder. A healthy adult Pembroke Welsh Corgi will normally weigh between 15 to 30 pounds (6.8 to 13.6kg). It is important to note that the weight of a healthy Pembroke Welsh Corgi depends on how large the Pembroke Welsh Corgi is – taller Pembroke Welsh Corgi should weigh more.

Breed Characteristics

The following section will give you a simplistic overview of the characteristics of a Pembroke Welsh Corgi. Our rating system is from 1 to 10 – with 1 being the lowest score and 10 being the highest.

- **Adaptability:** 8/10
- **Friendliness:** 8/10
- **Health:** 6/10
- **Ease of Grooming:** 9/10
- **Amount of Shedding:** 10/10
- **Trainability:** 7/10
- **Intelligence:** 10/10
- **Exercise Needed:** 8/10
- **Playfulness:** 8/10
- **Family Friendliness:** 10/10

THE PETIT BASSET GRIFFON VENDEEN

The Petit Basset Griffon Vendeen is a breed of scent hound that originates from the Vendee district of France. Due to the breed's long name it is commonly shortened to simply the PBGV. The breed is closely related to the other three Griffon Vendeen breeds: the Grand Griffon Vendeen, the Briquet Griffon Vendeen and the Grand Basset Griffon Vendeen. The PBGV has a solidly built body and a rough and unrefined appearance. The breed has short legs, a sturdy bone structure and is only slightly longer than it is tall at the withers. The PBGV has a profuse, long, harsh and rough double coat that gives the breed a tousled and 'messy' appearance. However despite the harsh coat, the PBGV has very soft facial hair. The hair on the PBGV's face gives it a very unique appearance as it makes it look like it has a moustache and beard! The PBGV's coat is always predominately white but will have sports of orange, lemon, black, sable and grizzle throughout its coat. The temperament of dogs is normally affected by the following factors: individual personality, heredity, training and socialization. It is therefore important to make sure that you meet the puppy's mother before purchasing a Petit Basset Griffon Vendeen. It is also important to make sure to thoroughly socialize your Petit Basset Griffon Vendeen with strangers, children and other animals during its puppyhood. Generally speaking, the PBGV is an extroverted, friendly and independent breed of hound. It has commonly been reffered to as the 'Happy Breed,' due to its constant state of friendly intrigue. The PBGV is known to wag its tail excessively to signify its happiness. The PBGV makes a perfect family pet for anyone with children as the breed is both playful and respectful. However the PBGV is known to 'play bite' other animals and may therefore not be suitable to be kept in a household with small animals. Despite being a small breed, the PBGV is not suited to apartment living for two reasons. Firstly it is a highly energetic and lively breed that enjoys having space to run around. Secondly the PBGV is a true hound and will 'give voice' frequently – which means that it is not uncommon for a PBGV to howl alone, or with companions, for no other reason that their own enjoyment. It is important to note that as a working breed, the Petit Basset Griffon Vendeen has a high amount of energy which needs to be expended. If the Petit Basset Griffon Vendeen has a buildup of energy it is likely to develop destructive behaviors due to boredom or hyperactivity.

Lifespan

A Petit Basset Griffon Vendeen will normally live to be between 12 and 14 years old. However it is not uncommon for a Petit Basset Griffon Vendeen to live to be as old as 15, providing that it does not develop any serious health issues.

Height and Weight

A fully grown Petit Basset Griffon Vendeen will normally stand between 12 to 15 inches (30.5 to 38.1cm) tall at the shoulder. A healthy adult Petit Basset Griffon Vendeen will normally weigh between 30 to 40 pounds (13.6 to 18.1kg). It is important to note that the weight of a healthy Petit Basset Griffon Vendeen depends on how large the Petit Basset Griffon Vendeen is – taller Petit Basset Griffon Vendeen should weigh more.

Breed Characteristics

The following section will give you a simplistic overview of the characteristics of a Petit Basset Griffon Vendeen. Our rating system is from 1 to 10 – with 1 being the lowest score and 10 being the highest.

- **Adaptability:** 6/10
- **Friendliness:** 10/10
- **Health:** 6/10
- **Ease of Grooming:** 6/10
- **Amount of Shedding:** 8/10

- **Trainability:** 8/10
- **Intelligence:** 8/10
- **Exercise Needed:** 10/10
- **Playfulness:** 10/10
- **Family Friendliness:** 10/10

THE PHARAOH HOUND

The Pharaoh Hound is a breed of dog that originates from Malta. In Malta the breed is known as 'Kelb tal-Fenek,' which translates to 'Rabbit Dog.' As the name suggests, the Pharaoh Hound was primarily used for the purpose of hunting rabbits in the Maltese islands. There is a popular belief that suggests that the Pharaoh Hound descends from the Tesem dog that originates from Egypt. The main reason for this belief is due to the fact that the two breeds look so similar and there are images painted on Egyptian tombs that seem to resemble the Pharaoh Hound. This myth suggests that the Pharaoh Hound was brought to the islands of Malta by the Phoenicians over 2000 years ago. However DNA analysis has proved this belief to be incorrect! The Pharaoh Hound was first introduced to Britain in the 1920s, but no litter was bred. Pharaoh Hounds were again brought into the country in 1960 and the first litter was born in 1963. The Pharaoh Hound breed standard was not recognized until 1974. The Pharaoh Hound has a elegant, athletic and powerful body structure. The Pharaoh Hound was developed to be a strong and fast breed due to its history in rabbit hunting. The Pharaoh Hound also has a long thin neck which helped it to reach rabbits during a hunt. The Pharaoh Hound has a short and fine haired coat with no feathering. The breed's coat can come in a variety of textures (from silky to hard) but should never stand off the dog's body. The only coat color that is accepted by Kennel Clubs is red – however multiple shade variations are accepted. Interestingly the Pharaoh Hound is born with blue eyes that slowly change colour to a golden amber as they age. The temperament of dogs is normally affected by the following factors: individual personality, heredity, training and socialization. It is therefore important to make sure that you meet the puppy's mother before purchasing a Pharaoh Hound. It is also important to make sure to thoroughly socialize your Pharaoh Hound with strangers, children and other animals during its puppyhood. Generally speaking, the Pharaoh Hound is an independent, confident and athletic breed. The Pharaoh Hound is prone to clownish behaviors and is more than capable of entertaining itself for hours. Due to their independence, the Pharaoh Hound is known to be very aloof with strangers however the Pharaoh Hound is known to be an extremely friendly breed once it has warmed up to people! The Pharaoh Hound is also known to be a highly emphatic breed and will easily become stressed in high-drama situations. It is important to note that as a working breed, the Pharaoh Hound has a high amount of energy which needs to be expended. If the Pharaoh Hound has a buildup of energy it is likely to develop destructive behaviors due to boredom or hyperactivity.

Lifespan

A Pharaoh Hound will normally live to be between 10 and 11 years old. However it is not uncommon for a Pharaoh Hound to live to be as old as 14, providing that it does not develop any serious health issues.

Height and Weight

A fully grown Pharaoh Hound will normally stand between 21 to 25 inches (53.3 to 63.5cm) tall at the shoulder. A healthy adult Pharaoh Hound will normally weigh between 45 to 55 pounds (20.5 to 25kg). It is important to note that the weight of a healthy Pharaoh Hound depends on how large the Pharaoh Hound is – taller Pharaoh Hound should weigh more.

Breed Characteristics

The following section will give you a simplistic overview of the characteristics of a Pharaoh Hound. Our rating system is from 1 to 10 – with 1 being the lowest score and 10 being the highest.

- **Adaptability:** 8/10
- **Friendliness:** 10/10
- **Health:** 9/10

- ➢ **Ease of Grooming:** 8/10
- ➢ **Amount of Shedding:** 3/10
- ➢ **Trainability:** 8/10
- ➢ **Intelligence:** 8/10
- ➢ **Exercise Needed:** 7/10
- ➢ **Playfulness:** 8/10
- ➢ **Family Friendliness:** 10/10

THE PLOTT

The Plott is a large breed of scent hound that originates from the United States of America, but has its ancestral roots in Germany, The breed is also commonly known as the 'Plotthund' in Germany. Despite knowing that the Plott's ancestry lies in Germany, it is unknown which hound breed the Plott descend from and it is likewise unknown who is responsible for the development of the breed. The Plott was developed for the purpose of hunting boars and bears. The Plott has been bred for its stamina and gameness which makes it a popular choice for hunting larger game. The Plott was first registered with the United Kennel Club in 1946 but was only officially recognized by the American Kennel Club in 2006! A typical Plott has an athletic, muscular and agile body of a medium build. The breeding standard states that a Plott's face should show an expression of intelligence, confidence and determination. The Plott's coat is made up of fine to medium in texture, short to medium in length hairs that have a smooth glossy appearance. The breeding standard states that a Plott's coat should be brindle in coloration and the following types of brindle are accepeted: yellow brindle, red brindle, tan brindle, brown brindle, black brindle, grey brindle and maltese (which is a mixture of a slate grey coloration and a blue brindle). The temperament of dogs is normally affected by the following factors: individual personality, heredity, training and socialization. It is therefore important to make sure that you meet the puppy's mother before purchasing a Plott. It is also important to make sure to thoroughly socialize your Plott with strangers, children and other animals during its puppyhood. Generally speaking, the Plott is known to be a highly confident, loyal and good natured breed. It is important to note that Plotts tend to be wary of unknown dogs and strangers, but will quickly warm up to new people if the Plott has been correctly socialized from its puppyhood. It is important to note that as a working breed, the Plott has a high amount of energy which needs to be expended. If the Plott has a buildup of energy it is likely to develop destructive behaviors due to boredom or hyperactivity.

Lifespan

A Plott will normally live to be between 12 and 13 years old. However it is not uncommon for a Plott to live to be as old as 14, providing that it does not develop any serious health issues.

Height and Weight

A fully grown Plott will normally stand between 20

to 27 inches (50.8 to 68.5cm) tall at the shoulder. A healthy adult Plott will normally weigh between 40 to 75 pounds (18 to 34kg). It is important to note that the weight of a healthy Plott depends on how large the Plott is – taller Plott should weigh more.

Breed Characteristics

The following section will give you a simplistic overview of the characteristics of a Plott. Our rating system is from 1 to 10 – with 1 being the lowest score and 10 being the highest.

- **Adaptability:** 5/10
- **Friendliness:** 8/10
- **Health:** 6/10
- **Ease of Grooming:** 10/10
- **Amount of Shedding:** 4/10
- **Trainability:** 8/10
- **Intelligence:** 7/10
- **Exercise Needed:** 8/10
- **Playfulness:** 6/10
- **Family Friendliness:** 9/10

THE POCKET BEAGLE

The Beagle is a small sized breed of scent hound that has been bred for the specific purpose of hunting hare. The Beagle has approximately 220 million scent receptors within its nose – which is over 40 times as many as humans! Due to their incredible sense of smell and ingrained ability to track, the Beagle is often employed as a detection dog within he agriculture and food industries. Breeds similar to the Beagle have existed for the last 2500 years, but the modern day Beagle was developed in the United Kingdom in the early 1800s. The Pocket Beagle is a variant and miniature version of the regular Beagle breed. The Pocket Beagle was developed during the reign of Queen Elizabeth I for the purpose of being small enough to be transported in a saddlebag. The Pocket Beagle would ride along on a hunt and while the larger hounds run the pretty to the ground, the Pocket Beagle was primarily used for the purpose of flushing prey out of dense underbrush. The Pocket Beagle went extinct during the First World War but has since been 'recreated' by groups of dedicated breeders. It is important to note that if you are purchasing a Pocket Beagle that the breed is not officially recognized by any of the Kennel Clubs and as such there is not solidified breed standard. The temperament of dogs is normally affected by the following factors: individual personality, heredity, training and socialization. It is therefore important to make sure that you meet the puppy's mother before purchasing a Pocket Beagle. It is also important to make sure to thoroughly socialize your Pocket Beagle with strangers, children and other animals during its puppyhood. Generally speaking, the Pocket Beagle tends to be a friendly, affectionate and playful breed. Queen Elizabeth I was known to let her Pocket Beagles roam around on her tables during banquets to entertain her guests. It is important to note that as a working breed, the Pocket Beagle has a high amount of energy which needs to be expended. If the Pocket Beagle has a buildup of energy it is likely to develop destructive behaviors due to boredom or hyperactivity.

Lifespan

A Pocket Beagle will normally live to be between 9 and 10 years old. However it is not uncommon for a Pocket Beagle to live to be as old as 12, providing that it does not develop any serious health issues.

Height and Weight

A fully grown Pocket Beagle will normally stand between 7 to 12 inches (17.75 to 30.5cm) tall at the shoulder. A healthy adult Pocket Beagle will normally weigh between 7 to 15 pounds (3 to 6.8kg). It is important to note that the weight of a healthy Pocket Beagle depends on how large the Pocket Beagle is – taller Pocket Beagle should weigh more.

Breed Characteristics

The following section will give you a simplistic overview of the characteristics of a Pocket Beagle. Our rating system is from 1 to 10 – with 1 being the lowest score and 10 being the highest.

- **Adaptability:** 6/10
- **Friendliness:** 10/10
- **Health:** 6/10
- **Ease of Grooming:** 10/10
- **Amount of Shedding:** 6/10
- **Trainability:** 8/10
- **Intelligence:** 8/10
- **Exercise Needed:** 8/10
- **Playfulness:** 8/10
- **Family Friendliness:** 10/10

THE POINTER

The Pointer is a medium to large sized breed of dog that was developed in England for the purposes of being a gun dog. The breed is also commonly known as the 'English Pointer' due to its place of origin. Records of the Pointer breed date back as far as 1650. Through anatomical evaluation it is clear that at least four different breeds appear to have been used in the development of the Pointer: Greyhounds, Foxhounds, Bull Terriers and Bloodhounds. Each of these four breeds have highly unique qualities that the Pointer could use to do its job. The Pointer was introduced to the United States of America in the early 19th century and the breed quickly flourished in the abundant open hunting lands of America. The Pointer quickly dethroner the Setter at being the best bird-hunting dog breed. The Pointer is used to hunt upland game and implements three key skills which lead it to great success: pointing, honor and retrieving. 'Pointing' is the process where the Pointer find the preys location and will 'point' to it using its body. 'Honor' is the process of the dog stopping immediately within a few steps, usually in a pointing stance, upon locating a bracemate on point. 'Retrieving' is the process of the Pointer retrieving the dead or wounded game – despite Pointers not being natural retrievers they are highly trainable and more than capable of fulfilling retrievers purpose. The Pointer has a short, densely packed and smooth coat with a sheen. The breed's coat is generally white with spots or either a liver, lemon, orange or black coloration. The temperament of dogs is normally affected by the following factors: individual personality, heredity, training and socialization. It is therefore important to make sure that you meet the puppy's mother before purchasing a Pointer. It is also important to make sure to thoroughly socialize your Pointer with strangers, children and other animals during its puppyhood. Generally speaking, the Pointer is known to be a even tempered breed with extremely high levels of energy. Despite their large size, the Pointer makes a good household pet due to their high levels of intelligent and trainability. The breed is not particularly territorial and will coexist happily with other animals but may be wary of strange people and animals. It is important to note that as a working breed, the Pointer has a high amount of energy which needs to be expended. If the Pointer has a buildup of energy it is likely to develop destructive behaviors due to boredom or hyperactivity.

Lifespan

A Pointer will normally live to be between 12 and 13 years old. However it is not uncommon for a Pointer to live to be as old as 15, providing that it does not develop any serious health issues.

Height and Weight

A fully grown Pointer will normally stand between 23 to 28 inches (58.5 to 71cm) tall at the shoulder. A healthy adult Pointer will normally weigh between 45 to 75 pounds (20.5 to 34kg). It is important to note that the weight of a healthy Pointer depends on how large the Pointer is – taller Pointer should weigh more.

Breed Characteristics

The following section will give you a simplistic overview of the characteristics of a Pointer. Our rating system is from 1 to 10 – with 1 being the lowest score and 10 being the highest.

- **Adaptability:** 5/10
- **Friendliness:** 10/10
- **Health:** 6/10
- **Ease of Grooming:** 10/10
- **Amount of Shedding:** 7/10
- **Trainability:** 10/10
- **Intelligence:** 10/10
- **Exercise Needed:** 10/10
- **Playfulness:** 10/10
- **Family Friendliness:** 10/10

THE POLISH LOWLAND SHEEPDOG

The Polish Lowland Sheepdog is a medium sized sheep dog that originates from Poland. The breed is known to have begun development during the thirteenth century and is believed to descend from the Pull, the Tibetan Terrier and other sheep herding breeds. The Polish Lowland Sheepdog was introduced to Scotland during the early 1500s and was bred with the local Scottish sheep dogs to create the Bearded Collie breed. The Polish Lowland Sheepdog went nearly extinct during the Second World War but was revitalized after the war by Dr. Danuta Hrynlewicz – who was the man who originally sired the first ten litters of Polish Lowland Sheepdog in the 1950s. The Polish Lowland Sheepdog has a thick double coat which gives it a uniquely shaggy appearance. The breed's coat can come in any coloration and with any pattern: but white, gray, brown and black are most common. The Polish Lowland Sheepdog's coat color is known to become faded as it ages. The breed's double coat is made up of a soft and densely packed undercoat, and a topcoat of rough and either straight or wavy hairs. The Polish Lowland Sheepdog is also a very athletic and muscular breed which is more than capable of herding sheep. The temperament of dogs is normally affected by the following factors: individual personality, heredity, training and socialization. It is therefore important to make sure that you meet the puppy's mother before purchasing a Polish Lowland Sheepdog. It is also important to make sure to thoroughly socialize your Polish Lowland Sheepdog with strangers, children and other animals during its puppyhood. Generally speaking, the Polish Lowland Sheepdog is known to be a self-confident, intelligent and adaptable breed. It is not uncommon for a Polish Lowland Sheepdog to dominate a weak-willed owner and it is therefore not a breed for beginner dog owners. It is important to note that as a working breed, the Polish Lowland Sheepdog has a high amount of energy which needs to be expended. If the Polish Lowland Sheepdog has a buildup of energy it is likely to develop destructive behaviors due to boredom or hyperactivity.

Lifespan

A Polish Lowland Sheepdog will normally live to be between 10 and 12 years old. However it is not uncommon for a Polish Lowland Sheepdog to live to be as old as 13, providing that it does not develop any serious health issues.

Height and Weight

A fully grown Polish Lowland Sheepdog will

normally stand between 17 to 20 inches (43.2 to 50.8cm) tall at the shoulder. A healthy adult Polish Lowland Sheepdog will normally weigh between 35 to 55 pounds (16 to 25kg). It is important to note that the weight of a healthy Polish Lowland Sheepdog depends on how large the Polish Lowland Sheepdog is – taller Polish Lowland Sheepdog should weigh more.

Breed Characteristics

The following section will give you a simplistic overview of the characteristics of a Polish Lowland Sheepdog. Our rating system is from 1 to 10 – with 1 being the lowest score and 10 being the highest.

- **Adaptability:** 8/10
- **Friendliness:** 8/10
- **Health:** 6/10
- **Ease of Grooming:** 3/10
- **Amount of Shedding:** 1/10
- **Trainability:** 6/10
- **Intelligence:** 8/10
- **Exercise Needed:** 8/10
- **Playfulness:** 8/10
- **Family Friendliness:** 10/10

THE POMERANIAN

The Pomeranian (commonly known as the 'Pom' or the 'Pom Pom') is a breed of dog of the Splitz type. The breed was named after the region in Poland named 'Pomerania.' The Pomeranian is a descendant of the large Splitz type dogs, specifically the German Splitz. However through selective breeding, the Pomeranian became smaller and smaller over the years and is now classified as a 'toy dog' due to its miniature size. The Pomeranian became very popular during the 18th century when it started to be owned by royal families around the world. Since 1998, the Pomeranian has ranked in the top 20 most popular dog breeds within the United States of America. Overall the Pomeranian is a sturdy, healthy and loving dog that makes a perfect companion or house hold pet. However it is important to note that the Pomeranian is not suitable for families with very small children. This is due to the small size of the breed which means that they can easily be injured.

Lifespan

The Pomeranian will normally live to be between 12 and 14 years old. However it is not uncommon for a Pomeranian to live to be as old as 16, providing they do not develop any serious health issues.

Height and Weight

A fully grown Pomeranian will normally be between a tiny 7 to 12 inches (17.75 to 30.5cm) tall at the shoulder! A healthy adult Pomeranian will normally weigh between 3 and 7 pounds (1.35 to 3.25kg) dependent upon its size.

Coat

The Pomeranian is famous for its beautiful coat. The Pomeranian's coat is a double coat that has a thick, fluffy and soft undercoat and a top coat made up of long, straight and shiny hair. The long hair around the Pomeranian's neck and chest forms a 'frill' that aids the Pomeranian royal appearance. The breed has a plumed tail cover in hair that fans out. The Pomeranian's coat can come in a wide variety of colors including: black, black and tan, tan, blue, chocolate, cream, cream and tan, orange, red, fawn, gold and many MANY other colors.

Breed Characteristics

The following section will give you a simplistic overview of the characteristics of a Pomeranian. Our rating system is from 1 to 10 – with 1 being the lowest score and 10 being the highest.

- **Adaptability:** 6/10
- **Friendliness:** 6/10
- **Health:** 6/10
- **Ease of Grooming:** 3/10
- **Amount of Shedding:** 8/10
- **Trainability:** 6/10
- **Intelligence:** 8/10
- **Exercise Needed:** 6/10
- **Playfulness:** 6/10
- **Family Friendliness:** 10/10

THE POODLE

The Poodle is a group of dog breeds, the Standard Poodle, Miniature Poodle and Toy Poodle. All three types of Poodle come in a wide variety of coat colorations. The Poodle has been ranked as the second most intelligent dog breed just behind the Border Collie. Due to its intelligence the Poodle is incredibly obedient and easy to train. Poodles also have a very strong and muscular body. Poodles have been used in all forms of work from helping the disabled to herding animals. Poodles generally get on very well with children and other household pets and have therefore become a very popular household breed. It is not uncommon for Poodles to develop destructive behaviors if they are not provided with enough exercise and mental stimulation.

Size Variants

As previously mentioned the Poodle comes in three size variants: Standard, Miniature and Toy. The Standard variant is considered to be the original Poodle breed that the two other variants come from. The following two sections will discuss the average height and weight of the three variants.

Height

A Toy Poodle will stand at a height of between 9.5 to 11 inches (24 to 28cm). Miniature Poodles are slightly taller and stand at a height of between 11 and 15 inches (28 to 38cm). Standard Poodles are the largest of the three variants. A Standard Poodle will normally stand at a height of between 15 and 22 inches (38 to 55cm).

Weight

An adult Toy Poodle will normally weigh between 6 and 9 pounds (3 to 4kg). Miniature Poodles are slightly heavier and normally weight between 15 and 17 pounds (7 to 8kg). Standard sizes Poodles will normally weigh between 45 and 70 pounds (20 to 31kg).

Lifespan

All three variants of Poodle normally live to be between 10 and 13 years of age. However it is not uncommon for a Poodle to live for up to 15 years if they do not develop any serious health issues.

Breed Characteristics

The following section will give you a simplistic overview of the characteristics of a Poodle. Our rating system is from 1 to 10 – with 1 being the lowest score

and 10 being the highest.

- **Adaptability:** 8/10
- **Friendliness:** 10/10
- **Health:** 4/10
- **Ease of Grooming:** 1/10
- **Amount of Shedding:** 10/10
- **Trainability:** 8/10
- **Intelligence:** 10/10
- **Exercise Needed:** 8/10
- **Playfulness:** 10/10
- **Family Friendliness:** 10/10

THE PORTUGUESE WATER DOG

The Portuguese Water Dog is a breed of working dog that originates from the Algarve region of Portugal. Historically the Portuguese Water Dog has been used to herd fish into fishermen's nets, to retrieve lost tackle and broken nets and to work as a courier from ship to ship, or from ship to shore. The Portuguese Water Dog traveled on fishing trawlers all the way from the Atlantic waters, off the shore of Portugal, to the waters off the coast of Iceland where the breed was tasked with catching cod. It is believed that the Portuguese Water Dog has been around since 400CE. It is also believed that the Portuguese Water Dog and the Poodle share a common ancestral history, as the longer coated Poodle looks very much like the Portuguese Water Dog. The Portuguese Water Dog breed is fairly rare; especially outside of continental Europe. Breeders will often claim that the Portuguese Water Dog is a low shedding hypoallergenic breed – but there is little to no scientific evidence of this, but their low shedding qualities has helped to boost the Portuguese Water Dog's popularity. The Portuguese Water Dog has recently gained more fame due to the fact that the Obama family adopted two Portuguese Water Dog. The temperament of dogs is normally affected by the following factors: individual personality, heredity, training and socialization. It is therefore important to make sure that you meet the puppy's mother before purchasing a Portuguese Water Dog. It is also important to make sure to thoroughly socialize your Portuguese Water Dog with strangers, children and other animals during its puppyhood. Generally speaking, the Portuguese Water Dog is known to make an excellent companion breed. They are loving, intelligent, independent and highly trainable. The Portuguese Water Dog is generally very good around strangers (both human strangers and animal strangers) and enjoys being petted, stroked and played with. It is important to note that as a working breed, the Portuguese Water Dog has a high amount of energy which needs to be expended. If the Portuguese Water Dog has a buildup of energy it is likely to develop destructive behaviors due to boredom or hyperactivity.

Lifespan

A Portuguese Water Dog will normally live to be between 10 and 12 years old. However it is not uncommon for a Portuguese Water Dog to live to be as old as 14, providing that it does not develop any serious health issues.

Height and Weight

A fully grown Portuguese Water Dog will normally

stand between 17 to 23 inches (43.2 to 58.5cm) tall at the shoulder. A healthy adult Portuguese Water Dog will normally weigh between 35 to 60 pounds (16 to 27.25kg). It is important to note that the weight of a healthy Portuguese Water Dog depends on how large the Portuguese Water Dog is – taller Portuguese Water Dog should weigh more.

Breed Characteristics

The following section will give you a simplistic overview of the characteristics of a Portuguese Water Dog. Our rating system is from 1 to 10 – with 1 being the lowest score and 10 being the highest.

- **Adaptability:** 6/10
- **Friendliness:** 10/10
- **Health:** 8/10
- **Ease of Grooming:** 5/10
- **Amount of Shedding:** 1/10
- **Trainability:** 8/10
- **Intelligence:** 8/10
- **Exercise Needed:** 10/10
- **Playfulness:** 10/10
- **Family Friendliness:** 10/10

THE PUG

The Pug is a small sized breed of companion dog that originates from China, dating back as far as 200 B.C! The breed was originally used by the Emperors of China as guard dogs. The Pug has a short muzzle, wrinkly face and a curly tail that normally curls over the dog's hip. They have square-shaped small compact bodies with a short, fine and glossy coat. The Pug's coat normally comes in the following color variations: fawn, black and apricot. Most Pug's will have a blackish muzzle which has become a trademark of the breed. The breed has two potential ear shapes: 'Button' and 'Rose.' 'Button' ears are considered the standard and tend to be slightly larger and flatter. 'Rose' ears are characterised by their smaller size and slightly folded appearance.

Lifespan

Most Pugs will live to be between 12 and 14 years old. However it is not uncommon for a Pug to live to be as old as 15 as long as it does not develop any serious health issues.

Height and Weight

An adult Pug will commonly be between 10 and 12 inches (25 to 30cm) tall at the shoulder. However it is not uncommon for males to grow to be as tall as 14 inches (35cm) tall at the shoulder. Pug should weigh between 14 and 18 pounds (6.25 to 8kg) depending on their height.

Company

Pugs have been bred to be companion dogs. For this reason they are extremely loyal but also extremely needy. It is very common for your Pug to follow you around your house at all times, sit in your lap whenever they are given the chance and to also want to sleep in your bed.

Obesity

Pugs are prone to be greedy and will over eat if they are given the chance. Due to the fact that they gain weight quickly, it is recommended to never feed your Pug from the table to avoid it gaining too much weight. It is important to also monitor your dog's food intake as closely as possible. Obesity in dogs, like in humans, can lead to a wide range of health issues spanning from arthritis to heart disease.

Eye Prolapse

Eye prolapse is a common problem for Pugs. A Pug's eyes may prolapse if they suffer any trauma to their neck or head. These traumas can occur easily – from an overly tight leash or harness, from a bump or fall or from being squeezed. A prolapse eye can normally be fixed by a swift trip to the vets. If your Pug has regular eye prolapses it may require eye surgery.

Breed Characteristics

The following section will give you a simplistic overview of the characteristics of a Pug. Our rating system is from 1 to 10 – with 1 being the lowest score and 10 being the highest.

- **Adaptability:** 6/10
- **Friendliness:** 8/10
- **Health:** 2/10
- **Ease of Grooming:** 10/10
- **Amount of Shedding:** 10/10
- **Trainability:** 4/10
- **Intelligence:** 4/10
- **Exercise Needed:** 6/10
- **Playfulness:** 10/10
- **Family Friendliness:** 10/10

THE PUGGLE

The Puggle is a cross breed of dog that is created by mixing a Beagle and a Pug. The breed's name is a portmanteau, following the trend set by other 'designer dog' crossbreeds such as the 'Labradoodle' and 'Cavapoo.' The Puggle is also commonly known as the 'Bug,' the 'Buggle' and the 'Peagle.' The first Puggle was bred by a Wisconsin breeder named Wallace Havens in the early 1980s. Havens is credited with creating the breed's name and was the first person to register the crossbreed to the American Canine Hybrid Club (an organization focused on tracking and recording crossbreeds). It is important to note that no major Kennel Clubs or other breed registries (such as the American Kennel Club and the United Kennel Club) recognize the Puggle as a dog breed. As a crossbreed, the Puggle has characteristics of both a Beagle and a Pug. The Beagle genetics generally lead the Puggle to have a love of sniffing things and makes the Puggle a relatively good jumper. The Pug genetics generally allows the Puggle to have a misleadingly fast land speed. The breed's coat coloration can be highly varied but will normally be found in the following colorations: tan, fawn and black. The Puggle can either have a short snout like a Pug or a longer snout like a Beagle. The temperament of dogs is normally affected by the following factors:

individual personality, heredity, training and socialization. It is therefore important to make sure that you meet the puppy's mother before purchasing a Puggle. It is also important to make sure to thoroughly socialize your Puggle with strangers, children and other animals during its puppyhood. Generally speaking, the Puggle tends to have an inquisitive and active nature. The Puggle also tends to love companionship and makes a great family dog. The Puggle is highly accepting and friendly towards children, strangers and strange dogs. Despite their small size, it is recommended to not keep a Puggle in an apartment environment due to the fact that Beagles enjoy howling and Pugs enjoy barking – the Puggle both howls and barks on a regular basis.

Lifespan

A Puggle will normally live to be between 10 and 12 years old. However it is not uncommon for a Puggle to live to be as old as 15, providing that it does not develop any serious health issues.

Height and Weight

A fully grown Puggle will normally stand between 12 to 15 inches (30.5 to 38.1cm) tall at the shoulder. A healthy adult Puggle will normally weigh between 15 to 30 pounds (6.8 to 13.6kg). It is important to note that the weight of a healthy Puggle depends on how large the Puggle is – taller Puggle should weigh more.

Breed Characteristics

The following section will give you a simplistic overview of the characteristics of a Puggle. Our rating system is from 1 to 10 – with 1 being the lowest score and 10 being the highest.

- **Adaptability:** 8/10
- **Friendliness:** 10/10
- **Health:** 8/10
- **Ease of Grooming:** 10/10
- **Amount of Shedding:** 6/10
- **Trainability:** 6/10
- **Intelligence:** 6/10
- **Exercise Needed:** 6/10
- **Playfulness:** 7/10
- **Family Friendliness:** 10/10

THE PULI

The Puli is a small-to-medium sized breed of dog that originates from Hungary. Within Hungary the Puli is known for its ability to easily herd and guard livestock and also for its unique coat. The Puli has a long, corded coat made up of tightly curling hairs that give the breed the appearance of having dreadlocks. The Puli is often compared to a much larger Hungarian breed, the 'Komondor,' as both breeds have the unique dreadlock coat. It is believed that the Puli was introduced into Hungary by the migration of the Magyars, from Central Asia, more than 1000 years ago. Traditionally the Puli was used to guard livestock and would normally work alongside other flock guardian breeds – but the Puli is more than capable of herding and guarding flock independently. If the Puli was working with other breeds, the Puli would normally be tasked with patrolling the area and barking at predators to alert larger guardian breeds (such as the Komondor) to the present danger. The Puli's coat gives it a great level of defense against predators such as bears and wolves, due to the fact that the predators cannot bite past the long corded coat. The Puli nearly also has a solidly colored coat and this solid color is most commonly black. Other less common coat colorations include: white, grey and cream. Due to the fact that the breed's coat mattes into long dreadlock-like cords, the Puli is actually considered to be a little to no shedding breed. The temperament of dogs is normally affected by the following factors: individual personality, heredity, training and socialization. It is therefore important to make sure that you meet the puppy's mother before purchasing a Puli. It is also important to make sure to thoroughly socialize your Puli with strangers, children and other animals during its puppyhood. Generally speaking, the Puli is known to be an intelligent, active, brave and adaptable breed. A working Puli will need obedience training during its early puppyhood to ensure that it is capable of herding and guarding flock independently. The Puli is a great family pet due to their love of children and a household environment. It is important to note that as a working breed, the Puli has a high amount of energy which needs to be expended. If the Puli has a buildup of energy it is likely to develop destructive behaviors due to boredom or hyperactivity.

Lifespan

A Puli will normally live to be between 10 and 12 years old. However it is not uncommon for a Puli to live to be as old as 15, providing that it does not develop any serious health issues.

Height and Weight

A fully grown Puli will normally stand between 16 to 18 inches (40.65 to 45.75cm) tall at the shoulder. A healthy adult Puli will normally weigh between 25 to 35 pounds (11.5 to 16kg). It is important to note that the weight of a healthy Puli depends on how large the Puli is – taller Puli should weigh more.

Breed Characteristics

The following section will give you a simplistic overview of the characteristics of a Puli. Our rating system is from 1 to 10 – with 1 being the lowest score and 10 being the highest.

- **Adaptability:** 6/10
- **Friendliness:** 8/10
- **Health:** 9/10
- **Ease of Grooming:** 1/10
- **Amount of Shedding:** 1/10
- **Trainability:** 8/10
- **Intelligence:** 8/10
- **Exercise Needed:** 10/10
- **Playfulness:** 10/10
- **Family Friendliness:** 10/10

THE PYRENEAN SHEPHERD

The Pyrenean Shepherd is a small-to-medium sized breed of dog that is native to the Pyrenees mountais located in southern France and northern Spain. The Pyrenean Shepherd breed is known by different names in both France and Spain. In France the breed is known as the 'Berger des Pyrenees,' and in Spain the breed is known as the 'Pastor de los Pirineos.' The breed was developed during medieval times for the purpose of herding livestock, especially sheep. The Pyrenean Shepherd worked in unison with other herding and flock guardian breeds of mountain dog, most notably the Great Pyrenees. The Pyrenean Shepherd saw wide use in the French military services during the first World War as it was employed as a courier, a search and rescue dog, as a company mascot and as a watch dog. The Pyrenean Shepherd in its harlequin or blue merle coloration is believed to be one of the breeds used in the development of the Australian Shepherd, when sheep herders brought their sheepdogs to the American West. The Pyrenean Shepherd's coat comes in two varieties: smooth-faced and rough-faced (demi-long or long-haired). The smooth-face variety has short, fine hairs on its muzzle, a larger haired ruff around its neck and a small amount of feathering on its belly, legs and tail. The rough-faced coat variation leads to the

Pyrenean Shepherd having long hairs on its muzzle and face with long coarse hairs covering the rest of its body. The rough-faced coat variety can lead the Pyrenean Shepherd to developing cord like mattes over its hindquarters and front legs. The temperament of dogs is normally affected by the following factors: individual personality, heredity, training and socialization. It is therefore important to make sure that you meet the puppy's mother before purchasing a Pyrenean Shepherd. It is also important to make sure to thoroughly socialize your Pyrenean Shepherd with strangers, children and other animals during its puppyhood. Generally speaking, the Pyrenean Shepherd is an independent and active breed. The Pyrenean Shepherd is also highly adaptable and can be taught a plethora of different skills. Interestingly, the Pyrenean Shepherd is known as a 'one man dog,' which means that they will generally form a very close attachment to one of their owners. It is important to note that as a working breed, the Pyrenean Shepherd has a high amount of energy which needs to be expended. If the Pyrenean Shepherd has a buildup of energy it is likely to develop destructive behaviors due to boredom or hyperactivity.

Lifespan

A Pyrenean Shepherd will normally live to be between 13 and 15 years old. However it is not uncommon for a Pyrenean Shepherd to live to be as old as 17, providing that it does not develop any serious health issues.

Height and Weight

A fully grown Pyrenean Shepherd will normally stand between 15 to 21 inches (38 to 53.5cm) tall at the shoulder. A healthy adult Pyrenean Shepherd will normally weigh between 25 to 30 pounds (11.3 to 13.6kg). It is important to note that the weight of a healthy Pyrenean Shepherd depends on how large the Pyrenean Shepherd is – taller Pyrenean Shepherd should weigh more.

Breed Characteristics

The following section will give you a simplistic overview of the characteristics of a Pyrenean Shepherd. Our rating system is from 1 to 10 – with 1 being the lowest score and 10 being the highest.

- **Adaptability:** 7/10
- **Friendliness:** 8/10
- **Health:** 5/10

- **Ease of Grooming:** 6/10
- **Amount of Shedding:** 5/10
- **Trainability:** 7/10
- **Intelligence:** 8/10
- **Exercise Needed:** 10/10
- **Playfulness:** 10/10
- **Family Friendliness:** 10/10

THE RAT TERRIER

The Rat Terrier is a small breed of dog that originates from America and is a member of the Terrier typing. The breed's name comes from the occupation of its earliest ancestors who were brought to the United States of America by British migrants. The Rat Terrier was mainly tasked with rat catching and rat baiting and was therefore developed to have a small and speedy build. Due to the breed's speed they have also often been used to catch other vermin such as hares and squirrels. During the 1890's the Beagle, Italian Greyhound and Miniature Pinscher were introduced into the Rat Terrier's development. Before the introduction of other breeds in the 1890's, the Rat Terrier was virtually indistinguishable from other small mixed-breed hunting known as 'Feists.' In the 20th century the Rat Terrier became extremely popular due to their loyalty, hunting ability and low maintenance. The Rat Terrier could be commonly found ratting on the farms across America. However in 1950 pesticides began being used to combat vermin infestations which made the Rat Terrier a redundant vermin catcher. The numbers of Rat Terrier across America dwindled due to this and it is now considered a rare breed. The temperament of dogs is normally affected by the following factors: individual personality, heredity, training and socialization. It is therefore important to make sure that you meet the puppy's mother before purchasing a Rat Terrier. It is also important to make sure to thoroughly socialize your Rat Terrier with strangers, children and other animals during its puppyhood. Generally speaking, the Rat Terrier is known to be an incredibly affectionate, loyal and empathetic breed and has in recent years been used as a service dog in hospices, depression clinics and in other fields of human care. The Rat Terrier has also seen a rise in popularity as a household pet due to its adaptability and friendly nature. It is important to note that as a working breed, the Rat Terrier has a high amount of energy which needs to be expended. If the Rat Terrier has a buildup of energy it is likely to develop destructive behaviors due to boredom or hyperactivity.

Lifespan

A Rat Terrier will normally live to be between 12 and 14 years old. However it is not uncommon for a Rat Terrier to live to be as old as 18, providing that it does not develop any serious health issues.

Height and Weight

A fully grown Rat Terrier will normally stand between 12 to 16 inches (30.5 to 40.5cm) tall at the shoulder. A healthy adult Rat Terrier will normally weigh between 10 to 25 pounds (4.5 to 11.3kg). It is important to note that the weight of a healthy Rat Terrier depends on how large the Rat Terrier is – taller Rat Terrier should weigh more.

Breed Characteristics

The following section will give you a simplistic overview of the characteristics of a Rat Terrier. Our rating system is from 1 to 10 – with 1 being the lowest score and 10 being the highest.

- **Adaptability:** 7/10
- **Friendliness:** 8/10
- **Health:** 9/10
- **Ease of Grooming:** 10/10
- **Amount of Shedding:** 7/10
- **Trainability:** 6/10
- **Intelligence:** 8/10
- **Exercise Needed:** 10/10
- **Playfulness:** 10/10
- **Family Friendliness:** 10/10

THE REDBONE COONHOUND

The Redbone Coonhound is a breed of dog that originates from America and was originally developed for the purposes of hunting both small game (such as raccoons) and larger game (such as bears, cougars and deer). The Redbone Coonhound breed was first recognized and registered by the United Kennel Club in 1902 and was later registered by the American Kennel Club in 2009. During the 18th century, many breeds of hunting dogs from Europe were imported into America – most notably the English Foxhound, the Bloodhound, the Harrier and the Welsh Hound. Over time, southern hunters selectively bred the imported breeds to create a fearless breed that would never back down during a hunt and hence the Redbone Coonhound was created. The Redbone Coonhound has incredible levels of stamina, independence and confidence and is known to 'hound' their prey until they are treed or cornered and exhausted. The Redbone Coonhound has a lean, muscular body with a build that is very typical of the coonhound subgroup. The breed also has long straight legs that allow it to easily keep a raccoon treed during a hunt. The temperament of dogs is normally affected by the following factors: individual personality, heredity, training and socialization. It is therefore important to make sure that you meet the puppy's mother before purchasing a Redbone Coonhound. It is also important to make sure to thoroughly socialize your Redbone Coonhound with strangers, children and other animals during its puppyhood. Generally speaking, the Redbone Coonhound is known to be an incredibly gentle, affectionate and friendly breed that gets along well with humans. It is important to note that as a hound, the Redbone Coonhound is incredibly vocal and it is therefore not recommended to be kept in an apartment environment. It is important to note that as a working breed, the Redbone Coonhound has a high amount of energy which needs to be expended. If the Redbone Coonhound has a buildup of energy it is likely to develop destructive behaviors due to boredom or hyperactivity.

Lifespan

A Redbone Coonhound will normally live to be between 10 and 11 years old. However it is not uncommon for a Redbone Coonhound to live to be as old as 12, providing that it does not develop any serious health issues.

Height and Weight

A fully grown Redbone Coonhound will normally stand between 21 to 27 inches (53.3 to 68.5cm) tall at the shoulder. A healthy adult Redbone Coonhound will normally weigh between 45 to 70 pounds (20.5 to 31.75kg). It is important to note that the weight of a healthy Redbone Coonhound depends on how large the Redbone Coonhound is – taller Redbone Coonhound should weigh more.

Breed Characteristics

The following section will give you a simplistic overview of the characteristics of a Redbone Coonhound. Our rating system is from 1 to 10 – with 1 being the lowest score and 10 being the highest.

- **Adaptability:** 6/10
- **Friendliness:** 8/10
- **Health:** 6/10
- **Ease of Grooming:** 10/10
- **Amount of Shedding:** 4/10
- **Trainability:** 8/10
- **Intelligence:** 8/10
- **Exercise Needed:** 10/10
- **Playfulness:** 10/10
- **Family Friendliness:** 10/10

THE RHODESIAN RIDGEBACK

The Rhodesian Ridgeback is a breed of dog that was named after its country of origin Rhodesia, which is now known as Zimbabwe. The Rhodesian Ridgeback is also commonly known as the 'African Lion Dog' and the 'African Lion Hound.' The breed's early ancestors can be traced back to the semi-domesticated ridged hunting dog brought into the Cape Colony by European pioneers. The Rhodesian Ridgeback has also been a difficult breed to categorizes as it could easily be placed in any of the following five cater gores: scent hound, sight hound, cur-dog, wagon dog and ridged primitive. However almost every major registry throughout the world categorizes the Rhodesian Ridgeback as a 'hound.' The British and the Canadian Kennel Clubs categorize the Rhodesian Ridgeback as simply a 'hound,' whereas the American Kennel Club further categorizes the Rhodesian Ridgeback as a 'sight hound.' The Rhodesian Ridgeback's main distinguishing feature is its large ridge of hair that runs along its back in the opposite direction to the rest of its coat. The ridge is formed by two fan-like crowns of hair and tapers from the dog's shoulders down to its hips. It is not uncommon for a Rhodesian Ridgeback's ridge to be as wide as 2 inches at its widest point! The breed is typically very muscular, lean and agile. Most Rhodesian Ridgeback's coats will come in a red wheaten coloration and be made up of short, dense and sleek hairs. The Rhodesian Ridgeback has mainly been used as a gundog, a sighthound, a scent hound and as a general purpose working dog through its history. The temperament of dogs is normally affected by the following factors: individual personality, heredity, training and socialization. It is therefore important to make sure that you meet the puppy's mother before purchasing a Rhodesian Ridgeback. It is also important to make sure to thoroughly socialize your Rhodesian Ridgeback with strangers, children and other animals during its puppyhood. Generally speaking, the Rhodesian Ridgeback is known to be a loyal, intelligent and strong willed breed. It is not uncommon for a Rhodesian Ridgeback to be extremely aloof with strangers but it should never appear to be aggressive. The Rhodesian Ridgeback is a highly protective breed and love spending time with its family unit. It is important to note that as a working breed, the Rhodesian Ridgeback has a high amount of energy which needs to be expended. If the Rhodesian Ridgeback has a buildup of energy it is likely to develop destructive behaviors due to boredom or hyperactivity.

Lifespan

A Rhodesian Ridgeback will normally live to be between 8 and 10 years old. However it is not uncommon for a Rhodesian Ridgeback to live to be as old as 12, providing that it does not develop any serious health issues.

Height and Weight

A fully grown Rhodesian Ridgeback will normally stand between 24 to 27 inches (61 to 68.5cm) tall at the shoulder. A healthy adult Rhodesian Ridgeback will normally weigh between 65 to 85 pounds (29.5 to 38.5kg). It is important to note that the weight of a healthy Rhodesian Ridgeback depends on how large the Rhodesian Ridgeback is – taller Rhodesian Ridgeback should weigh more.

Breed Characteristics

The following section will give you a simplistic overview of the characteristics of a Rhodesian Ridgeback. Our rating system is from 1 to 10 – with 1 being the lowest score and 10 being the highest.

- **Adaptability:** 6/10
- **Friendliness:** 6/10
- **Health:** 8/10
- **Ease of Grooming:** 10/10
- **Amount of Shedding:** 1/10
- **Trainability:** 6/10

- **Intelligence:** 8/10
- **Exercise Needed:** 10/10
- **Playfulness:** 10/10
- **Family Friendliness:** 10/10

THE ROTTWEILER

The Rottweiler is a breed of medium to large domestic dog. Rottweilers were originally used to herd animals and to pull carts laden with butchered meat. In the present day they are mainly used as rescue dogs, police dogs, military dogs, security dogs and dogs to aid the disabled. They are a calm, good natured, confident and intelligent breed of dog that has an ingrained instinct to protect its family unit. Rottweilers have a negative stigma attached to them due to irresponsible owners. Rottweilers rarely display dangerous and destructive behavior unless they have been neglected, abused or not socialized properly. However it is important to remember that Rottweilers are extremely powerful dogs which is a potential risk factor for a beginner owner.

Lifespan

Rottweilers normally live for between 8 and 10 years. However it is not uncommon for a Rottweiler to live to be as old as 11 if they do not develop any serious health issues.

Size

A fully grown male Rottweiler will typically grow to

be around 24 to 27 inches (61 to 68.5cm) tall at the shoulder. Adult females will normally grow to be 22 to 25 inches (56 to 63.5cm) tall at the shoulder. Males normally weigh between 95 and 130 pounds (43 to 59kg). Females weigh slightly less and normally weigh between 85 and 115 pounds (38.5 to 52kg).

Children

Due to their instinct to herd other animals it is not uncommon for a Rottweiler to attempt to herd small children. Your Rottweiler may 'bump' children with its head, in an attempt to herd them, which may cause small children to fall over. It is believed that Rottweilers exhibit this herding behavior around small children due to their size. If you are raising children around a Rottweiler it is important to properly socialize your dog with children from puppyhood. It is important to ALWAYS supervise your Rottweiler while it is around children due to its large size, powerful body and strong prey drive (it may become overly excited by children who are running and playing).

Introducing New Animals and Dogs

It is important to remember that Rottweilers are incredibly protective over their family unit. It is therefore important to introduce any new dogs, or animals, to your Rottweiler in a calm and positive environment. Rottweilers have a tendency to be aggressive towards strange dogs, especially if they are of the same sex. Under your leadership, your Rottweiler should be able to learn to coexist with new animals and dogs.

Breed Characteristics

The following section will give you a simplistic overview of the characteristics of a Rottweiler. Our rating system is from 1 to 10 – with 1 being the lowest score and 10 being the highest.

- **Adaptability:** 4/10
- **Friendliness:** 8/10
- **Health:** 8/10
- **Ease of Grooming:** 10/10
- **Amount of Shedding:** 8/10
- **Trainability:** 8/10
- **Intelligence:** 10/10
- **Exercise Needed:** 8/10
- **Playfulness:** 10/10
- **Family Friendliness:** 10/10

Encyclopedia of Dog Breeds

THE SAINT BERNARD

The Saint Bernard is a very large breed of working dog that originates from the western Alps in Switzerland, Italy and France. The breed is also commonly known as the 'Saint Bernhardshund,' the 'Bernhardiner,' and the now archaic 'Alpine Mastiff.' The Saint Bernard was originally bred at the 'Great and Little Saint Bernard Pass' for search and rescue purposes. The breed was developed by cross breeding the Sennenhund with other large molossers type dogs that were introduced to the Alps by the ancient Romans. The Sennenhund was traditionally used throughout the Alps for the purposes of hunting, flock guarding, search and rescue as well as being a family household dog. These traits have allowed the Saint Bernard to be one of the most intelligent, loyal and trainable breeds of dog that, when combined with the breed's enormous size, allow it to easily perform search and rescue related tasks. The Saint Bernard breed is internationally recognizes and categorized as a Molossid breed. The traditional Saint Bernard looked very different from the Saint Bernard of today. During the early 1800s there was a large increase of avalanches in the Alps area which lead to the death of many of the Saint Bernard dogs. The breed was then crossbred with the Newfoundland to increase breed numbers. However the new Saint Bernard inherited the

Newfoundland's longer coat which hinders its ability to perform search and rescue tasks. The reason for this is that in the freezing conditions of the Alps longer hairs are more likely to freeze and hinder the dog's ability to move. The temperament of dogs is normally affected by the following factors: individual personality, heredity, training and socialization. It is therefore important to make sure that you meet the puppy's mother before purchasing a Saint Bernard. It is also important to make sure to thoroughly socialize your Saint Bernard with strangers, children and other animals during its puppyhood. Generally speaking, the Saint Bernard breed is nicknamed the 'Gentle Giant' due to the fact that is in an incredibly friendly, gentle and affectionate breed of dog. The Saint Bernard is also incredibly respectful of smaller animals and children. However despite the Saint Bernard's calm, patient and sweet-natured disposition it is still important to make sure that you properly socialize your Saint Bernard during its puppyhood to avoid any chance of an accident occurring! The Saint Bernard was bred for the purpose of being a working dog and have developed a desire to please its owners which, when paired with the breed's high level of intelligence, makes the Saint Bernard a very trainable breed. It is important to note that as a working breed, the Saint Bernard has a high amount of energy which needs to be expended. If the Saint Bernard has a buildup of energy it is likely to develop destructive behaviors due to boredom or hyperactivity.

Lifespan

A Saint Bernard will normally live to be between 8 and 9 years old. However it is not uncommon for a Saint Bernard to live to be as old as 10, providing that it does not develop any serious health issues.

Height and Weight

A fully grown Saint Bernard will normally stand between 26 to 30 inches (66 to 76.2cm) tall at the shoulder. A healthy adult Saint Bernard will normally weigh between 120 to 180 pounds (54.4 to 81.6kg). It is important to note that the weight of a healthy Saint Bernard depends on how large the Saint Bernard is – taller Saint Bernard should weigh more.

Breed Characteristics

The following section will give you a simplistic overview of the characteristics of a Saint Bernard. Our rating system is from 1 to 10 – with 1 being the lowest score and 10 being the highest.

- **Adaptability:** 6/10
- **Friendliness:** 10/10

- ➢ **Health:** 5/10
- ➢ **Ease of Grooming:** 5/10
- ➢ **Amount of Shedding:** 8/10
- ➢ **Trainability:** 7/10
- ➢ **Intelligence:** 8/10
- ➢ **Exercise Needed:** 7/10
- ➢ **Playfulness:** 8/10
- ➢ **Family Friendliness:** 10/10

THE SALUKI

The Saluki is a breed of dog that originates from the Fertile Crescent, which is located in west Asia. The Saluki is also commonly known as the 'Persian Greyhound.' There are images of dogs, that look very similar to the modern day Saluki, adorning poetry that has been found in the Fertile Crescent which date back to nearly 6000 years ago which indicates that the Saluki is a very ancient breed. The Saluki rose to prominence during the Eighteenth dynasty of Egypt where it became one of the most popular breeds of dogs to be owned by Egyptian royalty. The Saluki was traditionally used for the purpose of hunting large quarry such as gazelles and jackals as well as smaller game such as hares and foxes. While the Greyhound is credited as being the world's fastest breed of dog over distances of around 800 meteres, both the Saluki and the Whippet breeds are thought to be faster over longer distances. In 1996, the Guinness Book of Records listed the Saluki as being the fastest breed of dog as it was capable of reaching speeds of over 68 kilometers per hour! The temperament of dogs is normally affected by the following factors: individual personality, heredity, training and socialization. It is therefore important to make sure that you meet the puppy's mother before purchasing a Saluki. It is also important to make sure to thoroughly socialize your

Saluki with strangers, children and other animals during its puppyhood. Generally speaking, the Saluki has retained most of the qualities of a hunting hound and is therefore extremely affectionate and loyal towards its handler but aloof, and ever wary, or strangers. Due to the breeds independent and aloof nature they are relatively hard to train and should only be owned by experience dog owners. The Saluki is also a highly empathetic breed and all training should therefore be administered in a clam, friendly and patient environment. It is important to properly socialize a Saluki during its puppyhood to minimize its chances of being shy, aloof and timid in later life. The Saluki as a sight hunting hound is also very prone to chasing moving objects! It is important to note that as a hunting breed, the Saluki has a high amount of energy which needs to be expended. If the Saluki has a buildup of energy it is likely to develop destructive behaviors due to boredom or hyperactivity.

Lifespan

A Saluki will normally live to be between 10 and 12 years old. However it is not uncommon for a Saluki to live to be as old as 14, providing that it does not develop any serious health issues.

Height and Weight

A fully grown Saluki will normally stand between 23 to 28 inches (58.5 to 71.1cm) tall at the shoulder. A healthy adult Saluki will normally weigh between 35 to 70 pounds (15.8 to 31.6kg). It is important to note that the weight of a healthy Saluki depends on how large the Saluki is – taller Saluki should weigh more.

Breed Characteristics

The following section will give you a simplistic overview of the characteristics of a Saluki. Our rating system is from 1 to 10 – with 1 being the lowest score and 10 being the highest.

- **Adaptability:** 4/10
- **Friendliness:** 6/10
- **Health:** 6/10
- **Ease of Grooming:** 8/10
- **Amount of Shedding:** 4/10
- **Trainability:** 8/10
- **Intelligence:** 8/10
- **Exercise Needed:** 8/10
- **Playfulness:** 10/10
- **Family Friendliness:** 10/10

THE SAMOYED

The Samoyed is a large breed of herding dog that is a member of the Spitz grouping. The breed's name is a reference to the Samoyedic people that originated in Serbia, as they are believed to have played a major part in the development of the Samoyed. The Samoyedic people where nomadic reindeer herders who used the Samoyed dog to help them with their herding, to pull sleds and to watch over livestock and encampments. The Samoyed is also common known as the 'Sobaka,' the 'Lafka,' and the 'Smiley' (due to its friendly disposition and 'smiling' face). The Samoyed has been recognized as a basal breed – which means that it predates the emergence of the modern breeds in the 19th century! The Samoyed has a thick, white, double layered coat which traditionally helped to protect it during the harsh weather conditions found in Russia. The Samoyed's coat is so long and fluffy that it has actually been used for knitting purposes as an alternative to wool. Once knit, a Samoyed has a similar texture to angora and Samoyed jumpers have been reported to handle temperatures well below freezing! The Samoyedic nomads were also known to use lumps of Samoyed fur as artificial flies for fly fishing. The temperament of dogs is normally affected by the following factors: individual personality, heredity, training and socialization. It is therefore important to make sure that you meet the puppy's mother before purchasing a Samoyed. It is also important to make sure to thoroughly socialize your Samoyed with strangers, children and other animals during its puppyhood. Generally speaking, the Samoyed has a friendly and affectionate disposition that makes it a perfect household pet as the breed gets along well with other animals, children and strangers. Aggression in Samoyed is considered very rare. While the Samoyed has a history of being used as a watchdog due to their tendency to bark at unknown noises, the Samoyed breed makes terrible guard dogs due to their friendly and socially curious nature. It is important to note that as a working breed, the Samoyed has a high amount of energy which needs to be expended. If the Samoyed has a buildup of energy it is likely to develop destructive behaviors due to boredom or hyperactivity.

Lifespan

A Samoyed will normally live to be between 10 and 12 years old. However it is not uncommon for a Samoyed to live to be as old as 14, providing that it does not develop any serious health issues.

Height and Weight

A fully grown Samoyed will normally stand between

18 to 24 inches (45.75 to 61cm) tall at the shoulder. A healthy adult Samoyed will normally weigh between 50 to 60 pounds (22.5 to 27.25kg). It is important to note that the weight of a healthy Samoyed depends on how large the Samoyed is – taller Samoyed should weigh more.

Breed Characteristics

The following section will give you a simplistic overview of the characteristics of a Samoyed. Our rating system is from 1 to 10 – with 1 being the lowest score and 10 being the highest.

- **Adaptability:** 6/10
- **Friendliness:** 10/10
- **Health:** 6/10
- **Ease of Grooming:** 3/10
- **Amount of Shedding:** 10/10
- **Trainability:** 8/10
- **Intelligence:** 7/10
- **Exercise Needed:** 8/10
- **Playfulness:** 10/10
- **Family Friendliness:** 10/10

THE SCHIPPERKE

The Schipperke is a small breed of dog that originated in Belgium during the 16th century. The breed is also commonly known as the 'Spitzke,' and the 'Spits.' There is a lot of debate throughout the Kennel Clubs of the world as to whether the Schipperke should be a member of the Spitz typing or of the Miniature Sheepdog typing. In the breed's country of origin, Belgium, the Schipperke is categorized as a Miniature Sheepdog. The Schipperke breed was first recognized in the early 1880s and the breed's first standard was written in 1889. Interestingly the breed's name, Schipperke, translates in English to mean 'little boatman.' However, while the Schipperke was occasionally seen on barges and small fishing ships it was not their primary function. The Schipperke has traditionally been used for flock herding purposes. The main reason for the discrepancy in translation is due to the fact that within the Brussels and Leuven region 'schipper' was the word for shepherd, making the breed's actual translated name 'Little Shepherd.' The Schipperke was used throughout World War II by the Belgian Resistance as messenger dogs that would secretly transport messages from hideout to hideout while avoiding detection from the occupying Nazi forces. The Schipperke has small, pointed ears that sit erect atop their head which gives the breed an alert expression. The Schipperke has a double coat with a soft, fluffy undercoat and a harsher and much longer outter coat. While the Schipperke's coat comes in a wide variety of solid colors, black has always been favored by the breed standard. The temperament of dogs is normally affected by the following factors: individual personality, heredity, training and socialization. It is therefore important to make sure that you meet the puppy's mother before purchasing a Schipperke. It is also important to make sure to thoroughly socialize your Schipperke with strangers, children and other animals during its puppyhood. Generally speaking, the Schipperke is an active, trainable and adaptable breed. While the Schipperke is highly affectionate towards its family unit it is slightly aloof and suspicious of strangers. The Schipperke gets along well with children as it is known to be both a highly respectful and playful breed. It is important to note that as a working breed, the Schipperke has a high amount of energy which needs to be expended. If the Schipperke has a buildup of energy it is likely to develop destructive behaviors due to boredom or hyperactivity.

Lifespan

A Schipperke will normally live to be between 12 and 13 years old. However it is not uncommon for a Schipperke to live to be as old as 15, providing that it does not develop any serious health issues.

Height and Weight

A fully grown Schipperke will normally stand between 10 to 15 inches (25.5 to 38.25cm) tall at the shoulder. A healthy adult Schipperke will normally weigh between 10 to 18 pounds (4.5 to 8kg). It is important to note that the weight of a healthy Schipperke depends on how large the Schipperke is – taller Schipperke should weigh more.

Breed Characteristics

The following section will give you a simplistic overview of the characteristics of a Schipperke. Our rating system is from 1 to 10 – with 1 being the lowest score and 10 being the highest.

- **Adaptability:** 6/10
- **Friendliness:** 6/10
- **Health:** 6/10
- **Ease of Grooming:** 10/10
- **Amount of Shedding:** 6/10

- ➢ **Trainability:** 6/10
- ➢ **Intelligence:** 8/10
- ➢ **Exercise Needed:** 10/10
- ➢ **Playfulness:** 10/10
- ➢ **Family Friendliness:** 10/10

THE SCHNOODLE

The Schnoodle is a cross breed of dog that was created by breeding a Schnauzer with a Poodle. It is important to note that a Schnoodle is a first-generation crossbreed and will therefore always have to purebred parents. The American Kennel Club, the United Kennel Club and the Canadian Kennel Club do not recognize the Schnoodle, or any other breed of designer dog, as a breed in their own right. As with many other popular breeds of designer dog, the Schnoodle's rise to popularity has led to many Schnoodles being bred in puppy mills. It is therefore very important to make sure where you are purchasing your Schnoodle from as it is not advisable to support the puppy mill industry due to its innate cruelness and care limitations. In terms of appearance, the Schnoodle can possess the curly haired coat and thin agile body of the Poodle or it can possess the rough haired coat and sturdily built body shape of the Schnauzer – or any combination of the traits of its parents. The temperament of dogs is normally affected by the following factors: individual personality, heredity, training and socialization. It is therefore important to make sure that you meet the puppy's mother before purchasing a Schnoodle. It is also important to make sure to thoroughly socialize your Schnoodle with strangers, children and other animals during its puppyhood. Generally speaking, the temperament of a Schnoodle will reflect the temperament of its Poodle and Schnauzer parents. The Poodle is a highly intelligent breed who excels in obedience training. The Schnauzer is known to be an intelligent, strong willed, highly affectionate and naturally protective of its family members. The Schnoodle can inherit any combination of its forbearer's personality traits. However the Schnoodle tends to be an intelligent and affectionate breed that loves spending time with its family unit. Like both of its parents breed, the Schnoodle also tends to be an incredibly active and athletic breed that will need extensive exercising to make sure that it does not develop any destructive behaviors due to being bored or having an abundance of unspent energy.

Lifespan

A Schnoodle will normally live to be between 10 and 12 years old. However it is not uncommon for a Schnoodle to live to be as old as 15, providing that it does not develop any serious health issues.

Height and Weight

A fully grown Schnoodle will normally stand between 15 to 26 inches (38.1 to 66cm) tall at the shoulder. A healthy adult Schnoodle will normally weigh between 20 to 75 pounds (9 to 34kg). It is important to note that the weight of a healthy Schnoodle depends on how large the Schnoodle is – taller Schnoodle should weigh more.

Breed Characteristics

The following section will give you a simplistic overview of the characteristics of a Schnoodle. Our rating system is from 1 to 10 – with 1 being the lowest score and 10 being the highest.

- **Adaptability:** 6/10
- **Friendliness:** 8/10
- **Health:** 6/10
- **Ease of Grooming:** 8/10
- **Amount of Shedding:** 5/10
- **Trainability:** 7/10
- **Intelligence:** 10/10
- **Exercise Needed:** 9/10
- **Playfulness:** 8/10
- **Family Friendliness:** 10/10

THE SCOTTISH DEERHOUND

The Scottish Deerhound is a large breed of hound that originates from Scotland. The breed is also commonly known as simply the 'Deerhound.' The Scottish Deerhound's ancestors existed in a time that predates recorded history. It is believed that the Scottish Deerhound's ancestors would have been kept by the Scots and used primarily for the purposes of hunting hoofed game, such as Deer, for dietary purposes. There is archaeological evidence which supports this belief as Roman pottery was found in Scotland that depicts a deerhunt using large rough hounds. The pottery has been dated to around the 1st Century AD and can be viewed in the National Museum of Scotland, in Edinburgh. The Scottish Deerhound highly resembles the Greyhound in physical appearance, but the Scottish Deerhound is much larger and has a heavier bone structure. While a Greyhound can outrun a Scottish Deerhound on a smooth flat surface, the Scottish Deerhound's heavy bone structure allows it to outrun most other breed's over rough and uneven terrain. The Scottish Deerhound's rough-coated appearance is believed to be a product of the environment in which the Scottish Deerhound traditionally hunted in – the rough coat protects the Scottish Deerhound from the cold, wet and rough terrain found around the Scottish

Highland glens. The Scottish Deerhound was developed for the purposes of hunting Red Deer by 'coursing' and 'deer-stalking,' and was employed for this purposes up until the end of the 19th century. The Scottish Deerhound was replaced by smaller and slower tracking dogs due to the fact that hunters began using modern rifles which allowed them to quickly take down deer, which made the far and fast running Scottish Deerhound obsolete. The temperament of dogs is normally affected by the following factors: individual personality, heredity, training and socialization. It is therefore important to make sure that you meet the puppy's mother before purchasing a Scottish Deerhound. It is also important to make sure to thoroughly socialize your Scottish Deerhound with strangers, children and other animals during its puppyhood. Generally speaking, the Scottish Deerhound is an extremely friendly and docile breed. The Scottish Deerhound is also known to be a breed that is incredibly eager to please its owners. It is important to note that as a working breed, the Scottish Deerhound has a high amount of energy which needs to be expended. If the Scottish Deerhound has a buildup of energy it is likely to develop destructive behaviors due to boredom or hyperactivity.

Lifespan

A Scottish Deerhound will normally live to be between 8 and 10 years old. However it is not uncommon for a Scottish Deerhound to live to be as old as 11, providing that it does not develop any serious health issues.

Height and Weight

A fully grown Scottish Deerhound will normally stand between 28 to 32 inches (71 to 81cm) tall at the shoulder. A healthy adult Scottish Deerhound will normally weigh between 75 to 110 pounds (34 to 50kg). It is important to note that the weight of a healthy Scottish Deerhound depends on how large the Scottish Deerhound is – taller Scottish Deerhound should weigh more.

Breed Characteristics

The following section will give you a simplistic overview of the characteristics of a Scottish Deerhound. Our rating system is from 1 to 10 – with 1 being the lowest score and 10 being the highest.

- **Adaptability:** 6/10
- **Friendliness:** 8/10
- **Health:** 6/10

- ➢ **Ease of Grooming:** 5/10
- ➢ **Amount of Shedding:** 10/10
- ➢ **Trainability:** 6/10
- ➢ **Intelligence:** 6/10
- ➢ **Exercise Needed:** 10/10
- ➢ **Playfulness:** 10/10
- ➢ **Family Friendliness:** 10/10

THE SCOTTISH TERRIER

The Scottish Terrier is a small breed of terrier type dog that originates from Scotland. The breed is also commonly known as the 'Scottie' and the 'Aberdeen Terrier.' The Scottish Terrier was initially considered to be one of the Highland breeds of terrier as it is one of the four modern terrier breeds that originates from Scotland. The other four modern terrier breeds are: the Dandie Dinmont, the Cairn, the Skye and the West Highland White Terrier. The Scottish Terrier has a soft undercoat made up of densely packed short hairs and a protective wiry overcoat that gives the Scottish Terrier a rugged appearance and physicality. The Scottish Terrier and the West Highland White Terrier are closely related as both of the breeds forefather's originate from the Perthshire and the Moor of Rannoch regions of Scotland. The Scottish Terrier was originally developed for the purpose of hunting and killing small vermin (such as mice and rats) on farms. However due to the breed's rugged coat and brave nature, the Scottish Terrier quickly began to be used to hunt both foxes and badger in the Highlands of Scotland. The temperament of dogs is normally affected by the following factors: individual personality, heredity, training and socialization. It is therefore important to make sure that you meet the puppy's mother before purchasing a Scottish Terrier. It is also important to make sure to thoroughly socialize your Scottish Terrier with strangers, children and other animals during its puppyhood. Generally speaking, the Scottish Terrier is a highly territorial, alert and feisty breed – the Scottish Terrier is actually commonly considered to be the feisty breed of Terrier! The Scottish Terrier has been nicknamed the 'Diehard,' due to its rugged nature and unyielding determination. However the Scottish Terrier is also known to be an affectionate, playful and intelligent breed that loves to interact with its owners and family unit. While the Scottish Terrier is very loving towards its family, the breed is also known to be aloof, wary and sometimes dismissive of strangers. The Scottish Terrier is not known to be an aggressive breed and can easily get along with children and other animals. However it is still considered best practice to make sure that your Scottish Terrier is properly and thoroughly socialized during its early puppyhood to avoid any potential accidents and bad behaviors. It is important to note that as a working breed, the Scottish Terrier has a high amount of energy which needs to be expended. If the Scottish Terrier has a buildup of energy it is likely to develop destructive behaviors due to boredom or hyperactivity.

Lifespan

A Scottish Terrier will normally live to be between 10 and 11 years old. However it is not uncommon for a Scottish Terrier to live to be as old as 13, providing that it does not develop any serious health issues.

Height and Weight

A fully grown Scottish Terrier will normally stand between 6 to 10 inches (15.25 to 25.5cm) tall at the shoulder. A healthy adult Scottish Terrier will normally weigh between 18 to 22 pounds (8 to 10kg). It is important to note that the weight of a healthy Scottish Terrier depends on how large the Scottish Terrier is – taller Scottish Terrier should weigh more.

Breed Characteristics

The following section will give you a simplistic overview of the characteristics of a Scottish Terrier. Our rating system is from 1 to 10 – with 1 being the lowest score and 10 being the highest.

- **Adaptability:** 6/10
- **Friendliness:** 8/10
- **Health:** 8/10
- **Ease of Grooming:** 4/10
- **Amount of Shedding:** 3/10

- **Trainability:** 6/10
- **Intelligence:** 8/10
- **Exercise Needed:** 8/10
- **Playfulness:** 8/10
- **Family Friendliness:** 10/10

THE SEALYHAM TERRIER

The Sealyham Terrier is a small to medium-sized breed of dog that is a member of the Terrier typing. The Sealyham Terrier is also commonly known as the 'Welsh Border Terrier' and the 'Cowley Terrier.' The Sealyham Terrier is considered to be one of the rarest breeds of dog that originates from Wales. The breed became extremely popular following the First World War due to its association with popular Hollywood stars and members of the British Royal Family. However in recent years the Sealyham Terrier's popularity plummeted to the point where it is actually now listed as a Vulnerable Native Breed by the Kennel Club. In 2008 the Sealyham Terrier saw an all-time low of only 43 new puppy registrations! It is believed that the Sealyham Terrier has lost popularity based upon fashion (there has been an influx of very popular 'Designer' dog breeds in recent years) and the fact that the Sealyham Terrier has reduced usefulness as a working dog. Traditionally the Sealyham Terrier was developed for the purpose of hunting small game and eliminating vermin – particularly badgers. During the period of 1850 to 1891, Wlesh Corgis, Fox Terriers and English White Terriers were mixed to create the Sealyham Terrier. The temperament of dogs is normally affected by the following factors: individual personality, heredity, training and socialization. It is therefore important to make sure that you meet the puppy's mother before purchasing a Sealyham Terrier. It is also important to make sure to thoroughly socialize your Sealyham Terrier with strangers, children and other animals during its puppyhood. Generally speaking, the Sealyham Terrier is known to be a highly loyal and affectionate pet that enjoys spending time with its family unit. However the Sealyham Terrier is also a very independent breed and can cope perfectly fine if it is left alone for extended periods of time. The Sealyham Terrier is known to be a highly adaptable breed that can live happily in countryside, town or city environments. Due to its history as a working dog, the Sealyham Terrier is a very obedient and trainable breed that makes it an easy to train working dog and an easy to socialize breed. It is important to note that as a working breed, the Sealyham Terrier has a high amount of energy which needs to be expended. If the Sealyham Terrier has a buildup of energy it is likely to develop destructive behaviors due to boredom or hyperactivity.

Lifespan

A Sealyham Terrier will normally live to be between 10 and 12 years old. However it is not uncommon for a Sealyham Terrier to live to be as old as 14, providing that it does not develop any serious health issues.

Height and Weight

A fully grown Sealyham Terrier will normally stand between 6 to 10 inches (15.25 to 25.5cm) tall at the shoulder. A healthy adult Sealyham Terrier will normally weigh between 22 to 24 pounds (10 to 11kg). It is important to note that the weight of a healthy Sealyham Terrier depends on how large the Sealyham Terrier is – taller Sealyham Terrier should weigh more.

Breed Characteristics

The following section will give you a simplistic overview of the characteristics of a Sealyham Terrier. Our rating system is from 1 to 10 – with 1 being the lowest score and 10 being the highest.

- **Adaptability:** 8/10
- **Friendliness:** 8/10
- **Health:** 9/10
- **Ease of Grooming:** 4/10
- **Amount of Shedding:** 8/10
- **Trainability:** 7/10
- **Intelligence:** 8/10
- **Exercise Needed:** 8/10
- **Playfulness:** 8/10
- **Family Friendliness:** 10/10

THE SHETLAND SHEEPDOG

The Shetland Sheepdog is a breed of herding dog that originates from Scotland. The breed is also commonly known as the 'Sheltie' and the 'Dwarf Scotch Shepherd.' The Shetland Sheepdog was actually originally called the 'Shetland Collie,' but this name causes controversy among the Rough Collie breeders, so the breed's name was formally changed to the Shetland Sheepdog. The Shetland Sheepdog was officially recognized, under its new name, by the Kennel Club in 1909. Unlike most miniature breeds, the Shetland Sheepdog was not developed by selectively breeding the smallest Rough Collies available. The Shetland Sheepdog is believed to be a mixture of the Rough Collie and a Icelandic Spitz type dog, the Pomeranian and the King Charles Spaniel. Ironically the Shetland Sheepdog in its modern form has never actually been used as working sheepdog and is actually a highly uncommon breed in its place of origin. The Shetland Sheepdog's general appearance is very similar to that of a miniature Rough Collie. The Shetland Sheepdog is a small, double coated dog with a study, athletic and agile body. The Shetland Sheepdog's double coat is a made up of an overcoat of long and rough hairs that sit on top of the breed's soft undercoat. Shetland Sheepdog with a blue merle coat are prone to having either blue eyes, or one blue eye and one brown eye, while all other colorations of Shetland Sheepdogs have dark eyes. The temperament of dogs is normally affected by the following factors: individual personality, heredity, training and socialization. It is therefore important to make sure that you meet the puppy's mother before purchasing a Shetland Sheepdog. It is also important to make sure to thoroughly socialize your Shetland Sheepdog with strangers, children and other animals during its puppyhood. Generally speaking, the Shetland Sheepdog is known to be an incredibly loyal and affectionate breed. The Shetland Sheepdog is known to love spending time with its family unit and is known to get along well with strangers, children and other animals. The Shetland Sheepdog is also an incredibly intelligent and trainable breed and it is actually ranked 6th most intelligent out of the 132 most common dog breeds. The average Shetland Sheepdog is known to be able to learn a new command after as little as five repetitions! It is important to note that as a breed developed for working purposes, the Shetland Sheepdog has a high amount of energy which needs to be expended. If the Shetland Sheepdog has a buildup of energy it is likely to develop destructive behaviors due to boredom or hyperactivity.

Lifespan

A Shetland Sheepdog will normally live to be

between 10 and 13 years old. However it is not uncommon for a Shetland Sheepdog to live to be as old as 15, providing that it does not develop any serious health issues.

Height and Weight

A fully grown Shetland Sheepdog will normally stand between 12 to 16 inches (30.5 to 40.6cm) tall at the shoulder. A healthy adult Shetland Sheepdog will normally weigh between 20 to 30 pounds (9 to 13.5kg). It is important to note that the weight of a healthy Shetland Sheepdog depends on how large the Shetland Sheepdog is – taller Shetland Sheepdog should weigh more.

Breed Characteristics

The following section will give you a simplistic overview of the characteristics of a Shetland Sheepdog. Our rating system is from 1 to 10 – with 1 being the lowest score and 10 being the highest.

- **Adaptability:** 6/10
- **Friendliness:** 10/10
- **Health:** 8/10
- **Ease of Grooming:** 5/10
- **Amount of Shedding:** 10/10

- ➢ **Trainability:** 8/10
- ➢ **Intelligence:** 10/10
- ➢ **Exercise Needed:** 8/10
- ➢ **Playfulness:** 8/10
- ➢ **Family Friendliness:** 10/10

THE SHIBA INU

The Shiba Inu is one of the six breeds of Spitz type dog that originate from Japan. The Shiba Inu is the smallest of the six breeds. The word 'Inu' in Japanese translates to 'dog.' However the origin of the prefix 'Shiba' is much less clear. The word 'Shiba' translates to 'Brushwood' in Japanese, and is in reference to a type of tree or shrub that has leaves that turn a red color in the fall. This prefix has lead there to be two different opinions as to why 'Shiba' is a part of the Shiba Inu's name. One school of thought suggests that the breed gained the prefix 'Shiba' due to the fact that the Shiba Inu was traditionally used to hunt small game in shrub land. The second school of thought suggests that the Shiba Inu gained the prefix 'Shiba' due to the fact that the breed's most common coloration is a similar red to that of a Shiba tree's leafs during fall. The Shiba Inu has a small compact body with a well-muscled and agile frame. The breed has a double coat which is a made up of an outer coat of stiff and straight hairs, and an undercoat of soft and thick fur. The Shiba Inu has short hair covering its face, legs and ears which gives the breed a fox-like appearance. The temperament of dogs is normally affected by the following factors: individual personality, heredity, training and socialization. It is therefore important to make sure that you meet the puppy's mother before purchasing a Shiba Inu. It is also important to make sure to thoroughly socialize your Shiba Inu with strangers, children and other animals during its puppyhood. Generally speaking, the Shiba Inu tends to exhibit an independent nature. The breed is also known to have a hard time getting along with smaller animals due to its extremely high prey drive but can happily get along with other dogs, strangers and small children. To minimize the chance of your Shiba Inu harassing other smaller animals, it is highly important to make sure that you properly socialize your Shiba Inu during its puppyhood. The Shiba Inu is an incredibly easy breed to housebreak due to their fastidious nature. The Shiba Inu is known to love to keep itself clean and will often lick its paws and legs in a very cat-like fashion. Due to their desire to remain as clean as possible at all times, it is not uncommon for a Shiba Inu to actually housebreak itself. It is important to note that as a working breed, the Shiba Inu has a high amount of energy which needs to be expended. If the Shiba Inu has a buildup of energy it is likely to develop destructive behaviors due to boredom or hyperactivity.

Lifespan

A Shiba Inu will normally live to be between 12 and 14 years old. However it is not uncommon for a Shiba Inu to live to be as old as 16, providing that it does not develop any serious health issues.

Height and Weight

A fully grown Shiba Inu will normally stand between 13 to 18 inches (33 to 45.75cm) tall at the shoulder. A healthy adult Shiba Inu will normally weigh between 17 to 23 pounds (7.7 to 10.5kg). It is important to note that the weight of a healthy Shiba Inu depends on how large the Shiba Inu is – taller Shiba Inu should weigh more.

Breed Characteristics

The following section will give you a simplistic overview of the characteristics of a Shiba Inu. Our rating system is from 1 to 10 – with 1 being the lowest score and 10 being the highest.

- **Adaptability:** 8/10
- **Friendliness:** 6/10
- **Health:** 6/10
- **Ease of Grooming:** 8/10
- **Amount of Shedding:** 8/10
- **Trainability:** 8/10
- **Intelligence:** 8/10
- **Exercise Needed:** 7/10
- **Playfulness:** 6/10
- **Family Friendliness:** 10/10

THE SHIH TZU

The Shih Tzu, commonly known as the 'Chrysanthemum Dog,' is a breed of toy dog that has uncertain origins. It is believed that the breed originates from Tibet and was developed in China. The Shih Tzu is a small dog with a short muzzle and large darkly colored eyes. The breed has dropped ears and an extremely long and fast growing coat which will need to be brushed daily. The Shih Tzu can come in a variety of different coat colors but it is most commonly found in white, black, grey and brown. The breed generally has a very loyal, affectionate, alert and loving temperament which has helped the Shih Tzu to become one of the most popular house hold pets in the United States of America and throughout Europe. The Shih Tzu is especially popular for city dwellers (owners who live in apartments or houses with small gardens) due to the fact that the breed needs minimal exercise.

Lifespan

A Shih Tzu will normally live to be between 10 and 14 years old. However it is not uncommon for a Shih Tzu to live to be as old as 16 as long as they do not develop and serious health issues.

Height and Weight

An adult Shih Tzu will normally grow to be between 9 and 10 inches (23 to 25.5cm) tall at the shoulder – however it is not uncommon for a Shih Tzu to grow to be as tall as 11 inches (28.5cm) tall at the shoulder. Males normally weigh more than females and will normally weigh between 14 and 16 pounds (6.25 to 7.25kg). Females will normally weigh between 9 and 14 pounds (4 to 6.25kg) but it is not uncommon for larger females to also weigh as much as 16 pounds.

The Tea Cup and Imperial Shih Tzu

It is important to note that there is no such breed as a "Teacup" or "Imperial" Shih Tzu. These terms are used by untrustworthy breeders as a marketing ploy. A "Teacup" Shih Tzu is just a small Shih Tzu. An "Imperial" Shih Tzu is simply a large Shih Tzu. Do not allow yourself to be swindled by dodgy breeders!

Breed Characteristics

The following section will give you a simplistic overview of the characteristics of a Shih Tzu. Our rating system is from 1 to 10 – with 1 being the lowest score and 10 being the highest.

➢ **Adaptability:** 6/10

- ➢ **Friendliness:** 10/10
- ➢ **Health:** 6/10
- ➢ **Ease of Grooming:** 2/10
- ➢ **Amount of Shedding:** 7/10
- ➢ **Trainability:** 6/10
- ➢ **Intelligence:** 8/10
- ➢ **Exercise Needed:** 6/10
- ➢ **Playfulness:** 8/10
- ➢ **Family Friendliness:** 10/10

THE SIBERIAN HUSKY

The Siberian Husky is a medium sized working dog that belongs to the Spitz genetic family. The breed originates from Siberia, Russia – hence the name 'Siberian Husky.' The Siberian Husky was originally bred to help the Chukchi people of Russia during their hunting expeditions. The breed has an incredibly thick double coat made up of a thick undercoat and much softer outer coat. The double coat was originally needed to combat the extremely cold weather present within the Siberian Artic. The breed is also incredibly active, energetic and resilient due to its place of origin being such a harsh environment. The Siberian Husky is highly recognizable due to its large erect triangular ear, 'almond' shaped eyes, double coat and facial distinctive markings.

Lifespan

Siberian Huskies normally live to be between 10 and 12 years old. However it is not uncommon for a Siberian Husky to live to be as old as 15, providing they do not develop any serious health issues.

Height and Weight

A fully grown Siberian Husky will normally grow to

be between 20 to 23 inches (51 to 59cm) tall at the shoulder. Males tend to be heavier than females. A fully grown male will normally weigh between 45 and 60 pounds (20 to 27kg). Fully grown females, on the other hands, will normally weigh between 35 and 50 pounds (16 to 22.5kg).

Coat

The Siberian Husky has a coat that is dramatically thicker than average. As previously mentioned the Siberian Husky's coat comprises of two layers: a dense undercoat and a longer topcoat of short hairs. The dual coat allows the Siberian Husky to withstand temperatures as low as -76 degrees Fahrenheit (-60 degrees Celsius)! Siberian Huskies come in a wide variety of coat colorations and patterns. The most common coat colors are black and white. However the Siberian Husky also comes in the following rarer colorations: silver, copper-red, pure white and blondish. Most Huskies will have some form of white facial markings, white feet and a white tipped tail.

Behavior

It is important to note that Siberian Huskies do not bark – they howl! The fact that they howl means that you need to carefully considered where you are living –

you do not want to disturb your neighbors. The Siberian Husky is also a breed known to escape gardens by either chewing through, digging under or jump over fences. It is recommended to have a 6ft (1.8m) metal fence in your garden to prevent your Siberian Husky from escaping. The breed has always been raised in family settings which makes the Siberian Husky extremely good around children. The Siberian Husky needs a lot of exercise and walking on a daily basis – they are known to develop destructive behaviors if they are not provided with enough exercise. It is recommend to take your Siberian Husky on at least one 30 minute walk a day – but it is considered best practice to take it on between 2 and 4 half an hour walks.

Breed Characteristics

The following section will give you a simplistic overview of the characteristics of a Siberian Husky. Our rating system is from 1 to 10 – with 1 being the lowest score and 10 being the highest.

- **Adaptability:** 6/10
- **Friendliness:** 10/10
- **Health:** 8/10
- **Ease of Grooming:** 4/10
- **Amount of Shedding:** 6/10
- **Trainability:** 8/10

- **Intelligence:** 6/10
- **Exercise Needed:** 10/10
- **Playfulness:** 10/10
- **Family Friendliness:** 10/10

THE SILKY TERRIER

The Silky Terrier is a small breed of dog that is a member of the Terrier typing. The breed is also commonly nicknamed the 'Silky' as well as being known as the 'Australian Silky Terrier,' which is a name that pays homage to the Silky Terrier's country of origin – Australia. Despite the breed being developed in Australia, the Silky Terrier's ancestral history originates in Great Britain as it is closely related to the Yorkshire Terrier. According to the American Kennel Club, the Silky Terrier came into existence during the early 19th century when the Yorkshire Terrier was bred with the Australian Terrier. Unlike most terrier breeds, the Silky Terrier was developed primarily for the purpose of being an urban pet and companion. However, the Silky Terrier has been known to be used as a working dog in specific parts of Australia where it is tasked with catching and killing snakes. The Silky Terrier has a small and compact body and small legs. The Silky Terrier has a very unique and distinct coat that is made up of long, silky hair that parts down the dog's back and hangs low to the floor. The breed standard describes the Silky Terrier's coat as being 'flat, fine and glossy.' The Silky Terrier's coat normally comes in either grey, white, tan or blue. The Silky Terrier should be slightly longer than it is tall and should be athletic enough to catch vermin and snakes if it is tasked to do so. The temperament of dogs is normally affected by the following factors: individual personality, heredity, training and socialization. It is therefore important to make sure that you meet the puppy's mother before purchasing a Silky Terrier. It is also important to make sure to thoroughly socialize your Silky Terrier with strangers, children and other animals during its puppyhood. Generally speaking, the Silky Terrier is known to be an alert, active and playful breed. Due to the breed's innate desire to hunt small animals it is highly recommended to have a securely fenced yard to allow your Silky Terrier to play and exercise in. It is important to note that as a working breed, the Silky Terrier has a high amount of energy which needs to be expended. If the Silky Terrier has a buildup of energy it is likely to develop destructive behaviors due to boredom or hyperactivity.

Lifespan

A Silky Terrier will normally live to be between 12 and 13 years old. However it is not uncommon for a Silky Terrier to live to be as old as 15, providing that it does not develop any serious health issues.

Height and Weight

A fully grown Silky Terrier will normally stand

between 9 to 10 inches (22.86 to 25.4cm) tall at the shoulder. A healthy adult Silky Terrier will normally weigh between 8 to 10 pounds (3.6 to 4.5kg). It is important to note that the weight of a healthy Silky Terrier depends on how large the Silky Terrier is – taller Silky Terrier should weigh more.

Breed Characteristics

The following section will give you a simplistic overview of the characteristics of a Silky Terrier. Our rating system is from 1 to 10 – with 1 being the lowest score and 10 being the highest.

- **Adaptability:** 6/10
- **Friendliness:** 6/10
- **Health:** 8/10
- **Ease of Grooming:** 8/10
- **Amount of Shedding:** 5/10
- **Trainability:** 8/10
- **Intelligence:** 8/10
- **Exercise Needed:** 8/10
- **Playfulness:** 8/10
- **Family Friendliness:** 8/10

THE SKYE TERRIER

The Skye Terrier is a small breed of dog that originates from Scotland. The Kennel Club states that the Skye Terrier is "one of the most endangered native dog breeds in the United Kingdom." Scotland has developed multiple breeds of Terrier type dogs, and the Skye Terrier is among the oldest of them. The Skye Terrier was developed along the west coast of Scotland and was used primarily for the purpose of hunting foxes and otter from among the rocky cairns. The breed is named after the Isle of Skye, where the purest Skye Terrier are believed to come from. The Skye Terrier rose to popularity after one accompanied Mary, Queen of Scots to her execution. The Skye Terrier's desirability grow further when, in 1840, Queen Victoria began keeping both drop and prick eared Skye Terrier. Due to its popularity, the Skye Terrier quickly got exported to America and was registered to the American Kennel Club for the first time in 1887. However despite the breed's popularity, the Skye Terrier is now considered to be one of the least known breeds within the Terrier typing. The Skye Terrier is actually under threat of extinction as only 30 were born in the United Kingdom in 2005 – which makes it the most vulnerable native breed in the country! The Skye Terrier has a unique double coat that is made up of a short, soft undercoat and a hard, straight topcoat. The Skye Terrier has short hairs on its head that veil its forehead and eyes, forming a mock beard. The temperament of dogs is normally affected by the following factors: individual personality, heredity, training and socialization. It is therefore important to make sure that you meet the puppy's mother before purchasing a Skye Terrier. It is also important to make sure to thoroughly socialize your Skye Terrier with strangers, children and other animals during its puppyhood. Generally speaking, the Skye Terrier is known to be a good natured, brave and loyal breed of dog. The Skye Terrier is known to be aloof and suspicious of strangers which makes it a perfect watchdog. The Skye Terrier is known to be a sensitive breed but not a submissive breed – and will often explore on its own if left to its own devices. It is important to note that as a working breed, the Skye Terrier has a high amount of energy which needs to be expended. If the Skye Terrier has a buildup of energy it is likely to develop destructive behaviors due to boredom or hyperactivity.

Lifespan

A Skye Terrier will normally live to be between 10 and 12 years old. However it is not uncommon for a Skye Terrier to live to be as old as 14, providing that it does not develop any serious health issues.

Height and Weight

A fully grown Skye Terrier will normally stand between 8 to 10 inches (20.3 to 25.5cm) tall at the shoulder. A healthy adult Skye Terrier will normally weigh between 25 to 40 pounds (11.3 to 18.15kg). It is important to note that the weight of a healthy Skye Terrier depends on how large the Skye Terrier is – taller Skye Terrier should weigh more.

Breed Characteristics

The following section will give you a simplistic overview of the characteristics of a Skye Terrier. Our rating system is from 1 to 10 – with 1 being the lowest score and 10 being the highest.

- **Adaptability:** 8/10
- **Friendliness:** 8/10
- **Health:** 9/10
- **Ease of Grooming:** 7/10
- **Amount of Shedding:** 7/10
- **Trainability:** 8/10
- **Intelligence:** 8/10
- **Exercise Needed:** 8/10
- **Playfulness:** 8/10
- **Family Friendliness:** 10/10

THE SLOUGHI

The Sloughi is a breed of sighthound that originates from North Africa. It is believed that the Sloughi originated from Ethiopia. It is also believed that the Sloughi, or its close ancestors, is an ancient breed as there are multiple tributes to the Pharaohs of Egypt that depict smooth coated, lop-eared sighthounds that highly resemble the Sloughi. The Sloughi is closely related to other breeds that have originated from Africa such as the Basenji, the Sica and the Nguni. The Sloughi was, and still is, used for hunting and guarding purposes in its native countries. In modern times, the Sloughi is mainly found in Morocco, Algeria, Tunisia and Libya. Morocco is actually responsible for creating the Sloughi's FCI breeding standard. Despite the fact that the Sloughi is an ancient breed, it only got recognized by the American Kennel Club as of January 1, 2016 when it became eligible to compete in the American Kennel Club Hound Group. The Sloughi is a medium-large, short-haired, smooth-coated breed of sighthound that has an extremely agile and athletic build. The Sloughi has always excelled at hunting hare, fox, jackal, wild pigs and gazelles due to its strength, speed and endurance. While the Sloughi is not a fragile breed it also has an heir of class and elegance. The temperament of dogs is normally affected by the following factors: individual personality, heredity, training and socialization. It is therefore important to make sure that you meet the puppy's mother before purchasing a Sloughi. It is also important to make sure to thoroughly socialize your Sloughi with strangers, children and other animals during its puppyhood. Generally speaking, the Sloughi, like most breeds of sighthound, is a highly loyal and sensitive breed that loves nothing more than spending time with its family unit. The Sloughi does not handle harsh criticism or negative tones very well and should therefore always be treated empathetically during training and day to day life. The breed is also known to be incredibly intelligent, athletic and conscientious. It is important to note that as a working breed, the Sloughi has a high amount of energy which needs to be expended. If the Sloughi has a buildup of energy it is likely to develop destructive behaviors due to boredom or hyperactivity.

Lifespan

A Sloughi will normally live to be between 12 and 13 years old. However it is not uncommon for a Sloughi to live to be as old as 16, providing that it does not develop any serious health issues.

Height and Weight

A fully grown Sloughi will normally stand between 24 to 29 inches (61 to 73.5cm) tall at the shoulder. A healthy adult Sloughi will normally weigh between 40 to 63 pounds (18 to 28.5kg). It is important to note that the weight of a healthy Sloughi depends on how large the Sloughi is – taller Sloughi should weigh more.

Breed Characteristics

The following section will give you a simplistic overview of the characteristics of a Sloughi. Our rating system is from 1 to 10 – with 1 being the lowest score and 10 being the highest.

- **Adaptability:** 6/10
- **Friendliness:** 8/10
- **Health:** 6/10
- **Ease of Grooming:** 10/10
- **Amount of Shedding:** 6/10
- **Trainability:** 6/10
- **Intelligence:** 8/10
- **Exercise Needed:** 9/10
- **Playfulness:** 6/10
- **Family Friendliness:** 10/10

THE SMALL MUNSTERLANDER POINTER

The Small Munsterlander Pointer is a versatile breed of hunting dog that was developed in Munster, Germany. The breed has traits of a retriever, a hunting dog and a pointer. The Large Small Munsterlander is of no relation to the Small Munsterlander Pointer as they share no common breeding stock – the two breed's share a similar name solely based upon the place of their development. The Small Munsterlander Pointer looks very similar to both spaniels and setters but is a much more versatile hunting breed that is capable of easily hunting on land and in water. The Small Munsterlander Pointer is a relatively rare breed in the United States of America, with only around 2000 registered to the Kennel Club. There is a high demand from American hunters and breeders typically give newly born Small Munsterlander Pointer to hunters rather than to family for companionship purposes. However the Small Munsterlander Pointer is dramatically more common throughout Germany, Belgium, Denmark, the Czech Republic and the Netherlands where they are bred, trained and tested to a high standard to ensure that the Small Munsterlander Pointer remains one of the most versatile breeds of hunting dogs in existence. The Small Munsterlander Pointer is an agile, athletic and well-muscled breed that has an heir of elegance. The Small

Munsterlander Pointer should appear to be an equal mix of both strong and graceful. The breed's coat is of a medium length and is made up of densely packed glossy hairs of either a wavy or straight texture. The Small Munsterlander Pointer's coat should be of a white or ticked coloration with large patches of brown. The temperament of dogs is normally affected by the following factors: individual personality, heredity, training and socialization. It is therefore important to make sure that you meet the puppy's mother before purchasing a Small Munsterlander Pointer. It is also important to make sure to thoroughly socialize your Small Munsterlander Pointer with strangers, children and other animals during its puppyhood. Generally speaking, the Small Munsterlander Pointer is a highly intelligent breed that is incredibly trainable and attentive to the wishes of its owners. The Small Munsterlander Pointer is also a highly empathetic breed and therefore does not cope well with negative training, aggressive tones or scolding. It is very important to create a relaxed and friendly environment while training your Small Munsterlander Pointer. It is important to note that as a working breed, the Small Munsterlander Pointer has a high amount of energy which needs to be expended. If the Small Munsterlander Pointer has a buildup of energy it is likely to develop destructive behaviors due to boredom or hyperactivity.

Lifespan

A Small Munsterlander Pointer will normally live to be between 11 and 12 years old. However it is not uncommon for a Small Munsterlander Pointer to live to be as old as 14, providing that it does not develop any serious health issues.

Height and Weight

A fully grown Small Munsterlander Pointer will normally stand between 19 to 22 inches (48 to 56cm) tall at the shoulder. A healthy adult Small Munsterlander Pointer will normally weigh between 40 to 60 pounds (18 to 27kg). It is important to note that the weight of a healthy Small Munsterlander Pointer depends on how large the Small Munsterlander Pointer is – taller Small Munsterlander Pointer should weigh more.

Breed Characteristics

The following section will give you a simplistic overview of the characteristics of a Small Munsterlander Pointer. Our rating system is from 1 to 10 – with 1 being the lowest score and 10 being the highest.

- **Adaptability:** 6/10
- **Friendliness:** 10/10
- **Health:** 10/10

- ➢ **Ease of Grooming:** 7/10
- ➢ **Amount of Shedding:** 7/10
- ➢ **Trainability:** 9/10
- ➢ **Intelligence:** 10/10
- ➢ **Exercise Needed:** 10/10
- ➢ **Playfulness:** 8/10
- ➢ **Family Friendliness:** 10/10

THE SOFT COATED WHEATEN TERRIER

The Soft Coated Wheaten Terrier is a pure breed of dog that originates from Ireland. The breed is also commonly known as the 'Irish Soft Coated Terrier,' the 'Wheaten' and the 'Wheatie.' The Soft Coated Wheaten Terrier has a single coat which shed very lightly, so they can easily be tolerated by people who have an allergy to dog hair. The Soft Coated Wheaten Terrier has two coat types: Irish and American. The Irish coat variation is considered to be the breed standard and is made up of silky, wavy hair. The American coat variation is made up of much thicker hairs that give the coat a wooly texture. The Soft Coated Wheaten Terrier was originally developed in Ireland for the purpose of being an all-purpose farm dog. The breed was mainly tasked with herding, guarding livestock, watching over the farm and family home, and vermin hunting and killing. The Soft Coated Wheaten Terrier shares a very similar ancestral history to the Kerry Blue Terrier and the Irish Terrier but was not owned by gentry and the middle class. The fact that the Soft Coated Wheaten Terrier was owned by the lower classes gained it the nickname of the 'Poor Man's Wolfhound.' In modern times the Soft Coated Wheaten Terrier is mainly kept as a companion breed but is also used in obedience, tracking and agility competitions as well as being used as a therapy dog. Puppies are born with dark coats of either a red, brown, mahogany or white coloration. As the puppies age their coats gradually turn into a wheat coloration but it is not uncommon for an adult Soft Coated Wheaten Terrier to have darker guard hairs scattered around its coat. The temperament of dogs is normally affected by the following factors: individual personality, heredity, training and socialization. It is therefore important to make sure that you meet the puppy's mother before purchasing a Soft Coated Wheaten Terrier. It is also important to make sure to thoroughly socialize your Soft Coated Wheaten Terrier with strangers, children and other animals during its puppyhood. Generally speaking, the Soft Coated Wheaten Terrier is an incredibly playful and energetic breed. The breed is also known to be very intelligent and head strong, so it is considered best practice to train a Soft Coated Wheaten Terrier in a very friendly, clam and patient environment. As previously mentioned the Soft Coated Wheaten Terrier is used as a therapy dog due to its empathetic nature – this empathetic nature means that the Soft Coated Wheaten Terrier does not do well with harsh or unfriendly training. The Soft Coated Wheaten Terrier is also known to be incredibly loving, affectionate and protective towards its family unit. This sometimes leads the Soft Coated Wheaten Terrier to be highly suspicious of strangers – but aggression is considered to be incredibly rare. It is important to note that as a working breed, the Soft Coated Wheaten Terrier has a high amount of energy which needs to be expended. If the Soft Coated Wheaten Terrier has a buildup of energy it is likely to develop destructive behaviors due to boredom or hyperactivity.

Lifespan

A Soft Coated Wheaten Terrier will normally live to be between 12 and 13 years old. However it is not uncommon for a Soft Coated Wheaten Terrier to live to be as old as 15, providing that it does not develop any serious health issues.

Height and Weight

A fully grown Soft Coated Wheaten Terrier will normally stand between 17 to 19 inches (43.2 to 48.25cm) tall at the shoulder. A healthy adult Soft Coated Wheaten Terrier will normally weigh between 30 to 40 pounds (13.6 to 18.1kg). It is important to note that the weight of a healthy Soft Coated Wheaten Terrier depends on how large the Soft Coated Wheaten Terrier is – taller Soft Coated Wheaten Terrier should weigh more.

Breed Characteristics

The following section will give you a simplistic overview of the characteristics of a Soft Coated Wheaten Terrier. Our rating system is from 1 to 10 – with 1 being the lowest score and 10 being the highest.

- **Adaptability:** 6/10
- **Friendliness:** 10/10
- **Health:** 8/10
- **Ease of Grooming:** 7/10
- **Amount of Shedding:** 3/10
- **Trainability:** 7/10
- **Intelligence:** 8/10
- **Exercise Needed:** 8/10
- **Playfulness:** 10/10
- **Family Friendliness:** 10/10

THE STABYHOUN

The Stabyhoun is one of the top five rarest breeds of dog in the world as of 2013! The Stabyhoun originates from the Frisian forest area located in the south east of Friesland. The Stabyhoun is also commonly known as the 'Stabij,' the 'Beike' and the 'Friese Stabij.' The breed has been mentioned in Dutch literature since the early 1800s but the breed was not exported to outside of the Netherlands until the 1960s. The breed's name roughly translates to mean 'stand by me.' There are only a few thousand Stabyhouns in existence today despite the breed being considered a national treasure in the Netherlands. Historically the Stabyhoun was only owned by farmers who has limited financial means and thus needed a breed of dog that was capable of executing multiple farm jobs such as guarding livestock, hunting and watching over the farm house. The Stabyhoun was also commonly as a vermin catcher and exterminator. The Stabyhoun also has an incredibly adept sense of smell that also lead it to be used as a retreiver and pointer during hunts. In modern times the Stabyhoun has a small dedicated following of Dutch sportsmen and homeowners who are working on increasing the breed's numbers. The Stabyhoun has recently become of interest to dog enthusiast in the United Kingdom, Scandinavia and North America. The Stabyhoun has a long, soft and silky coat that covers its sturdily built frame. The Stabyhoun is a perfectly built all-purpose farm dog as it is neither muscular nor slender. The temperament of dogs is normally affected by the following factors: individual personality, heredity, training and socialization. It is therefore important to make sure that you meet the puppy's mother before purchasing a Stabyhoun. It is also important to make sure to thoroughly socialize your Stabyhoun with strangers, children and other animals during its puppyhood. Generally speaking, the Stabyhoun is a good natured breed that has a friendly and gentle disposition. The breed is sensitive, intelligent, patient and highly eager to please its owners. The Stabyhoun makes a perfect household pet due to its high tolerance of children, strangers and other animals. It is important to note that as a working breed, the Stabyhoun has a high amount of energy which needs to be expended. If the Stabyhoun has a buildup of energy it is likely to develop destructive behaviors due to boredom or hyperactivity.

Lifespan

A Stabyhoun will normally live to be between 12 and 13 years old. However it is not uncommon for a Stabyhoun to live to be as old as 14, providing that it does not develop any serious health issues.

Height and Weight

A fully grown Stabyhoun will normally stand between 18 to 20 inches (45.75 to 51cm) tall at the shoulder. A healthy adult Stabyhoun will normally weigh between 40 to 50 pounds (18 to 22.5kg). It is important to note that the weight of a healthy Stabyhoun depends on how large the Stabyhoun is – taller Stabyhoun should weigh more.

Breed Characteristics

The following section will give you a simplistic overview of the characteristics of a Stabyhoun. Our rating system is from 1 to 10 – with 1 being the lowest score and 10 being the highest.

- **Adaptability:** 6/10
- **Friendliness:** 8/10
- **Health:** 10/10
- **Ease of Grooming:** 7/10
- **Amount of Shedding:** 6/10
- **Trainability:** 8/10
- **Intelligence:** 10/10
- **Exercise Needed:** 8/10
- **Playfulness:** 10/10
- **Family Friendliness:** 10/10

THE STAFFORDSHIRE BULL TERRIER

The Staffordshire Bull Terrier (commonly known as a 'Staffy') is a medium-sized, short-coated breed of dog that originated in England. The Staffordshire Bull Terrier was originally developed, in the 19th century, to be used in fights against bulls and bears. Due to its history in 'Blood Sports,' the Staffordshire Bull Terrier is a sturdily built and muscular breed. The breed has become an excellent companion dog due to its loving and loyal temperament. A Staffordshire Bull Terrier should not be left to live alone outside as they thrive on the presence and companionship of a family unit. The breed love children, but due to their strength they should not be left alone with small children. It is important to always supervise your children around your dog. Overall the Staffordshire Bull Terrier is a very intelligent, loyal, free thinking and loving breed that would make a great addition to any family unit. Due to the breeds tendency to be 'free thinking' it is recommended that the Staffordshire Bull Terrier should only be owned by experienced and confident dog owners.

Lifespan

A Staffordshire Bull Terrier will normally live for between 10 and 12 years. However it is not uncommon for a Staffordshire Bull Terrier to live to be as old as 14, providing they do not develop any serious health issues.

Height and Weight

A fully grown Staffordshire Bull Terrier will normally be between 14 and 16 inches (35.5 to 40.5cm) tall at the shoulder. A healthy adult Staffordshire Bull Terrier should weigh between 24 and 38 pounds (11 to 17kg), dependent on their respective size.

Socialization

The Staffordshire Bull Terrier is known to have a tendency to be aggressive towards unknown dogs and other animals. It is therefore important to socialize your Staffordshire Bull Terrier at an early age. If properly socialized a Staffordshire Bull Terrier can do well with other dogs and animals. However it is considered best practice to never walk your Staffordshire Bull Terrier off its leash as a precaution.

Breed Characteristics

The following section will give you a simplistic overview of the characteristics of a Staffordshire Bull Terrier. Our rating system is from 1 to 10 – with 1 being the lowest score and 10 being the highest.

- **Adaptability:** 3/10
- **Friendliness:** 8/10
- **Health:** 6/10
- **Ease of Grooming:** 10/10
- **Amount of Shedding:** 6/10
- **Trainability:** 6/10
- **Intelligence:** 6/10
- **Exercise Needed:** 8/10
- **Playfulness:** 10/10
- **Family Friendliness:** 10/10

THE STANDARD SCHNAUZER

The Standard Schnauzer is a breed of dog that originated in Germany during the 15th and 16th centuries. The breed is also commonly known as the 'Wirehair Pinscher,' the 'Mittleshnauzer' and as simply the 'Schnauzer.' The name Schnauzer translates to 'Snouter,' as the German word for 'Snout' colloquially means 'moustache,' which is a reference to the Standard Schnauzer's distinctively bearded snout. The Standard Schnauzer was developed for the purpose of being a medium sized breed that is capable of both herding flocks of sheep and cattle, guarding cattle and also as an all-purpose farm house ratter. The original Standard Schnauzer stock was mixed with the German Black Standard Poodle to give the Standard Schnauzer a more 'regal' appearance and a higher level of trainability and intelligence. The Standard Schnauzer is easily distinguishable due to their long bearded snout and low hanging eyebrows. The breed's coat will normally come in a salt and pepper coloration. However the breed's coat can also come in a solid black coloration – but this is much rarer than the standard salt and pepper coat. The Standard Schnauzer's coat is made up of long wiry hairs that lie flat to the dog's body. The temperament of dogs is normally affected by the following factors: individual personality, heredity, training and socialization. It is therefore important to make sure that you meet the puppy's mother before purchasing a Standard Schnauzer. It is also important to make sure to thoroughly socialize your Standard Schnauzer with strangers, children and other animals during its puppyhood. Generally speaking, the temperament of a Standard Schnauzer is that of an incredibly loyal, protective and family orientated dog. The Standard Schnauzer is known to 'protect' its home from intruders with a loud and deep bark. Due to this fact the Standard Schnauzer makes a perfect watchdog as it is highly suspicious of all strangers and unknown noises. The Standard Schnauzer is also a highly intelligent and trainable breed. However the Standard Schnauzer has also been known to have a strong-willed personality which means that all training sessions should be administered by a strong-willed and confident owner. It is also important to remember that as a working breed, the Standard Schnauzer also tends to be an incredibly active and athletic breed. It is therefore incredibly important to provide your Standard Schnauzer with adequate exercise to make sure that it does not develop any destructive behaviors due to being bored or having an abundance of unspent energy.

Lifespan

A Standard Schnauzer will normally live to be between 13 and 14 years old. However it is not uncommon for a Standard Schnauzer to live to be as old as 16, providing that it does not develop any serious health issues.

Height and Weight

A fully grown Standard Schnauzer will normally stand between 16 to 20 inches (40.5 to 51cm) tall at the shoulder. A healthy adult Standard Schnauzer will normally weigh between 30 to 50 pounds (13.6 to 22.6kg). It is important to note that the weight of a healthy Standard Schnauzer depends on how large the Standard Schnauzer is – taller Standard Schnauzer should weigh more.

Breed Characteristics

The following section will give you a simplistic overview of the characteristics of a Standard Schnauzer. Our rating system is from 1 to 10 – with 1 being the lowest score and 10 being the highest.

- **Adaptability:** 6/10
- **Friendliness:** 6/10
- **Health:** 9/10

- ➢ **Ease of Grooming:** 5/10
- ➢ **Amount of Shedding:** 1/10
- ➢ **Trainability:** 8/10
- ➢ **Intelligence:** 10/10
- ➢ **Exercise Needed:** 10/10
- ➢ **Playfulness:** 10/10
- ➢ **Family Friendliness:** 9/10

THE SUSSEX SPANIEL

The Sussex Spaniel is a breed of dog that was originally developed in Sussex, which is located in the south of England. The Sussex Spaniel is commonly nicknamed simply the 'Sussex.' The Sussex Spaniel has a compact body that lies relatively low to the ground and is incredibly similar in appearance to the Clumber Spaniel. The Sussex Spaniel was originally developed in the last 1700s for the specific purpose of hunting and working in the rough terrain and large amount of undergrowth found in Sussex. The Sussex Spaniel was bred to be loyal, hardy and vocal – as when it was hunting, the Sussex Spaniel was tasked with alerting the hunter of quarry with short sharp barks. The Sussex Spaniel was bred specifically for its barking ability, as most of the other Spaniels at the time (such as the Norfolk Spaniel, the Field Spaniel and the English Springer Spaniel) were mainly quiet breeds. The Sussex Spaniel almost went extinct during the Second World War but was saved by a single dedicated breed named Joy Freer. All modern Sussex Spaniel as directly descended from the dogs Freer saved, raised and bred. In 2004 the Sussex Spaniel was classified as a 'Vulnerable native breed,' which means that under 300 new Sussex Spaniel are registered to the English Kennel Club – in 2008 only 56 Sussex Spaniel puppies were registered! Despite the Sussex Spaniel not being an overly popular breed in the United Kingdom, they have gained popularity in the United States of America and are recognized by all the world's major Kennel Clubs. The Sussex Spaniel has a unique golden liver-colored coat – however the Sussex Spaniel can also have a black or sand colored coat but these colorations are much rarer. The breed has a silky thick top coat, feathering on its legs, chest and ears and a water-resistant undercoat. The temperament of dogs is normally affected by the following factors: individual personality, heredity, training and socialization. It is therefore important to make sure that you meet the puppy's mother before purchasing a Sussex Spaniel. It is also important to make sure to thoroughly socialize your Sussex Spaniel with strangers, children and other animals during its puppyhood. Generally speaking, the temperament of a Sussex Spaniel is calm, loyal and respectful. The Sussex Spaniel is a highly energetic breed but will keep itself in check around smaller animals, children and strangers. The Sussex Spaniel is also known to be a people orientated breed that loves nothing more than spending time with its close family. It is also important to remember that as a working breed, the Sussex Spaniel also tends to be an incredibly active and athletic breed. It is therefore incredibly important to provide your Sussex Spaniel with adequate exercise to make sure that it does not develop any destructive behaviors due to being bored or having an abundance of unspent energy.

Lifespan

A Sussex Spaniel will normally live to be between 10 and 12 years old. However it is not uncommon for a Sussex Spaniel to live to be as old as 14, providing that it does not develop any serious health issues.

Height and Weight

A fully grown Sussex Spaniel will normally stand between 12 to 15 inches (30.5 to 38cm) tall at the shoulder. A healthy adult Sussex Spaniel will normally weigh between 30 to 45 pounds (13.5 to 20.5kg). It is important to note that the weight of a healthy Sussex Spaniel depends on how large the Sussex Spaniel is – taller Sussex Spaniel should weigh more.

Breed Characteristics

The following section will give you a simplistic overview of the characteristics of a Sussex Spaniel. Our rating system is from 1 to 10 – with 1 being the lowest score and 10 being the highest.

- **Adaptability:** 8/10
- **Friendliness:** 10/10

- ➢ **Health:** 6/10
- ➢ **Ease of Grooming:** 8/10
- ➢ **Amount of Shedding:** 5/10
- ➢ **Trainability:** 6/10
- ➢ **Intelligence:** 10/10
- ➢ **Exercise Needed:** 6/10
- ➢ **Playfulness:** 8/10
- ➢ **Family Friendliness:** 10/10

THE SWEDISH VALLHUND

The Swedish Vallhund is a small breed of dog that originates from Sweden. The Swedish Vallhund is also commonly known as the 'Swedish Cattle Dog' and the 'Swedish Shepherd.' The Swedish Vallhund originates from the Vastergotland county of Sweden and is therefore also commonly known as the 'Vastgotaspets.' The Swedish Vallhund was developed over 1,000 years ago for the purpose of herding and driving cattle as well as guarding and watching over human settlements. The breed was introduced to the United Kingdom during the Viking invasion and settling during the eighth and ninth centuries. It is believed that the Swedish Vallhund played a part in the development of the modern Lancashire Heeler and the Welsh Corgi – as the three breeds are very similar both in terms of personality and appearance. The Swedish Vallhund is related to larger Spitz type dogs and moose hunting dogs that originated in Scandinavia. The skeleton of a Swedish Vallhund is remarkably similar to that of the much larger Norwegian Elkhound. The Swedish Vallhund has a large wedge shaped head, with large pricked ears and brown oval shaped eyes. The breed's coat is made up of a short, harsh and tightly packed topcoat and a soft, dense undercoat. The Swedish Vallhund coat comes in a wide variety of greys, browns and reds. It is very common for a Swedish Vallhund to have light markings on its shoulders and chest. The temperament of dogs is normally affected by the following factors: individual personality, heredity, training and socialization. It is therefore important to make sure that you meet the puppy's mother before purchasing a Swedish Vallhund. It is also important to make sure to thoroughly socialize your Swedish Vallhund with strangers, children and other animals during its puppyhood. Generally speaking, the temperament of a Swedish Vallhund is that of an intelligent, loyal, athletic and friendly breed. The Swedish Vallhund is highly trainable and can adapt to new situations quickly. The Swedish Vallhund is known to love nothing more than spending time with its direct family unit. The Swedish Vallhund makes a perfect playmate for a child due to its playful and respectful nature. The Swedish Vallhund also has a small compact body which makes it relatively hardy – which again makes it a perfect pet for a family with small children. It is also important to remember that as a working breed, the Swedish Vallhund also tends to be an incredibly active and athletic breed. It is therefore incredibly important to provide your Swedish Vallhund with adequate exercise to make sure that it does not develop any destructive behaviors due to being bored or having an abundance of unspent energy.

Lifespan

A Swedish Vallhund will normally live to be between 10 and 12 years old. However it is not uncommon for a Swedish Vallhund to live to be as old as 15, providing that it does not develop any serious health issues.

Height and Weight

A fully grown Swedish Vallhund will normally stand between 11 to 14 inches (? to ?cm) tall at the shoulder. A healthy adult Swedish Vallhund will normally weigh between 22 to 35 pounds (? to ?kg). It is important to note that the weight of a healthy Swedish Vallhund depends on how large the Swedish Vallhund is – taller Swedish Vallhund should weigh more.

Breed Characteristics

The following section will give you a simplistic overview of the characteristics of a Swedish Vallhund. Our rating system is from 1 to 10 – with 1 being the lowest score and 10 being the highest.

- **Adaptability:** 7/10
- **Friendliness:** 8/10
- **Health:** 8/10
- **Ease of Grooming:** 10/10

- ➢ **Amount of Shedding:** 1/10
- ➢ **Trainability:** 8/10
- ➢ **Intelligence:** 10/10
- ➢ **Exercise Needed:** 10/10
- ➢ **Playfulness:** 10/10
- ➢ **Family Friendliness:** 10/10

Encyclopedia of Dog Breeds

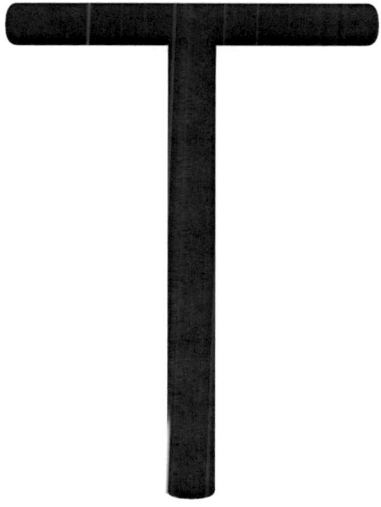

THE TIBETAN MASTIFF

The Tibetan Mastiff is a large breed of dog that originates from Tibet. The Tibetan Mastiff was developed by the nomadic cultures found throughout Tibet, India, Mongolia and Nepal and is known to have diverged from the gray wolf over 42,000 years ago. The Tibetan Mastiff is related to the Great Pyrenees, Bernese Mountain Dog, the Rottweiler and the Saint Bernard – all of these breeds are believed to have descended from the ancient Tibetan Mastiff. The Tibetan Mastiff was originally used by nomadic tribes for the purpose of protecting their sheep from wolves, leopard, tigers, bears and other large predators. The breed was also kept in encampments as a watchdog and a protective guardian. The Tibetan Mastiff has a much lower hemoglobin level compared to low-altitude dog breeds and thus has a very low chance of developing hypoxia. It is believed that the Tibetan Mastiff's low hemoglobin level is due to the breed's prehistoric interbreeding with Tibetan Wolves. The Tibetan Mastiff is split into two different variants: the 'Dokhyi' and the 'Tsang-khyi.' The 'Tsang-khyi,' also commonly known as the 'Monestary' variant, is generally larger, more heavily boned and has a more face wrinkling and haw than the 'Dokhyi' variant. Due to its larger size, the 'Tsang-khyi,' was traditionally tasked with more stationary jobs such as encampment or monetary guarding. The 'Dokhyi,' also commonly known as the 'Nomad' variant, was generally tasked with more active jobs such as flock driving, herding and hunting. Both the 'Dokhyi' and the 'Tsang-khyi' variants can occur in the same litter. The Tibetan Mastiff has a large, well-muscled and hardy body. It's body is covered in a long, thick double coat which comes in a wide variety of colorations, including solid black, solid white, black and tan, and various shades of 'red.' The temperament of dogs is normally affected by the following factors: individual personality, heredity, training and socialization. It is therefore important to make sure that you meet the puppy's mother before purchasing a Tibetan Mastiff. It is also important to make sure to thoroughly socialize your Tibetan Mastiff with strangers, children and other animals during its puppyhood. Generally speaking, the temperament of a Tibetan Mastiff reflects its ancient origins. The Tibetan Mastiff is at its happiest if it has a canine companion as it has a strong sense of pack living. Due to its history as a flock guardian, the Tibetan Mastiff is a highly intelligent, self-assured, strong-willed and loyal to its family. Due to its independent nature it is recommended to start obedience training with a Tibetan Mastiff during its very early puppyhood. Due to its history as a flock guardian, the Tibetan Mastiff is also known to sleep throughout the day and become most active at night. It is also important to remember that as a working breed, the Tibetan Mastiff also tends to be an incredibly active and athletic breed. It is therefore incredibly important to provide your Tibetan Mastiff with adequate exercise to make sure that it does not develop any destructive behaviors due to being bored or having an abundance of unspent energy.

Lifespan

A Tibetan Mastiff will normally live to be between 10 and 12 years old. However it is not uncommon for a Tibetan Mastiff to live to be as old as 14, providing that it does not develop any serious health issues.

Height and Weight

A fully grown Tibetan Mastiff will normally stand between 20 to 26 inches (51 to 66cm) tall at the shoulder. A healthy adult Tibetan Mastiff will normally weigh between 75 to 160 pounds (34 to 72.5kg). It is important to note that the weight of a healthy Tibetan Mastiff depends on how large the Tibetan Mastiff is – taller Tibetan Mastiff should weigh more.

Breed Characteristics

The following section will give you a simplistic overview of the characteristics of a Tibetan Mastiff. Our

rating system is from 1 to 10 – with 1 being the lowest score and 10 being the highest.

- **Adaptability:** 5/10
- **Friendliness:** 8/10
- **Health:** 6/10
- **Ease of Grooming:** 8/10
- **Amount of Shedding:** 4/10
- **Trainability:** 6/10
- **Intelligence:** 10/10
- **Exercise Needed:** 7/10
- **Playfulness:** 10/10
- **Family Friendliness:** 10/10

THE TIBETAN SPANIEL

The Tibetan Spaniel is a small breed of dog that shares a lot of its ancestral history with the Pekingese, the Japanese Chin, the Shih Tzu, the Pug and the Tibetan Terrier. As the breed's name suggests, the Tibetan Spaniel originates from Tibet, more specifically the Himalayan mountains. Despite having 'Spaniel' in its name, the Tibetan Spaniel is not actually considered to be a true Spaniel. Spaniels are gun dogs whereas the Tibetan Spaniel was traditionally employed as a watchdog at monasteries or as a companion dog. It is believed that the Tibetan Spaniel gained the 'Spaniel' name due to its resemblance to lap-dogs that descended from Spaniels – such as the King Charles Spaniel. While acting as a monastery watchdog, the Tibetan Spaniel would sit atop the walls of the monetary and keep watch over the countryside. The Tibetan Spaniel has incredibly keen eye sight that allows it to easily spot any threat. If a threat was spotted, the Tibetan Spaniel would bark loudly to alert the monks and the Tibetan Mastiffs of the incoming danger. The Tibetan Spaniel breed is believed to have originated over 2,500 years ago! The Tibetan Spaniel is also commonly known as the 'Simkhyi' and the 'Tibbie.' The small Tibetan Spaniel also gained the nickname of 'Little Lion,' due to its resemblance to the Chinese guardian lions. The Tibetan

Spaniel has a relatively small head in comparison to its body, a short blunt muzzle, no wrinkled skin and either an under-bite or an end-to-end bite. The breed's neck is covered in a mane of hair, which is dramatically more notable in the males of the breed. The breed has a silky double coat made up of medium-to-long hairs that lie flat the dog's body. The Tibetan Spaniel face and front legs are covered in much shorter hairs. The Tibetan Spaniel's coat comes in a wide variety of colors that includes white, fawn, red, cream black and tan, and gold. It is not uncommon for a Tibetan Spaniel's coat to contain multiple different colors. The temperament of dogs is normally affected by the following factors: individual personality, herecity, training and socialization. It is therefore important to make sure that you meet the puppy's mother before purchasing a Tibetan Spaniel. It is also important to make sure to thoroughly socialize your Tibetan Spaniel with strangers, children and other animals during its puppyhood. Generally speaking, the temperament of a Tibetan Spaniel is similar to most cat-like dog breeds. The Tibetan Spaniel is a lap dog at heart and loves spending time in contact with its owner. They are known to climb onto tables, chairs and sofas to get a better view of what is going on. The Tibetan Spaniel is also known to be an incredibly intelligent breed and do not respond well to being alone for long periods of time. Due to the fact that the Tibetan Spaniel was primarily developed for companion purposes, it is also a highly empathetic breed. The Tibetan Spaniel is also known to be incredibly protective of its family unit and it is therefore important to properly socialize your Tibetan Spaniel during its puppyhood to minimize its suspicion of strangers.

Lifespan

A Tibetan Spaniel will normally live to be between 10 and 12 years old. However it is not uncommon for a Tibetan Spaniel to live to be as old as 15, providing that it does not develop any serious health issues.

Height and Weight

A fully grown Tibetan Spaniel will normally stand between 10 to 12 inches (25.5 to 30.5cm) tall at the shoulder. A healthy adult Tibetan Spaniel will normally weigh between 9 to 15 pounds (4 to 6.8kg). It is important to note that the weight of a healthy Tibetan Spaniel depends on how large the Tibetan Spaniel is – taller Tibetan Spaniel should weigh more.

Breed Characteristics

The following section will give you a simplistic overview of the characteristics of a Tibetan Spaniel. Our rating system is from 1 to 10 – with 1 being the lowest score and 10 being the highest.

- ➤ **Adaptability:** 6/10
- ➤ **Friendliness:** 8/10
- ➤ **Health:** 6/10
- ➤ **Ease of Grooming:** 8/10
- ➤ **Amount of Shedding:** 6/10
- ➤ **Trainability:** 8/10
- ➤ **Intelligence:** 8/10
- ➤ **Exercise Needed:** 8/10
- ➤ **Playfulness:** 8/10
- ➤ **Family Friendliness:** 10/10

THE TIBETAN TERRIER

The Tibetan Terrie is a medium-sized breed of dog that originates Tibet. The Tibetan Terrier is also commonly known as the 'Tsnag Apso' and the 'Dokhi Apso.' Despite the breed's name including the term 'Terrier,' the Tibetan Terrier is not actually classified as a member of the Terrier grouping. The Tibetan Terrier was given its English name by European travelers who named the 'Tibetan Terrier' based upon its country of origin and the fact that the breed highly resembles the Terries found in Europe. The Tibetan Terrier is considered to be an ancient breed and has been in existence for over 1,000 years! The Tibetan Terrier was traditionally kept as either a good luck charm, a mascot, a watchdog or as a companion. The Tibetan Terrier breed is also known as the 'Holy Dogs of Tibet,' due to the fact that they were never sold but were rather given to people by monks to promote good fortune. The Tibetan Terrier has a powerful, square proportioned and athletic body that is covered in a long, profuse and shaggy double coat. The Tibetan Terrier's coat has an incredibly long growth cycle that is more similar in length to human hair rather than dog hair. The breed's double coat is made up of a warm undercoat and a topcoat which has a texture similar to that of human hair. All coat colorations are permissible, except liver and chocolate. The temperament of dogs is normally affected by the following factors: individual personality, heredity, training and socialization. It is therefore important to make sure that you meet the puppy's mother before purchasing a Tibetan Terrier. It is also important to make sure to thoroughly socialize your Tibetan Terrier with strangers, children and other animals during its puppyhood. Generally speaking, the temperament of a Tibetan Terrier is considered to be its most attractive quality. The Tibetan Terrier breed is known to be amiable, affectionate, gentle, respectful and family orientated. The Tibetan Terrier makes a perfect companion dog for any family as long as it is properly socialized during its puppyhood. Due to its history as a watchdog, the Tibetan Terrier is suspicious of strangers but should never be shy or aggressive.

Lifespan

A Tibetan Terrier will normally live to be between 10 and 12 years old. However it is not uncommon for a Tibetan Terrier to live to be as old as 15, providing that it does not develop any serious health issues.

Height and Weight

A fully grown Tibetan Terrier will normally stand between 14 to 16 inches (35.5 to 40.5cm) tall at the shoulder. A healthy adult Tibetan Terrier will normally weigh between 20 to 25 pounds (9 to 11.25kg). It is important to note that the weight of a healthy Tibetan Terrier depends on how large the Tibetan Terrier is – taller Tibetan Terrier should weigh more.

Breed Characteristics

The following section will give you a simplistic overview of the characteristics of a Tibetan Terrier. Our rating system is from 1 to 10 – with 1 being the lowest score and 10 being the highest.

- **Adaptability:** 8/10
- **Friendliness:** 8/10
- **Health:** 10/10
- **Ease of Grooming:** 3/10
- **Amount of Shedding:** 10/10
- **Trainability:** 7/10
- **Intelligence:** 8/10
- **Exercise Needed:** 8/10
- **Playfulness:** 10/10
- **Family Friendliness:** 10/10

THE TOY FOX TERRIER

The Toy Fox Terrier is a small breed of dog that is a member of the Terrier typing. The Toy Fox Terrier is a direct descendant of the larger Fox Terrier but is considered to be a separate breed. The breed is also commonly known as the 'American Toy Terrier' and the 'Amertoy.' The Toy Fox Terrier is believed to have been developed by systematically breeding the smallest Fox Terriers available as there is no DNA evidence to suggest that the breed was crossed with any miniature breeds: such as the Manchester Terrier or the Chihuahua. The Toy Fox Terrier was recognized as its own breed by the United Kennel Club in 1936 and was place in the Terrier grouping. The breed was later recognized by the American Kennel Club in 2003 where it was placed in the Toy group. The Toy Fox Terrier is a small breed but has a muscular and athletic build. The breed's most notable features are its short high-set tail, its large V-shaped ears, its large eyes and its short glossy coat. The Toy Fox Terrier's coat is normally of a predominantly white coloration with patches of other colors. The temperament of dogs is normally affected by the following factors: individual personality, heredity, training and socialization. It is therefore important to make sure that you meet the puppy's mother before purchasing a Toy Fox Terrier. It is also important to make sure to thoroughly socialize your Toy Fox Terrier with strangers, children and other animals during its puppyhood. Generally speaking, the temperament of a Toy Fox Terrier is that of an active and intelligent breed. The Toy Fox Terrier is known to be able to easily learn and follow a large number of word based commands. Traditionally the Toy Fox Terrier was primarily used in circuses to entertain crowds with athletic tricks which suggests that the breed is highly trainable. The Toy Fox Terrier is also known to be an incredibly loyal and affectionate breed and is commonly found as a companion breed for the elderly or disabled. The Toy Fox Terrier's small size makes it very adaptable to apartment living but it is important to also remember that the Toy Fox Terrier is a highly athletic breed that revels in running and physical exertion.

Lifespan

A Toy Fox Terrier will normally live to be between 10 and 12 years old. However it is not uncommon for a Toy Fox Terrier to live to be as old as 14, providing that it does not develop any serious health issues.

Height and Weight

A fully grown Toy Fox Terrier will normally stand between 8 to 11 inches (20.3 to 28cm) tall at the shoulder. A healthy adult Toy Fox Terrier will normally weigh between 3 to 7 pounds (1.3 to 3.175kg). It is important to note that the weight of a healthy Toy Fox Terrier depends on how large the Toy Fox Terrier is – taller Toy Fox Terrier should weigh more.

Breed Characteristics

The following section will give you a simplistic overview of the characteristics of a Toy Fox Terrier. Our rating system is from 1 to 10 – with 1 being the lowest score and 10 being the highest.

- **Adaptability:** 7/10
- **Friendliness:** 8/10
- **Health:** 10/10
- **Ease of Grooming:** 10/10
- **Amount of Shedding:** 8/10
- **Trainability:** 8/10
- **Intelligence:** 8/10
- **Exercise Needed:** 8/10
- **Playfulness:** 10/10
- **Family Friendliness:** 10/10

THE TREEING TENNESSEE BRINDLE

The Treeing Tennessee Brindle is a breed of dog that is a member of the Cur grouping. The Treeing Tennessee Brindle was developed in the early 1960s by Reverend Earl Philips. Philips was in the process of writing a column for a hunting dog magazine which lead to him becoming aware of the existence of 'brindle curs.' A 'brindle cur' is a hunting and treeing dog that has a brown coat, with tiger-like stripes of a black coloration. Philips researched the 'brindle cur' and found that they were highly regarded for their hunting and treeing abilities. Philips started an organization in 1967 for the purpose of preserving and promoting the brindle cur. The Treeing Tennessee Brindle was established on March 21st of 1967. However since 1995 records concerning the Treeing Tennessee Brindle have been maintained by the American Kennel Club's Foundation Stock Service Program. The Treeing Tennessee Brindle is the epitome of a brindle cur and therefore obviously has a brindle coat made up of short and soft hairs. The Treeing Tennessee Brindle standard allows for small white markings on a dog's chest and feet. The temperament of dogs is normally affected by the following factors: individual personality, heredity, training and socialization. It is therefore important to make sure that you meet the puppy's mother before purchasing a Treeing Tennessee Brindle. It is also important to make sure to thoroughly socialize your Treeing Tennessee Brindle with strangers, children and other animals during its puppyhood. Generally speaking, the temperament of a Treeing Tennessee Brindle is that of an intelligent hunting dog. The Treeing Tennessee Brindle has a strong propensity for scent based hunting and its strong athletic body allows it to easily tree prey. The Treeing Tennessee Brindle was developed for the purpose of hunting and it therefore is most content while hunting. It is also important to remember that as a working breed, the Treeing Tennessee Brindle also tends to be an incredibly active and athletic breed. It is therefore incredibly important to provide your Treeing Tennessee Brindle with adequate exercise to make sure that it does not develop any destructive behaviors due to being bored or having an abundance of unspent energy.

Lifespan

A Treeing Tennessee Brindle will normally live to be between 9 and 10 years old. However it is not uncommon for a Treeing Tennessee Brindle to live to be as old as 12, providing that it does not develop any serious health issues.

Height and Weight

A fully grown Treeing Tennessee Brindle will normally stand between 16 to 24 inches (40.5 to 61cm) tall at the shoulder. A healthy adult Treeing Tennessee Brindle will normally weigh between 30 to 45 pounds (13.6 to 20.4kg). It is important to note that the weight of a healthy Treeing Tennessee Brindle depends on how large the Treeing Tennessee Brindle is – taller Treeing Tennessee Brindle should weigh more.

Breed Characteristics

The following section will give you a simplistic overview of the characteristics of a Treeing Tennessee Brindle. Our rating system is from 1 to 10 – with 1 being the lowest score and 10 being the highest.

- **Adaptability:** 4/10
- **Friendliness:** 8/10
- **Health:** 8/10
- **Ease of Grooming:** 10/10
- **Amount of Shedding:** 7/10
- **Trainability:** 7/10
- **Intelligence:** 8/10
- **Exercise Needed:** 9/10
- **Playfulness:** 6/10
- **Family Friendliness:** 9/10

THE TREEING WALKER COONHOUND

The Treeing Walker Coonhound is a breed of dog that is a member of the Hound grouping. The Treeing Walker Coonhound is a direct descendant of the English and American Foxhound. The breed is commonly referred to as either one of its nicknames which are the 'TWC' and the 'Walker.' The breed was developed during the Colonial era by two breeders from Kentucky, John W. Walker and George Washington Maupin. The two breeders created the Treeing Walker Coonhound by crossing the English Foxhound, the American Foxhound and the Tennessee Lead (which is of unknown origin). The Treeing Walker Coonhound was first recognized by the United Kennel Club in 1905 as a subsection of the English Coonhound. However in 1945 it was recognized as a separate breed due to its name change to the 'Treeing Walker Coonhound' (the breed had previous been known as the 'Walker Hound'). The Treeing Walker Coonhound has a broad head, with a long muzzle and long low-hanging ears. The breed's body is muscular and athletically built. The Treeing Walker Coonhound's coat is smooth, fine and glossy and comes in either a tri-color or bi-color pattern. Both the tri-colored and bi-colored patterns are made up of either white, black or tan coloration. The temperament of dogs is normally affected by the following factors: individual personality, heredity, training and socialization. It is therefore important to make sure that you meet the puppy's mother before purchasing a Treeing Walker Coonhound. It is also important to make sure to thoroughly socialize your Treeing Walker Coonhound with strangers, children and other animals during its puppyhood. Generally speaking, the temperament of a Treeing Walker Coonhound is that of a loving, intelligent, confident and loyal hunting dog. Due to the fact that the breed was developed for hunting purposes, the Treeing Walker Coonhound has a high prey drive. The breed's high prey drive leads it to be tirelessly alert if they pick up on a scent that they find interesting. However while they are not 'hunting,' the Treeing Walker Coonhound is known to be a very mellow, sensitive and empathetic breed. The Treeing Walker Coonhound is a highly even tempered breed and should never show signs of aggression or annoyance towards people or other dogs. It is also important to remember that as a working breed, the Treeing Walker Coonhound also tends to be an incredibly active and athletic breed. It is therefore incredibly important to provide your Treeing Walker Coonhound with adequate exercise to make sure that it does not develop any destructive behaviors due to being bored or having an abundance of unspent energy.

Lifespan

A Treeing Walker Coonhound will normally live to be between 11 and 12 years old. However it is not uncommon for a Treeing Walker Coonhound to live to be as old as 13, providing that it does not develop any serious health issues.

Height and Weight

A fully grown Treeing Walker Coonhound will normally stand between 20 to 27 inches (50.8 to 68.5cm) tall at the shoulder. A healthy adult Treeing Walker Coonhound will normally weigh between 45 to 80 pounds (20.4 to 36.25kg). It is important to note that the weight of a healthy Treeing Walker Coonhound depends on how large the Treeing Walker Coonhound is – taller Treeing Walker Coonhound should weigh more.

Breed Characteristics

The following section will give you a simplistic overview of the characteristics of a Treeing Walker Coonhound. Our rating system is from 1 to 10 – with 1 being the lowest score and 10 being the highest.

- **Adaptability:** 6/10
- **Friendliness:** 8/10
- **Health:** 8/10

- **Ease of Grooming:** 10/10
- **Amount of Shedding:** 6/10
- **Trainability:** 8/10
- **Intelligence:** 8/10
- **Exercise Needed:** 8/10
- **Playfulness:** 6/10
- **Family Friendliness:** 9/10

Encyclopedia of Dog Breeds

THE VIZSLA

The Vizsla is a breed of dog that originates from Hungary and is a member of the Pointer grouping. The Vizsla's ancestors were favored by the Magyar tribes, who lived in the Carpathian Basin in the 10th century, as competent and loyal hunting dogs. There are primitive stone etchings that are over a thousand years old that depict a Magyar hunter with his falcon and his Vizsla. The Vizsla was preserved as a pure breed hunting dog for centuries as it was also highly favored by the warlords and barons of Hungary. The warlords and barons guarded their stocks of Vizsla jealously as they aimed to continue developing the hunting ability of the Vizsla. Despite being incredibly popular in its country of origin, the Vizsla nearly went extinct twice: once during the 1800s and once during World War II. The reason the Vizsla nearly went extinct during the 1800s is due to the fact that the English Pointer and the German Shorthair Pointer were introduced into Hungary and the Vizsla went out of fashion. After World War II there were only twelve recorded Vizsla left in Hungary. From this minimum stock, the Vizsla breed rose to prominence once again due to the dedicated work of a few breeders. The Vizsla is a medium-sized dog with a short haired coat. The Vizsla is known to be a robust but also lightly built breed which gives it incredible speed and athleticism. The breed's standard states that a Vizsla coat should be of a solid golden-rust color. However the Vizsla's coat is also known to come in browns, sandy gold, pale yellow and mahogany. The temperament of dogs is normally affected by the following factors: individual personality, heredity, training and socialization. It is therefore important to make sure that you meet the puppy's mother before purchasing a Vizsla. It is also important to make sure to thoroughly socialize your Vizsla with strangers, children and other animals during its puppyhood. Generally speaking, the temperament of a Vizsla is that of a loyal and respectful hunting dog. The Vizsla is known to be very energetic, gentle, caring and highly affectionate that has also lead the breed to be kept as much for companionship as for hunting purposes. It is also important to remember that as a working breed, the Vizsla also tends to be an incredibly active and athletic breed. It is therefore incredibly important to provide your Vizsla with adequate exercise to make sure that it does not develop any destructive behaviors due to being bored or having an abundance of unspent energy.

Lifespan

A Vizsla will normally live to be between 10 and 12 years old. However it is not uncommon for a Vizsla to live to be as old as 14, providing that it does not develop any serious health issues.

Height and Weight

A fully grown Vizsla will normally stand between 21 to 24 inches (53.35 to 61cm) tall at the shoulder. A healthy adult Vizsla will normally weigh between 45 to 65 pounds (20.4 to 29.5kg). It is important to note that the weight of a healthy Vizsla depends on how large the Vizsla is – taller Vizsla should weigh more.

Breed Characteristics

The following section will give you a simplistic overview of the characteristics of a Vizsla. Our rating system is from 1 to 10 – with 1 being the lowest score and 10 being the highest.

- **Adaptability:** 6/10
- **Friendliness:** 10/10
- **Health:** 8/10
- **Ease of Grooming:** 10/10
- **Amount of Shedding:** 4/10
- **Trainability:** 8/10
- **Intelligence:** 8/10
- **Exercise Needed:** 10/10
- **Playfulness:** 10/10
- **Family Friendliness:** 10/10

THE WEIMARANER

The Weimaraner is a large breed of dog that originates from Germany. The Weimaraner is commonly nicknamed the 'Weim' or the 'Grey Ghost.' The Weimaraner was originally developed for the purpose of being able to easily hunt large game such as boar, bear and deer. However once big game hunting declined, the Weimaraner was mainly employed for the purpose of hunting smaller prey such as fowl, rabbits and foxes. The Weimaraner was developed and owned exclusively by German royalty. The breed was developed to have a noble appearance and to be an all-purpose and reliable gun dog. The exclusivity of the Weimaraner made it a prized possession which normally lead to the Weimaraner being housed inside with its owners – it was common practice for hunting dogs to be kenneled outside in packs. This practice resulted in the Weimaraner being dependent on the company of humans. The Weimaraner proved to be a highly adaptable breed and was commonly used to protect the family home, watch over sleeping children and complete any other household task as well as being an adept hunting breed. The Weimaraner has an athletic build and a long legged frame. The Weimaraner has webbed paws which makes it an incredibly proficient swimmer. The breed's short coat and distinctive amber, grey, or blue eyes give the Weimaraner its noble appearance. The Weimaraner's coat should always be of a grey coloration: however this grey can range from silvery to charcoal-blue. The temperament of dogs is normally affected by the following factors: individual personality, heredity, training and socialization. It is therefore important to make sure that you meet the puppy's mother before purchasing a Weimaraner. It is also important to make sure to thoroughly socialize your Weimaraner with strangers, children and other animals during its puppyhood. Generally speaking, the temperament of a Weimaraner is that of an energetic hunting dog. The breed thrives in a physical environment and love exercising. The Weimaraner is known to be an incredibly intolerant breed of small animals – the Weimaraner will normally be overcome by the urge to hunt which normally results in the injury, or death, of small animals (such as cats). It is important to properly socialize your Weimaraner during its early puppyhood to ensure that it has a calm and controlled demeanor. The Weimaraner is also an incredible affectionate, loyal and loving companion. It is also important to remember that as a working breed, the Weimaraner also tends to be an incredibly active and athletic breed. It is therefore incredibly important to provide your Weimaraner with adequate exercise to make sure that it does not develop any destructive behaviors due to being bored or having an abundance of unspent energy.

Lifespan

A Weimaraner will normally live to be between 10 and 11 years old. However it is not uncommon for a Weimaraner to live to be as old as 13, providing that it does not develop any serious health issues.

Height and Weight

A fully grown Weimaraner will normally stand between 23 to 27 inches (23.5 to 68.5cm) tall at the shoulder. A healthy adult Weimaraner will normally weigh between 55 to 85 pounds (25 to 38.5kg). It is important to note that the weight of a healthy Weimaraner depends on how large the Weimaraner is – taller Weimaraner should weigh more.

Breed Characteristics

The following section will give you a simplistic overview of the characteristics of a Weimaraner. Our rating system is from 1 to 10 – with 1 being the lowest score and 10 being the highest.

- **Adaptability:** 6/10
- **Friendliness:** 8/10

- ➢ **Health:** 6/10
- ➢ **Ease of Grooming:** 10/10
- ➢ **Amount of Shedding:** 8/10
- ➢ **Trainability:** 8/10
- ➢ **Intelligence:** 10/10
- ➢ **Exercise Needed:** 10/10
- ➢ **Playfulness:** 10/10
- ➢ **Family Friendliness:** 10/10

THE WELSH SPRINGER SPANIEL

The Welsh Springer Spaniel is a breed of dog that is a member of the Spaniel typing. The breed is also commonly known as the 'Welsh Cocker Spaniel' and the 'Welsh Starter.' The Welsh Springer Spaniel's origin cannot be pin pointed, however dogs that highly resemble the Welsh Springer Spaniel in old pictures and prints. These depicted dogs are known as the 'Land Spaniel' and are considered to have play some part in the ancestry of the Welsh Springer Spaniel. The Welsh Springer Spaniel was traditionally used to 'spring' game into the open to allow a hunter's falcon to catch it. The Welsh Springer Spaniel breed nearly went extinct during World War I and there were actually no registered dogs whose parents were both registered pedigrees. The Welsh Springer Spaniel breed was restarted with the remaining and unregistered dogs – and these dogs form the basis of the modern breed. The Welsh Springer Spaniel has a compact, solidly built body that is capable of enduring hours or hard work. The Welsh Springer Spaniel's coat is always white with patches of reddish brown scattered across its body and face. The temperament of dogs is normally affected by the following factors: individual personality, heredity, training and socialization. It is therefore important to make sure that you meet the puppy's mother before purchasing a Welsh Springer Spaniel. It is also important to make sure to thoroughly socialize your Welsh Springer Spaniel with strangers, children and other animals during its puppyhood. Generally speaking, the temperament of a Welsh Springer Spaniel is that of an affectionate and loyal hunting dog. The breed is known to be incredible affectionate towards its direct family unit but aloof and suspicious of strangers. It is therefore incredibly important to make sure that you properly socialize your Welsh Springer Spaniel during its early puppyhood to ensure that it is friendly towards newcomers. It is also important to remember that as a working breed, the Welsh Springer Spaniel also tends to be an incredibly active and athletic breed. It is therefore incredibly important to provide your Welsh Springer Spaniel with adequate exercise to make sure that it does not develop any destructive behaviors due to being bored or having an abundance of unspent energy.

Lifespan

A Welsh Springer Spaniel will normally live to be between 10 and 12 years old. However it is not uncommon for a Welsh Springer Spaniel to live to be as old as 15, providing that it does not develop any serious health issues.

Height and Weight

A fully grown Welsh Springer Spaniel will normally stand between 16 to 19 inches (40.5 to 48.25cm) tall at the shoulder. A healthy adult Welsh Springer Spaniel will normally weigh between 35 to 55 pounds (16 to 25kg). It is important to note that the weight of a healthy Welsh Springer Spaniel depends on how large the Welsh Springer Spaniel is – taller Welsh Springer Spaniel should weigh more.

Breed Characteristics

The following section will give you a simplistic overview of the characteristics of a Welsh Springer Spaniel. Our rating system is from 1 to 10 – with 1 being the lowest score and 10 being the highest.

- **Adaptability:** 8/10
- **Friendliness:** 8/10
- **Health:** 68/10
- **Ease of Grooming:** 8/10
- **Amount of Shedding:** 6/10
- **Trainability:** 8/10
- **Intelligence:** 8/10
- **Exercise Needed:** 10/10
- **Playfulness:** 8/10
- **Family Friendliness:** 10/10

THE WELSH TERRIER

The Welsh Terrier is a breed of dog that is a member of the Terrier typing. As the breed's name suggests, the Welsh Terrier originates from Wales. According to research, the Welsh Terrier is the oldest existing breed of dog within the United Kingdom. The Welsh Terrier was developed for the purpose of hunting and exterminating rodents, badgers and foxes. Traditionally the Welsh Terrier was mainly kept on farmhouses and large estates for rodent killing purposes. In modern times, the Welsh Terrier is mainly found as a show dog or as a household companion dog. The Welsh Terrier has a tan colored head, legs and underbelly while all other parts of its coat are of a black or grizzle coloration. The Welsh Terrier has a sturdily built body with a relatively large and 'brick' shaped head. The Welsh Terrier's coat is made up of two layers, an undercoat, which helps to insulate and regulate the dog's core body temperature, and an abrasive overcoat that protects the breed from rain, dirt and wind. The Welsh Terrier's coat does not shed and will therefore need to be groomed on a regular basis. The temperament of dogs is normally affected by the following factors: individual personality, heredity, training and socialization. It is therefore important to make sure that you meet the puppy's mother before purchasing a Welsh Terrier. It is also important to make sure to thoroughly socialize your Welsh Terrier with strangers, children and other animals during its puppyhood. Generally speaking, the temperament of a Welsh Terrier a typical Terrier. The Welsh Terrier is known to be confident, head strong and proud. The Welsh Terrier was developed to be able to hunt alone and is therefore very assertive and self-assured. However, the Welsh Terrier is also known to be a perfect household companion as it has a happy, lively and outgoing personality. It is also important to remember that as a working breed, the Welsh Terrier also tends to be an incredibly active and athletic breed. It is therefore incredibly important to provide your Welsh Terrier with adequate exercise to make sure that it does not develop any destructive behaviors due to being bored or having an abundance of unspent energy.

Lifespan

A Welsh Terrier will normally live to be between 10 and 12 years old. However it is not uncommon for a Welsh Terrier to live to be as old as 14, providing that it does not develop any serious health issues.

Height and Weight

A fully grown Welsh Terrier will normally stand

between 13 to 15 inches (33 to 38cm) tall at the shoulder. A healthy adult Welsh Terrier will normally weigh between 14 to 20 pounds (6.35 to 9kg). It is important to note that the weight of a healthy Welsh Terrier depends on how large the Welsh Terrier is – taller Welsh Terrier should weigh more.

Breed Characteristics

The following section will give you a simplistic overview of the characteristics of a Welsh Terrier. Our rating system is from 1 to 10 – with 1 being the lowest score and 10 being the highest.

- **Adaptability:** 6/10
- **Friendliness:** 10/10
- **Health:** 10/10
- **Ease of Grooming:** 3/10
- **Amount of Shedding:** 1/10
- **Trainability:** 8/10
- **Intelligence:** 10/10
- **Exercise Needed:** 10/10
- **Playfulness:** 10/10
- **Family Friendliness:** 10/10

THE WHIPPET

The Whippet is a breed of medium-sized dog that originates from England. The Whippet is a member of the sighthound grouping and is a direct descendant of the Greyhound. Whippets were originally Greyhound that were deemed unsuitable for hunting purposes due to their smaller than average size. These unsuitable Greyhound were maimed (so the breeders could not use the small Greyhounds to break forest law, which stated that only nobility could hunt) and returned to their breeders. The breeders began to breed the small Greyhounds together which lead to creation of the Whippet! Traditionally the Whippet was used for the purposes of hunting small prey – such as rats and rabbits. The Whippet retained much on the Greyhounds physical capabilities and 'Whippet Racing' soon became very popular, which lead to the Whippet being nicknamed the 'Poor Mans' Racehorse.' In modern times the Whippet is still used in dog races as it has the highest running speed of any breed of their weight: 64 kilometers per hour (40mph)! The temperament of dogs is normally affected by the following factors: individual personality, heredity, training and socialization. It is therefore important to make sure that you meet the puppy's mother before purchasing a Whippet. It is also important to make sure to thoroughly socialize your

Whippet with strangers, children and other animals during its puppyhood. Generally speaking, the temperament of a Whippet is that of a gentle, quiet and respectful dog. The Whippet will spend much of its day resting but will still need regular exercise. The Whippet breed is known to be highly affectionate towards its owners and likes nothing more than sitting on its owner's lap. A properly socialized Whippet has no trouble getting along with strangers, children or other animals. However a untrained, or poorly socialized, Whippet may chase small animals (such as cats) due to its high prey drive. It is also important to remember that as a racing breed, the Whippet also tends to be an incredibly active and athletic breed. It is therefore incredibly important to provide your Whippet with adequate exercise to make sure that it does not develop any destructive behaviors due to being bored or having an abundance of unspent energy.

Lifespan

A Whippet will normally live to be between 12 and 13 years old. However it is not uncommon for a Whippet to live to be as old as 15, providing that it does not develop any serious health issues.

Height and Weight

A fully grown Whippet will normally stand between 18 to 22 inches (45.75 to 56cm) tall at the shoulder. A healthy adult Whippet will normally weigh between 18 to 48 pounds (8.1 to 21.75kg). It is important to note that the weight of a healthy Whippet depends on how large the Whippet is – taller Whippet should weigh more.

Breed Characteristics

The following section will give you a simplistic overview of the characteristics of a Whippet. Our rating system is from 1 to 10 – with 1 being the lowest score and 10 being the highest.

- **Adaptability:** 6/10
- **Friendliness:** 10/10
- **Health:** 8/10
- **Ease of Grooming:** 10/10
- **Amount of Shedding:** 4/10
- **Trainability:** 8/10
- **Intelligence:** 8/10
- **Exercise Needed:** 8/10
- **Playfulness:** 10/10
- **Family Friendliness:** 10/10

THE WEST HIGHLAND WHITE TERRIER

The West Highland White Terrier is a breed of dog that originates from Scotland. The West Highland White Terrier is commonly known by its two nicknames: the 'Westie' and the 'Scotty Dog.' The modern West Highland White Terrier descends from the numerous breeding programs of white Terriers in Scotland that occurred before the 20th century. The West Highland White Terrier has been a highly popular breed ever since its development. The West Highland White Terrier has won Cruft's twice and has been ranked in the top third of most popular dog breeds in America since the 1960s. Like most Terriers, The West Highland White Terrier was developed for the purpose of hunting and exterminating small rodents. Due to this, traditionally The West Highland White Terrier was mainly found working on small farms. However in modern times, The West Highland White Terrier has become a very popular companion breed. The West Highland White Terrier has a small compact body that is cover in a bright white coat. The breed has bright, deep-set, almond-shaped eyes that are dark in color and a pair of pointed and erect ears. The West Highland White Terrier's feet are slightly turned outwards which gives the breed good grip over rocky surfaces. The West Highland White Terrier has a soft, densely packed and thick undercoat and a rough outer coat which normally grows to about two inches in length. The temperament of dogs is normally affected by the following factors: individual personality, heredity, training and socialization. It is therefore important to make sure that you meet the puppy's mother before purchasing a West Highland White Terrier. It is also important to make sure to thoroughly socialize your West Highland White Terrier with strangers, children and other animals during its puppyhood. Generally speaking, the temperament of a West Highland White Terrier can vary greatly. Some West Highland White Terrier are highly affectionate and friendly towards children, strangers and other animals. While others tend to prefer solitude or the company of one or two family members. The West Highland White Terrier can also be a very generous breed that is willing to share its food and toys or an incredibly possessive breed that will aggressively defend what it believes to be its property. However, the breed is a Terrier and shares many common Terrier traits such as stubbornness, self-assurance, independence and having a high prey drive. If a West Highland White Terrier is properly socialized during its puppyhood it will normally have a happy and jolly temperament. The West Highland White Terrier has been used throughout history as a watchdog due to its likelihood to bark at an suspicious noises or strangers.

Lifespan

A West Highland White Terrier will normally live to be between 12 and 14 years old. However it is not uncommon for a West Highland White Terrier to live to be as old as 16, providing that it does not develop any serious health issues.

Height and Weight

A fully grown West Highland White Terrier will normally stand between 9 to 11 inches (23 to 28cm) tall at the shoulder. A healthy adult West Highland White Terrier will normally weigh between 12 to 22 pounds (5.4 to 10kg). It is important to note that the weight of a healthy West Highland White Terrier depends on how large The West Highland White Terrier is – taller West Highland White Terrier should weigh more.

Breed Characteristics

The following section will give you a simplistic overview of the characteristics of a West Highland White Terrier. Our rating system is from 1 to 10 – with 1 being the lowest score and 10 being the highest.

- **Adaptability:** 8/10
- **Friendliness:** 8/10
- **Health:** 6/10

- ➢ **Ease of Grooming:** 6/10
- ➢ **Amount of Shedding:** 7/10
- ➢ **Trainability:** 8/10
- ➢ **Intelligence:** 8/10
- ➢ **Exercise Needed:** 8/10
- ➢ **Playfulness:** 8/10
- ➢ **Family Friendliness:** 10/10

THE WIREHAIRED POINTING GRIFFON

The Wirehaired Pointing Griffon is a medium sized breed of dog that is a member of the gundog grouping. The Wirehaired Pointing Griffon's country of origin is a highly debated topic amongst Wirehaired Pointing Griffon enthusiasts. Many believe that the Wirehaired Pointing Griffon originated in the Netherlands as the breed's founder, Eduard Karei Korthals, is of Dutch origin. However records indicate that the Wirehaired Pointing Griffon breed was mainly developed in Germany at the Ipenwound kennel. Others believe that the Wirehaired Pointing Griffon true country of origin is France due to the fact that the French Kennel Club was the first kennel club to recognize the Wirehaired Pointing Griffon as a legitimate breed. The breed's founder aimed to develop a versatile gun dog that was resilient, highly trainable, vigorous and dedicated to its master. The Wirehaired Pointing Griffon has a harsh wiry outercoat and a soft undercoat. The breed standard prefers a Wirehaired Pointing Griffon's coat to be of a steel gray coloration with brown markings. However the Wirehaired Pointing Griffon's coat comes in a widew variety of other colors such as: all white, white and orange, white and brown, and roan. The temperament of dogs is normally affected by the following factors: individual personality, heredity, training and socialization. It is therefore important to make sure that you meet the puppy's mother before purchasing a Wirehaired Pointing Griffon. It is also important to make sure to thoroughly socialize your Wirehaired Pointing Griffon with strangers, children and other animals during its puppyhood. Generally speaking, the temperament of a Wirehaired Pointing Griffon is that of a devoted companion. The Wirehaired Pointing Griffon is intelligent, willing to please and has a very soft and gentle temperament. The breed is also incredibly empathetic and thus does not react well to harsh training methods. It is also important to remember that as a working breed, the Wirehaired Pointing Griffon also tends to be an incredibly active and athletic breed. It is therefore incredibly important to provide your Wirehaired Pointing Griffon with adequate exercise to make sure that it does not develop any destructive behaviors due to being bored or having an abundance of unspent energy.

Lifespan

A Wirehaired Pointing Griffon will normally live to be between 10 and 12 years old. However it is not uncommon for a Wirehaired Pointing Griffon to live to be as old as 14, providing that it does not develop any serious health issues.

Height and Weight

A fully grown Wirehaired Pointing Griffon will normally stand between 20 to 24 inches (50.8 to 61cm) tall at the shoulder. A healthy adult Wirehaired Pointing Griffon will normally weigh between 50 to 60 pounds (22.7 to 27.25kg). It is important to note that the weight of a healthy Wirehaired Pointing Griffon depends on how large the Wirehaired Pointing Griffon is – taller Wirehaired Pointing Griffon should weigh more.

Breed Characteristics

The following section will give you a simplistic overview of the characteristics of a Wirehaired Pointing Griffon. Our rating system is from 1 to 10 – with 1 being the lowest score and 10 being the highest.

- **Adaptability:** 6/10
- **Friendliness:** 10/10
- **Health:** 8/10
- **Ease of Grooming:** 5/10
- **Amount of Shedding:** 1/10
- **Trainability:** 8/10
- **Intelligence:** 10/10
- **Exercise Needed:** 8/10
- **Playfulness:** 10/10
- **Family Friendliness:** 10/10

Dog Care Professionals

THE XOLOITZCUINTLI

The Xoloitzcuintli is a small hairless breed of dog that originates from Mexico. The breed is also commonly known as the 'Xolo' and the 'Mexican Hairless Dog.' The Xoloitzcuintli comes in three size variations: toy, miniature and standard. Despite it being nicknamed the 'Mexican Hairless Dog,' the Xoloitzcuintli can actually come in a coated variety. All three size variations and both coat variations can occur in the same litter of puppies. The Xoloitzcuintli is very similar in appearance to the Pharaoh Hound, with its sleek body, almond-shaped eyes, relatively long neck and large ears. The Xoloitzcuintli has an athletic build which gives it an heir of elegance, agility and strength. The remains of Xoloitzcuintli have been found in the tombs of Mayan, Aztec and Tollec nobility as they believed that the Xoloitzcuintli would protect and safeguard spirits in the afterlife. In ancient times the Xoloitzcuintli would actually be sacrificed to accompany their owners into the afterlife. The temperament of dogs is normally affected by the following factors: individual personality, heredity, training and socialization. It is therefore important to make sure that you meet the puppy's mother before purchasing a Xoloitzcuintli. It is also important to make sure to thoroughly socialize your Xoloitzcuintli with strangers, children and other animals during its puppyhood. Generally speaking, the temperament of a Xoloitzcuintli is that of a highly intelligent, sensitive, energetic and inquisitive companion breed. Adult Xoloitzcuintli are known to have an incredibly calm demeanor that allows them to get along easily with children and strangers. Due to their inquisitive nature the Xoloitzcuintli is an expert escape artist and will frequently find its way out of fenced gardens. Due to their inquisitive nature it in incredibly important to train your Xoloitzcuintli to a high standard to ensure that it does not get lost. Overall the Xoloitzcuintli can make a perfect addition to any household.

Lifespan

A Xoloitzcuintli will normally live to be between 12 and 14 years old. However it is not uncommon for a Xoloitzcuintli to live to be as old as 20, providing that it does not develop any serious health issues.

Height and Weight

A fully grown Xoloitzcuintli will normally stand between 18 to 23 inches (45.75 to 58.5cm) tall at the shoulder. A healthy adult Xoloitzcuintli will normally weigh between 10 to 50 pounds (4.5 to 22.5kg). It is important to note that the weight of a healthy

Xoloitzcuintli depends on how large the Xoloitzcuintli is – taller Xoloitzcuintli should weigh more.

Breed Characteristics

The following section will give you a simplistic overview of the characteristics of a Xoloitzcuintli. Our rating system is from 1 to 10 – with 1 being the lowest score and 10 being the highest.

- **Adaptability:** 6/10
- **Friendliness:** 6/10
- **Health:** 6/10
- **Ease of Grooming:** 10/10
- **Amount of Shedding:** 1/10
- **Trainability:** 8/10
- **Intelligence:** 10/10
- **Exercise Needed:** 6/10
- **Playfulness:** 5/10
- **Family Friendliness:** 10/10

Dog Care Professionals

Y

THE YORKSHIRE TERRIER

The Yorkshire Terrier (commonly nicknamed 'Yorkie') is a small breed of dog within the Terrier grouping. The breed was developed in Yorkshire during the 19th century for the purpose of catching rats. The Yorkshire Terrier is placed within the Toy Terrier section of the Terrier group and will normally not exceed a weigh of 7 pounds (3.2kg). Due to their cute appearance and small size the Yorkshire Terrier has become one of the most popular breeds of companion dog. The breed is considered to be intelligent, confident and self-assured – Yorkshire Terriers have been known to start fights with dogs dramatically larger than them! The Yorkshire Terrier is a long haired breed but some owners choose to cut their pet's fur into a short coat for convenience of grooming. Their coats come in three main colorations: tan, grey and black.

Lifespan

Yorkshire Terriers will normally live for between 10 and 13 years. However it is not uncommon for a Yorkshire Terrier to live to be as old as 15 if they do not develop any serious health issues.

Size

An adult Yorkshire Terrier should be around 8 to 9 inches (20 to 23cm) tall at the shoulder and weigh no more than 7 pounds (3kg). Most Yorkshire Terriers will weigh between 4 and 6 pounds (1.8 to 2.75kg). Yorkshire Terriers are an inconsistently sized breed. A litter will commonly contain a range of sizes and weights. You should not purchase a 'tea cup' Yorkshire Terrier as they are prone to genetic disorders and have a much higher risk of general health issues.

Hypoallergenic Coat

The Yorkshire Terrier is considered to be a hypoallergenic breed. Despite having long coats, Yorkies do not shed very much hair. It is believe that they only shed hair when bathed, brushed or if the hair is broken. However Yorkshire Terriers will still trigger saliva and dander related allergies.

Yorkie Clubs

There are many Yorkshire Terrier clubs throughout the world. We recommended bringing your Yorkie to a gathering while it is a puppy to help socialize it with other dogs. Yorkshire Terrier clubs are also a great way to meet other owners and gain first hand grooming tips.

Breed Characteristics

The following section will give you a simplistic overview of the characteristics of a Yorkshire Terrier. Our rating system is from 1 to 10 – with 1 being the lowest score and 10 being the highest.

- **Adaptability:** 6/10
- **Friendliness:** 6/10
- **Health:** 4/10
- **Ease of Grooming:** 2/10
- **Amount of Shedding:** 4/10
- **Trainability:** 6/10
- **Intelligence:** 6/10
- **Exercise Needed:** 8/10
- **Playfulness:** 10/10
- **Family Friendliness:** 8/10

ABOUT THE AUTHOR

Here at Dog Care Professionals we are passionate about dog care. As a brand we have a strong idea of what makes up a good pet care book. We consult with multiple experts in multiple different fields to allow us to create a book filled with cumulative opinions and best practices. The experts we consult range from veterinarians to every day pet keepers who have had years of experience caring for the specific breed each book is on. Our aim, and mission, is to produce the best possible dog care books that are a great value for money.

Encyclopedia of Dog Breeds

OTHER POPULAR BOOKS BY DOG CARE PROFESSIONALS

The Chesapeake Bay Retriever

A Complete and Comprehensive Owners Guide to: Buying, Owning, Health, Grooming, Training, Obedience, Understanding and Caring for Your Chesapeake Bay Retriever

Dog Care Professionals

The German Shorthaired Pointer

A Complete and Comprehensive Owners Guide to: Buying, Owning, Health, Grooming, Training, Obedience, Understanding and Caring for Your German Shorthaired Pointer

Encyclopedia of Dog Breeds

The Miniature Pinscher

A Complete and Comprehensive Owners Guide to: Buying, Owning, Health, Grooming, Training, Obedience, Understanding and Caring for Your Miniature Pinscher

DOG Care Professionals

The Shih Tzu

A Complete and Comprehensive Owners Guide to: Buying, Owning, Health, Grooming, Training, Obedience, Understanding and Caring for Your Shih Tzu

Encyclopedia of Dog Breeds

The Harrier

A Complete and Comprehensive Owners Guide to: Buying, Owning, Health, Grooming, Training, Obedience, Understanding and Caring for Your Harrier

Dog Care Professionals

Encyclopedia of Dog Breeds

Dog Care Professionals

CPSIA information can be obtained
at www.ICGtesting.com
Printed in the USA
LVOW10s2240010118
561469LV00041B/3166/P

9 781546 526766